THE SOVIET UNION AND CENTRAL EUROPE
IN THE POST-WAR ERA

The Soviet Union and Central Europe in the Post-War Era: A Study in Precarious Security.

KRISTIAN GERNER

St. Martin's Press   New York

© Swedish Institute of International Affairs, 1985
All rights reserved. For information, write:
St. Martin's Press, Inc., 175 Fifth Avenue, New York, NY 10010
Printed in Great Britain
First published in the United States of America in 1985

Library of Congress Cataloging in Publication Data

Gerner, Kristian, 1942–
   The Soviet Union and Central Europe in the post-war era.
   Bibliography: p.
   Includes index.
   1. Europe, Eastern—Foreign relations—Soviet Union.
   2. Soviet Union—Foreign relations—Europe, Eastern.
   3. Europe, Eastern—Politics and government—1945–
   4. Europe, Eastern—National security.
   5. Soviet Union—National security.
   I. Title.
   DJK45.S65G47   1985   327'.0947   84-24780

ISBN 0-312-74905-8

To Annika

Cemeteries grow larger the number of defenders shrinks
but the defense continues and will last to the end
and even if the City falls and one of us survives
he will carry the City inside him on the roads of exile
he will be the City

we look at the face of hunger the face of fire the face of death
and the worst of them all — the face of treason

and only our dreams have not been humiliated

(Zbigniew Herbert, 'Warsaw 1982')

Just frontiers were secured for Poland through the resolute
support of the Soviet Union. Its help facilitated the postwar
restoration and industrialisation of Poland. In our present
difficulties, Soviet help is again invaluable to us. We will never
forget this.

(Wojciech Jaruzelski in Moscow, December 1982)

Contents

Abbreviations

English abbreviations are used when commonly accepted in the literature. In a number of cases, Polish abbreviations have been used as they have gained acceptance also in English.

CC	Central Committee
CMEA	Council for Mutual Economic Assistance
CPCS	Communist Party of Czechoslovakia
CPSU	Communist Party of the Soviet Union
DiP	Doswiadczenie i Przyszlosc (Experience and Future)
HSWP	Hungarian Socialist Workers' Party
KOR	Komitet Obrony Robotników (Workers' Defence Committee)
KSS	Komitet Samoobrony Spolecznej (Committee for Social Self Defence)
NATO	North Atlantic Treaty Organisation
ND	Narodowa Demokracja (National Democracy)
NEM	New Economic Mechanism
PPN	Polskie Porozumienie Niepodleglosciowe (Polish Association for Independence)
PPS	Polska Partja Socjalistyczna (Polish Socialist Party)
PUWP	Polish United Workers' Party
SDKPiL	Socjal-Demokracja Królestwa Polskiego i Litwy (Social Democracy of the Polish Kingdom and Lithuania)
WTO	Warsaw Treaty Organisation

Because of technical limitations, diacritical marks are not printed in Polish and Czech consonants (Pilsudski — Piłsudski, Solidarnosc — Solidarność, Mlynár — Mlynář etc.)

Acknowledgements

This study is the posthumous child of Professor Sven Tägil's research project on Boundary Conflicts at the Department of History at the University of Lund. I am grateful to Sven Tägil for his magnanimity in allowing me to depart from the Teschen conflict in the interwar era to the relations between the Soviet Union and Central Europe in the postwar era.

Sven Tägil has been a source of inspiration and support during my many years of conflict studies. He has read the manuscript of this work and offered valuable criticism.

My gratitude goes also to the other members of the Boundary Project, Göran Henrikson, Rune Johansson, Jan B. Molander, Ingmar Oldberg and Kim Salomon for criticism and rewarding discussions at earlier stages of my research work.

Within the community of Sovietologists I wish to express my gratitude to Christer Jönsson, whose thorough criticism of the first edition of the study has been of great help in preparing this book, and Stefan Hedlund and Kerstin Nyström, who have both read the manuscript and carried on lengthy discussions with me about it.

Professors Birgitta Odén and Göran Rystad have both read the manuscript and offered valuable criticism. Claes Peterson and Jyrki Iivonen have both been helpful in arranging seminars, where I could discuss methodological questions at a crucial stage of my work.

I have also received inspiration and help in different ways from colleagues and friends in the Soviet Union, Poland and Hungary. I am grateful to them, although they do not bear any responsibility for my conclusions. None of them has read my manuscript.

My thanks go also to Ingrid Gustafsson for typing my study and to Alan Harkess for correcting my English.

Last but not least I would like to thank the personnel at the Swedish Institute of International Affairs. The Institute gave me the opportunity, by way of a research semester, to start working on this study, and Atis Lejins and Margaretha Dufwa of the Institute have edited it.

Stockholm, 23 May, 1984.

Kristian Gerner

1 Introduction

The context

This is a study of certain aspects and parts of the Soviet bloc. The bloc is viewed as a political system established by the Soviet leaders after World War II in order to make the Soviet Union militarily secure and practically invulnerable from attack from the West. It is taken for granted, and thus not examined in this study, that the Soviet leaders view obedience to Soviet political demands as a precondition, without which the other Warsaw Pact (WTO) countries would be unable to fulfil their task of making the Soviet Union and the Soviet leaders themselves safe against any military threat from the West in Europe. Soviet security is built upon Soviet influence and assurance that the West cannot use the Central European countries against the USSR.

It is an empirical fact that not all the European WTO states have been politically stable at all points of time. The strikes and demonstrations in Berlin, capital of the GDR, on 17 June 1953, may be interpreted as proof that the GDR had not become politically stable. However, the upheaval was crushed with the help of Soviet tanks before any questioning of the loyalty of the GDR toward the Soviet Union had been voiced. After that, the GDR has been politically stable and has not undergone any structural economic change. The strikes and demonstrations of Polish workers in 1956 and the subsequent reshuffle among the Polish communist leaders

1

showed beyond doubt that Poland had not become politically stable. The lack of stability was even more evident in the same year in Hungary, where political turmoil was accompanied by the Nagy government's professed secession from the WTO. In 1968, the attempt at democratisation in Czechoslovakia endangered the political status quo as it implied a significant reduction in the power of the governing Communist Party, and hence was a threat to political stability. In 1980–81, the emergence and establishment of the Solidarity movement in Poland was a clear expression of political instability in a WTO state.

As the individual bloc countries are members of the WTO and form integrated parts of the Soviet defence and security system, political instability in any of the countries concerned obviously affects, indirectly, the military security of the Soviet Union and its leaders. Hence political instability in any of the countries is a potential threat to Soviet security. During all of the events mentioned above, the Soviet leaders have shown their apprehension and made clear that they see things this way.

The Polish 'self-limiting revolution'[1] in 1980–81 has been described as the first nonviolent mass movement to question the Soviet post World War II security system in Central Europe.[2] The economic breakdown in Poland,[3] and the open conflict between, on the one hand, organised labour, intellectuals and peasants and, on the other hand, the central apparatus of the ruling Communist Party (PUWP) and the state security forces were phenomena with wider implications. The Soviet leaders, in their letter to the PUWP leadership on 5 June 1981, declared that the events in Poland were a threat to the interests, cohesion, integrity and frontiers of the socialist bloc, to its security.[4] From a different perspective, political scientists in the West came to similar conclusions, asserting that the Polish turmoil constituted 'a critical turning point in the history of the Soviet imperium',[5] 'the most serious challenge' to Soviet rule after World War II,[6] and a 'strategic, politico-ideological and economic' threefold challenge at that.[7] Such assertions are based on notions such as that 'Poland is crucial to the USSR's ability to maintain the post World War II division of Europe',[8] that she is of 'unique strategic importance' to the USSR,[9] has a 'key role' in the latter's defence policy[10] and 'top priority' in Soviet security planning,[11] and that a neutralised Poland would render the whole WTO strategically worthless.[12] It is evident from their letter of 5 June 1981, that the Soviet leaders reached a corresponding conclusion. According to this letter, 'imperialist reaction' was supporting and encouraging the 'Polish counter-revolution' in order to try to change to its own advantage 'the balance of forces in Europe and in the world'.[13]

What happened in Poland was not just an indirect threat to Soviet security policies. Oppositional forces in Poland tended to depict the economic shortcomings and the social misery in Poland as a partial consequence of the country's relationship with the USSR. Consequently, the role of the USSR was brought into the heated discussion on the causes of the crisis in Poland. The connection between the domestic political crisis in Poland and Soviet influence was put forward by some informed Polish intellectuals already before the event, in 1979.

With the encouragement of some of the PUWP leaders, a committee of experts — economists and social scientists — was appointed in the autumn of 1978. Its task would be to inquire about the causes of the mounting economic and social crisis. The findings of the committee were such, however, that it had to go into opposition and publish its first report illegally in May, 1979.

The committee, which called itself 'Experience and Future' (abbreviated 'DiP' in Polish), based its conclusions on a survey of the opinion of top administrators and intellectuals. It pointed out that the Polish economy could not be brought into order if the people did not feel morally motivated to work effectively. Such motivation could emerge only if the relationship between Poland and the USSR was changed from one of subordination into one of equality. Polish public opinion did not question the necessity of the alliance with the Soviet Union, DiP observed, but it did demand Soviet acknowledgment of Poland's specific economic, political and cultural needs and traditions. DiP asserted that the Polish view was connected with a need of self-esteem and self-assertion in face of the powerful neighbour:

> In terms of its size and potential Poland is the second most important socialist country in Europe. In the estimation of Polish public opinion, this fact is not adequately reflected in the nature of our relationship with the Soviet Union. — We Poles can be valuable and trustworthy partners only when we are treated as partners. Then we repay friendship with friendship.[14]

The Polish revolution thus was not only a local reaction against material hardships. It had a supranational aspect as well, as it questioned the basic principles on which the Soviet security system in Central Europe was based. The broader international political implications of this were and are apparent. It raises questions of historical importance for Soviet security policy.

Questions and concepts

To understand the significance of the Polish events in 1980–81 for the Soviet security system, it is necessary to compare them with what must be said to be the other major challenges to it — by impairing its political stability — in Hungary and Czechoslovakia. In Hungary there was the revolt in 1956 and in Czechoslovakia the reform movement in 1968. It is

3

also necessary to compare the events in Czechoslovakia and Poland with the development in Hungary *after* 1956, as this development bears some important similarities to what was going on, but apparently not tolerated by the Soviet leaders, in Czechoslovakia in 1968. It is exactly in these three countries in the Soviet bloc that a 'continuous legitimation crisis' has been most persistent over the years.[15]

The central question of this study, then, is: *why have the constituent parts of the security system erected by the Soviet leaders in Central Europe not been politically stable?* The focus of interest will be on the period from 1968 onwards, as this period has offered examples of societal or economic changes within the sub-parts of the system Czechoslovakia, Hungary, and Poland, which in some cases have upset the political stability and in others not. Hence a second question to be investigated in this study is: *which methods have been adopted by those in power in order to achieve political stability in these states?*

It will not be questioned but serve as a postulate of this study that the non-Soviet members of the WTO and the Council of Mutual Economic Assistance (CMEA) in Central Europe are politically subordinated to the Soviet Union and that political stability, when the system was being established in the late 1940s, was upheld by direct Soviet military and police coercion. The alliance that took shape here has been labelled, in earlier research, an 'Al Capone alliance'. This means that the alliance is unequal, asymmetrical, that one strong part forces the weaker ones into submission, and that the stronger part exacts a price from the weaker ones in exchange for the 'protection' imposed upon the latter. The weaker members are being protected not only against the external enemies of the 'Al Capone state' but also against obliteration by the same 'Al Capone state'. It belongs to the logic of the 'Al Capone alliance' that the weaker parts are not allowed to opt out of it even though they do not perceive themselves in need of protection.[16]

When the Soviet Union under Stalin extended its empire to Central Europe (and part of the Balkans), it was according to the 'Al Capone' model. 'Liberated' states such as Poland and Czechoslovakia were treated as harshly as the conquered ones, i.e., the Soviet zone in Germany, Hungary, Romania (which changed sides late in the war) and Bulgaria. These countries were apparently regarded as a legitimate Soviet prey, or so Stalin and his men chose to interpret the Yalta agreement. The Soviet leaders chose to subordinate all the states associated with the USSR and make them vassals. In 1948 this process was completed. The Soviet Union had established a 'cordon sanitaire' of communist ruled, so called people's democracies, between itself and the adversaries, i.e., the democracies of Western Europe.

As the Cold War developed, the CPSU increased terror in the USSR and forced the vassal states to conform strictly to the Soviet pattern

4

politically, economically, ideologically and culturally. The military organisations of the vassal states became infiltrated and controlled by the Soviet military. The same was true of the security services.[17] All the subordinate states and especially the Soviet zone in Germany — from 1949 the GDR — were being exploited economically by the USSR. Calculations made by the American economist Paul Marer have shown that the magnitude of the net flow of resources from Central and South Eastern Europe to the Soviet Union in this period was of the same order as that from the United States to Western Europe under the Marshall plan.[18]

The political system of Stalinism was introduced into the states dependent on the USSR. The concept 'Stalinism' is clear regarding its denotation, and there is also, probably, a good deal of consensus among Sovietologists in the West concerning its connotation. Stalinism is seen as a variety of totalitarianism. The definition put forward by Zdenek Mlynár appears to be appropriate in the context of this study. 'Stalinism' is a societal system where:

> political and economical power is completely merged;
> the social position of both individuals and groups is defined exclusively by the relation to the central power;
> all power is concentrated in the Communist Party, all decision making is centralised;
> there is a lack of spontaneous information to the centre from below, i.e., a lack of feedback in the political system;
> political and police mass terror is part of the order;
> the society as such is living in what amounts to an 'informational vacuum';
> ideological conformity is decreed and controlled by the centre;
> the superiority of the Soviet system — and of **Russia** — is part of the 'self-understanding' of the doctrine.[19]

In specific circumstances, I will refer to 'high Stalinism' when all these characteristics are regarded as being present, and to 'de-Stalinisation' when one or several of them are being eroded. However, it does not seem necessary to discuss the inner relationship and interdependence between these different characteristics on the theoretical level.

To be able to analyse the processes leading up to the political crises in the Soviet bloc one must have some idea of what constitutes political stability as well as certain concepts, suitable for the investigation of the chosen problems.

Political stability is a state when the rulers are not openly challenged by their subjects, when there is not any gross or rapid turnover of the former and when the succession of rulers takes place in a regular and orderly way. However, what is strictly political cannot be defined once and for all. Suffice it to say at this stage of the investigation that political power can be first acquired and then maintained either with the help of physical violence and coercion or by voluntary submission and consent on the part of the subjects. At the end of the scale, one would get a condominium of equals, of citizens all striving for a *bonum commune*. Consent and condominium both denote legitimacy of political power. A political regime is legitimate when there is a community of values regarding the hierarchy of goals between the central powers (or power), the administrators of public affairs, and the governed population. Political legitimacy prevails when those who govern believe and feel that they are entitled to do so and those who are governed agree.[20]

Under Khrushchev, the CPSU made an obvious attempt to replace its habitual bases of power — coercion and terror — both at home and in the vassal states, by popular support and cooperation. The leadership was apparently striving for voluntary obedience and support from the population, i.e., some kind of legitimacy for its rule.[21] The previous terror had brought at least temporary stability, but it is incomprehensible to regard terror as a principle of legitimation. Even if outright physical coercion is abandoned but the population obeys and keeps quiet out of fear of reprisals, it would be strange to talk of legitimate authority.[22] But legitimacy can obviously be of different kinds.

Max Weber's classification of 'pure' types of legitimation of political regimes is also useful for an analysis of political stability in communist states.[23] Weber speaks of three inner legitimations of domination (authority):

> First, the authority of 'eternal yesterday', i.e., of the mores sanctified through the unimaginably ancient recognition and habitual orientation to conform. This is the 'traditional' domination exercised by the patriarch and the patrimonial prince of yore.
> There is the authority of the extraordinary and personal gift of grace (charisma), the absolutely personal devotion and personal confidence in revelation, heroism, or other qualities of individual leadership. This is 'charismatic' domination, as exercised by the prophet or — in the field of politics — by the elected war lord, the plebiscitarian ruler, the great demagogue, or the political party leader.
> Finally, there is domination by virtue of 'legality', by virtue of the belief in the validity of legal statute and functional 'competence' based on rationally created rules. In this case, obedience is expected in discharging statutory obligations. This is domination as exercised by the modern 'servant of the state' and by all those bearers of power who in this respect resemble him.[24]

As the communist regimes in Central Europe are not totally independent it is difficult for them to acquire legitimation in any of the Weberian senses. On the other hand, it is evident that these regimes sometimes do obtain some support from their subjects, a support which is not solely based on fear. A regime with semisovereignty, i.e., with a master above it to placate, can act according to the rule 'give to the emperor what belongs to the emperor' and still try to court its own subjects and take care of the population's culture and material well being. The counterpart to charisma would be an attempt at utilizing 'personality cult' of the leader. But while charisma is an erratic and inherently or potentially unstable state, even if 'routinized' and attributed to the Communist Party[25] and hardly may become a permanent, structural foundation of legitimacy, something resembling traditional or legal domination (authority) may be achieved. I will use the concepts 'protection of the national culture' and 'economic compensation', respectively, to denote situations when a semisovereign regime either tries to acquire or succeeds in obtaining stability without recourse to terror and in spite of its ultimate dependence on a foreign power. These devices may be viewed as functional equivalents to traditional or legal legitimation, although it is a peculiar, basically 'negative' kind of legitimation. A legitimation of this kind remains 'goal rational' and the regime is dependent on its subjects perceiving it as fulfilling the goals tacitly or openly agreed upon.[26] One may speak of an 'auxiliary legitimation'.[27] I will treat it as such, aware of the fact that it can be hard to tell when, with the strength of tradition or factual legality in societal life, the 'auxiliary' status is transcended. The sociologist of the Budapest school Maria Markus has noted that certain pragmatic or, as she calls them, 'covert' modes of legitimation of communist regimes, may appear to have a role which is more than auxiliary:

> . . . appealing as it usually does to more popular, sometimes traditional, sometimes 'external', so called 'petty-bourgeois' values. Thus internationalist references in overt legitimation are replaced within the system of covert legitimation by nationalist ones . . .[28]

The revised Weberian legitimation classification presented above is the theoretical framework of my analysis. However, this choice of framework is not only of theoretical significance. It is normative as well. It has as a premise that the Central European Communist regimes should be viewed as willing and even trying to acquire legitimation, be it purely of an 'auxiliary' character. An alternative approach would be to hypothesise that the regimes are not really interested in acquiring any kind of legitimation but only in preserving power with the help of refined oppression, of more subtle means of repression than was the case in the original Stalinist system. This is, for example, the gist of the criticism directed by the Swedish economist Anders Åslund against a study of Poland's economic predicament made by myself and another Swedish economist, Stefan Hedlund. Åslund's argument is that profound economic reform was incomprehensible in Gierek's Poland, as such a reform would have endangered the political power of the party apparatus of the PUWP.[29]

One of those taking part in the Czechoslovak reform movement in 1968, Zdenek Mlynár, has made an analysis of '*Crises and Crisis Management in the Soviet Bloc, 1953 – 1982*', which treats economic factors as important for political stabilisation, but not as a foundation of legitimacy. According to Mlynár, 'relative political stabilisation' is the effect of an 'economic-security and social welfare package' in combination with the 'unofficial economy'; the latter serves to make good the unavoidable shortages in the official economy. An additional factor behind the relative stabilisation is 'systematic and painful discrimination' against 'groups and individuals who are a potential opposition to the existing sociopolitical system'. Political purges are, Mlynár argues, indispensable for the political structure to regain stability whenever reformist tendencies have grown and taken on political significance. These purges may be 'inconspicuous', but they are necessary.[30]

While the approaches chosen by analysts such as Åslund and Mlynár are reasonable, they seem to presuppose that political stability is unattainable. What may be achieved is relative stabilisation. This judgment is corroborated by the conclusion of Karel Kaplán, a compatriot and also scientific collaborator of Mlynár. Analysing Czechoslovak politics 1948 – 1972, Kaplán concludes:

> During the twenty-five years of existence of the regime the forms of political persecution and the social function of the various degrees of this persecution have changed. But they have also become stabilised. Political persecution has remained the constant instrument of governing and totalitarian domination, but also both the source of crises of the system and an instrument to overcome them.[31]

In contrast to these approaches, which rule out the possibility of genuine political stability, my approach should be regarded as one that gives the Communist regimes in Central Europe the opportunity to show — theoretically — what they may be said to have been doing to overcome their political instability. My normative approach thus rests on the postulate that stability, if terror is significantly slackened, can only be achieved by making the regimes seem legitimate in the eyes of their subjects. My main focus of interest is neither on the mechanisms of repression nor on the phenomenon 'stability through apathy' but on the possible positive side of politics in the states under scrutiny.

However, if repression and apathy are to a certain degree left out of the analysis and the focus on legitimation is accepted, in the semisovereign states investigated, where real traditional, charismatic, or legal/rational legitimation all seem farfetched, the concepts 'protector of national culture' and 'economic compensation' acquire crucial importance.

Legitimation or auxiliary legitimation cannot be sought for in a vacuum. In order to understand the actual processes to be analysed with the help of this approach, one has to introduce a concept which can gear the analysis towards the empirical reality. The concept 'political culture' is useful for this purpose.[32]

It should be underlined at the outset that 'political culture' is a vague concept. It is more than just 'politics' and less than 'culture' in the broad sense. It refers to more than the so-called operational code of decision makers or temporary public opinion, as these may both be interpreted as dependent on or expressions of the political culture. The concept can hardly be used in nomothetically conceived tests of causes and effects. Due to the broad range of factors to take into consideration, the ambition must be restricted to one of 'broadening our understanding' of the interaction of factors.[33] 'Political culture' can be used to clarify the context and meaning of certain political processes, to show how something happens and to elucidate its significance.[34]

Reviewing the history of the concept 'political culture' in anthropology and political science, respectively, and discussing the relevance of the concept for communist studies, Robert Tucker has pointed to its different use by anthropologists and political scientists. While the former have treated it as a psychological as well as a behavioural concept, the latter have tended to regard it as (only) a psychological one, denoting values and subjective orientation. Tucker himself opted for the 'anthropologist' view, arguing that while the explanatory capacity of the concept might be thereby hampered, it could instead make studies of 'the political life of a society' more fruitful. According to Tucker, the political culture should not be seen as just 'an attribute of a political system' but as 'a complex of real and ideal culture patterns, including political roles and their inter-relations, political structures, and so on'.[35]

A comprehensive volume exploiting the concept 'political culture' in communist studies was a collection of conference papers published in 1977. Solid monographs on single countries were Stephen White's study of the USSR and David W. Paul's of Czechoslovakia, both published in 1979.[36]

Archie Brown, in his introduction to the collection of papers in 1977, asserted that it was the consensus of the nine authors of the volume 'that political culture may best be *operationalized* in the study of communist politics if its scope is defined in terms of subjective orientation and if its characteristics are not derived by generalising from observed behaviour.'

9

Brown thus defined the concept as 'the subjective perception of history and politics, the fundamental beliefs and values, the foci of identification and loyalty, and the political knowledge and expectations which are the product of the specific historical experience of nations and groups'. His argument was that it is useful to keep beliefs and values apart from behaviour in order not to 'jettison an analytical distinction which is useful if political culture is ever to play a part in the explanation of political behaviour'.[37]

Brown's distinction between beliefs-values and behaviour is not necessary, however, if the aim is not to explain political behaviour in a cause-effect way, but to try to elucidate how certain historically specific ways of ruling a population work or do not work. The behaviour of the population is then viewed as a clue to its values, its subjective orientation. This is a position similar to the one adopted later by one of the participants in Brown's own volume, i.e., Stephen White in his book on the USSR. Referring to Tucker (and some others), White defines political culture as 'the attitudinal and behavioural matrix within which the political system is located'. Dynamic processes within the political system and not its formal institutions thus come into the focus of interest.[38]

Mass—in distinction to individual—public behaviour which is politically relevant, i.e. which in an unambiguous way expresses attitudes to those in power in the society, I regard as an expression of the political culture of the collective actor in question. Strictly speaking one is referring to a political subculture as there is not in any society 'a single uniform political culture'.[39]

It is obvious that it is a question of at least two political cultures in Central European societies. H. Gordon Skilling, for example, writes of 'Stalinism and Czecholovak political culture'. Skilling takes care to note that the term 'political culture' is neither a 'magic formula' nor a 'precise theoretical concept'. It is, however, 'a notion useful in clarifying the meaning of Stalinism and the Czechoslovak setting into which it was introduced'.[40] As indicated above, this last assertion holds true also for other states in a position similar to that of Czechoslovakia. It must also be deemed valid for the post-Stalin era. To be able to capture the whole spectrum of political sub-cultures in a Stalinised society it is advisable, as Skilling and White have done, to take into consideration not just values, but also behaviour. This is also a help in discerning both continuity and change in a given society's political culture (or sub-cultures). As Skilling rightly observes, in each country within the Soviet empire, 'the emerging political culture was a complex one of many diverse elements, differing between countries and nations as to the relative continuity of the old and the degree of change'.[41] However, what remains of the old, dominant political culture, what is absorbed by the imposed new system (Stalinism), and what is distinctly novel, a developmental outcome, a new political culture, cannot be established once and for all. It emerges only in the course of history, not least in actions such as political upheavals, i.e., in behaviour.

After taking stock of the discussion of the concept 'political culture', I have chosen to use it for both attitudes — towards the real, existing, or towards an ideal political system — and behaviour which is politically relevant. I take the same eclecticist stand as David W. Paul and my analysis will rest on the definition of 'political culture' as 'an observable configuration of values, symbols, orientations and behaviour patterns related to the politics of a given society'.[42] As I understand the concept, 'political culture' generates a set of rules for actions that are permissible or nonpermissible — legitimate or illegitimate as it were — for the rulers in the eyes of the subjects. Incidentally, this definition comes very close to what Carl J. Friedrich calls 'political tradition' when he states that 'political tradition states how rule is conducted and how those who are being ruled behave towards the rulers'. But while Friedrich argues that political tradition is the main source of political legitimacy[43] — and he criticises Weber for missing a point here — I am using 'political culture' as a concept denoting the conditions or circumstances under which political legitimacy can be acquired. This use of the concept is to treat it as an intervening variable, as Lowell Dittmer defines it for cases when political culture is 'mediating between a political actor and an audience in a dynamic process'. In this perspective, a certain political culture is not regarded as a given constant but as something that is in the process of regeneration in political life.[44] The actual, empirical content of the concept in this view cannot be stated 'a priori' but will become apparent in the course of the analysis of the states under investigation.

It should be mentioned that there is quite another tradition of using the concept 'political culture' than the one I have discussed and will adhere to, namely one that sees the concept as expressing a norm, a condition for which a society should strive. In this tradition, which is upheld by some Soviet and Polish researchers, 'culture', and hence 'political culture', is defined according to the norm that 'culture' equals decency and orderly behaviour. This is evident in the statement, made in 1983 by a Polish political scientist, Czeslaw Mojsiewicz: 'The progress of that (political) culture is what Poland needs for today and for tomorrow'.[45]

The notion that there is a certain political culture determining the possibilities of legitimacy or, rather, of 'auxiliary legitimation', will serve as the structuring principle of my analysis and as the basis for comparison between the developments within Poland, Hungary and Czechoslovakia as well as for the analysis of the relations between these three countries and the USSR.

The method will be a qualitative-interpretative analysis of empirical facts and events. The developments in the respective states will be analysed with a view to their significance for political stability and Soviet security. As indicated above, the analysis will be couched in the terms 'political culture' and 'legitimation', referring, of course, to the same concepts.

Before entering the analysis, however, it is necessary to state the general epistemological and theoretical background of the study, its methodological principles and the criteria for the choice of source material.

Approach, method and sources

The concept 'political culture' refers partly to tradition. It is obvious that the political culture of the Soviet Union is significantly influenced by the Russian heritage. The Russian tradition is different from the Western one, which has set its imprint on the nations of today's Hungary, Poland, and Czechoslovakia. The political traditions of the past cannot be said to wholly determine the present political culture, but the latter can be understood as one of many possible outcomes of the former, and as its actual continuation. This is the premise upon which the following outline of salient features in the tradition is built.

The Russian state emerged in the 9th century. In 988 the ruling Prince in the capital Kiev, Vladimir, adopted Christianity from Constantinople (Byzantium). In contrast to the nations to the West, which became christianised from Rome, Russia, where the liturgical language was Church Slavonic, did not inherit the spirit of the rationalist Greek and Latin culture, nor did she inherit the notion of a distinction between secular and spiritual power, which became the norm in the Roman Catholic parts of Europe.

Russia was, with the exception of Novgorod in the north, separated from Europe from the early 13th to the late 15th century. During this period, she was part of the Mongol empire. Now Moscow became the capital of the Russian Great Prince, who acted as a plenipotentiary of the Mongol Khan. The subsequent political history of Russia became rather different from the Central and Western European varieties of feudalism. The common explanation is that the Russian rulers simply learnt from the Mongols. Against this view, the French historian Alain Besançon has objected that later Russian and Soviet despotism has been simply charged, in retrospect and with no historical grounds, on the noble and brave Mongols. The American historian Charles J. Halperin has underlined that the Mongols were hardly capable of 'isolating' Russia completely from the West. It was the Russian leaders who actively chose what to use: 'Russia did borrow from the Horde, copying military, political, and administrative techniques . . .'. Two other American historians, David MacKenzie and Michael W. Curran, have observed that Novgorod, which retained contact with the West, none-the-less 'in 1450 had advanced little beyond its status in 950', which was a marked contrast to the developments in the West. When one speaks of the 'Mongol heritage' one should keep in mind, then, that the Russian leaders could theoretically have chosen a Western and not a Mongol political culture. Apparently, the Mongol one was the one best suited to the Byzantine. The resulting despotism was a mixture of both traditions.

When Moscow liberated herself from the Mongol rule and gradually 'gathered the Russian lands' around herself, it was already with the help of despotic means. The Great Prince — who in 1547, under Ivan IV, adopted the title Tsar — was the Lord of the Church as well, according to the caesaropapist Byzantine tradition. Thus despotism and the amalgamation of political and spiritual power became part of the historical Russian political culture.

Russia in the Middle Ages and during the 16th and 17th centuries was a country without any significant secularised or profane culture above the popular level, i.e., a culture capable of assimilating the ideas of first the Renaissance and then the Enlightenment. There was neither an autonomous feudal aristocracy nor a domestic bourgeoisie to inspire cultural and political changes and reforms. It was not just a mere coincidence that the three major attempts to 'modernise' Tsarist Russia were initiated from above, by Peter I, Catherine II, and Alexander II, respectively.

Political power in the country remained autocratic, notwithstanding the attempts of the rulers to make Russia more 'European'. Not even in the 18th century, when Catherine II tolerated the influx of some of the ideas of the Enlightenment, did Russia have a modern legal system in the Western sense, i.e., with orderly judicial procedures, security of person and property, and politically independent courts of justice. It was on this political culture that Lenin and his Bolsheviks chose to build, when they introduced their 'democratic centralism' under 'the dictatorship of the proletariat'.[46]

The February revolution in 1917 constituted a break with the despotic political culture and the tradition of caesaropapism. The pluralist political sub-culture, which had emerged at the turn of the century, now seemed to become dominant. The October revolution in the very same year, 1917, actually meant a return to the old political culture, i.e., despotic rule by an autocracy and a merger of political and ideological power.

Important symbolistic traits of the Byzantine heritage in Tsarist Russia were the icons and the liturgy. These were preserved, although in a secularised form, after the October revolution. An icon is not a portrait, but a representation. The icon is not the saint but reminds one of him or her. Hence the faithful is assured that Heaven is with him and waits for him. In the same way, the pictures of the Soviet leaders carried in the processions on 1 May and 7 November every year should not be interpreted as portraits but as representations of the power which they embody — that of the Communist Party. Similarly, the ritualised participation by the audience in the speeches of the Soviet leaders with applauses, ovations, and genuflexes has its parallel in the singing and the rituals of the Russian Orthodox mass. This is a central part of Russian political culture which is alien to nations steeped in European, Roman Catholic and Protestant traditions.[47]

The Western tradition is far from uniform. Basically, though, it is one of competition, political pluralism, and civil rights. Today we equate pluralism with a democratic society, although Western feudal society was also pluralist, in a corporativist fashion. The estates had both rights and obligations to each other and to the central authority. The terrestrial centre of the Church was either separated from the local secular power, in the Roman Catholic countries, or nationalised and not regarded as universal, in the Protestant countries. In Central Europe — today's Hungary, Poland, and Czechoslovakia — society was dominated by the state. However, the Hapsburg emperor ruled with the help of a bureaucracy which more often than not applied legal rules and allowed both the courts and local interests to assert themselves. The gentry was a political force both in Poland and Hungary. Parliamentarism and universal suffrage were introduced into Poland and Czechoslovakia after the First World War. Nor was Hungary completely unaffected by such Western influences although fully fledged democracy did not establish itself there.[48]

One can regard the political traditions of Central Europe, in the area between the Germans and the eastern Slavs, as a distinct culture that naturally contained local characteristics. In the interwar years, it was markedly different from the Russian Soviet variety, and this difference was able to draw on a common heritage. The traditions which established themselves in the Middle Ages and became part of the political culture had their own characteristics that were different from Russian Byzantine and Mongol traditions. Viewing developments in Central Europe as a response to pressures from the German Empire, the Hungarian historian György Györffy has summarised what happened:

> The history of three neighbouring peoples shows marked similarities: the Czechs, Poles and Hungarians established their state and organized their church structure not only at the same time, but also in a very similar way: in Bohemia, the dynasty of the Premyslids, in Poland the Piasts, and in Hungary the Arpáds suppressed revolts by chieftains and those clans which were opposed to centralization, confiscated their castles and used these to construct coherent lines of fortifications.
>
> The princes also built an organization of agricultural and industrial servants around their scattered courts and mansions.

Rome encouraged the missionary bishops, and rulers obtained their own, more or less autonomous, church organizations.[49]

It is evident that Czechs, Hungarians, Poles and Slovaks, share a common or at least similar historical tradition. It is not necessary to go into the details of this history here. Suffice it to emphasise that any careful scrutiny of politically relevant statements and rituals in the Central European countries of today will clarify the significance of the perceptions of historical traditions and the presence of certain characteristics belonging to the inherited national political cultures. It cannot be said that the past exerts influence on the present in any direct, causal way, nor that the peoples in question believe that history will repeat itself. What is important is that contemporary Central Europeans show, both in stated arguments and in collective public behaviour, that they are conscious of and affected by the historical experiences of their respective nations. Contemporary problems are seen in the light of historical — or mythological — knowledge and understood as cases that are analogous to events in the past. Perceived history is a frame of reference.[50]

The above represents my 'pre-understanding' of the political culture of the countries being studied. These notions serve as my point of departure for an analysis of the political development within the states and the relations between them and the Soviet Union. It is important to point out that I am referring to my approach rather than my methods. I am sharing the view of Paul that this kind of study, based on the concept of 'political culture':

> . . . must proceed from a broadly based familiarity with the history, politics, sociology, economics, and intellectual patterns of that society — just as anthropological studies of specific cultures must proceed from a similar familiarity.[51]

My approach thus differs from the conventional historical one, as my pre-understanding is also based on my general personal experience of the countries in question, which I have acquired on the spot. Theoretically, personal experience might be compensated for by literature. In practice, however, it certainly does influence the researcher's perceptions and understanding.

My approach is hermeneutic in the sense that I view the behaviour and actions as meaningful and possible to interpret with the help of specific questioning. My kind of hermeneutics is 'semiotic', as I regard as meaningful messages or signs to be interpreted not only texts, statements in the natural languages, but also manners, rituals and symbolic corporal behaviour in general. One effect of this approach is that the question of validity cannot be solved once and for all, as the researcher/interpreter will remain the guarantor of truth, so to speak. This has to do with the nature of the sign:

> Semiotics — indeed the very definition of the sign — includes the interpreter (perceiver, addressee) as a constitutive component of meaning.[52]

According to this approach, there is no immanent meaning to be found in a human action or in an event. The concept of truth is pragmatic as the aim is not to find 'the essence' of something but to have actions and events make sense. The sense sought, in its turn, is not necessarily that of the individual actor — in that case, we would be dealing in psychology — but that of the culture of which the individual is part.[53]

Incidentally, the suggestion that a study in terms of 'political culture' should use a hermeneutic approach has also been put forward by two Finnish political scientists in relation to the analysis of one of the Central European countries, i.e., Poland. Ilkka Heiskanen notes that all politically relevant actions have got a 'symbolic' aspect, which demands interpretation. The researcher of a certain political culture has thus to consider not only written texts and orations but also institutional conduct and standard social practices:

> Thus a speech by a political leader may affirm the constitution, follow a ritualistic pattern, reflect the 'character' of the head of the State and/or display the expected features of a charismatic leader.[54]

Proceeding from this assumption, one will acknowledge that the range of 'objects of interpretation' is, potentially, very wide. Heiskanen's compatriot and colleague Erkki Berndtson has underlined the need for a hermeneutic approach by stating that to understand the different political development of different countries,

> one must . . . interpret the culture of these societies as texts in order to be able to see the real movement behind the structure.

Berndtson underlines that this implies that the researcher is also 'constructing a meaning into a society'.[55]

This hermeneutic approach is structural. The objects of research are not actors, but mentalities or collective minds. The level of analysis is supraindividual which means that the individuals, with their statements and actions, are viewed as representatives of their culture. What is sought is the typical and not the unique. The statements and actions registered and analysed are supposed to make sense, to be comprehensible, to the compatriots of the individual or individuals speaking or acting.

The study is not an analysis of the formal aspects of politics. Politics in

16

communist states cannot be approached through an investigation of formal institutions. These states are not governed, but ruled. Politics is not institutionalised but 'flourishes covertly in the "informal organization" of the system'.[56]

One effect of both the Soviet political system, which is also imposed upon the other WTO states, and the ideological notions and prescriptions of Marxism-Leninism, the state ideology which states that the policy of the ruling Communist Party may not be questioned, is that there is practically no access, for any researcher, to documents from the diplomatic sphere or from the decision making processes. The researcher has to use sources of different kinds that emanate from the societies in question in order to be able to learn something about, for example, political stability/instability.

This study postulates that political stability, when not accomplished through terror, is an effect of political legitimation, or of a functional equivalent to legitimation. Accordingly, the empirical investigation must pin-point the prevalent political attitudes of the population. In the societies under scrutiny, however, the political attitudes cannot be expressed either in free elections or through the free establishment of political organisations. Consequently, the researcher has to infer attitudes and values from data in areas of life that are not obviously political. In these societies, 'almost anything may take on political significance', as Paul observes, mentioning as examples religious beliefs, public gatherings, literature and the colour red.[57] Thus these and related phenomena acquire political significance, and the researcher may, by taking into consideration the context of their occurrence as well as his own pre-understanding of the culture in question, impute a certain meaning to them.

One aspect of politics is communication. There is a relationship between rulers and ruled, a process of outputs and inputs, actions and reactions. In a democracy with freedom of information the process is fairly transparent. In a dictatorship of the Stalinist type this is not the case. Thus our knowledge of the workings of the political process, and hence of one important factor behind stability/instability, in the Soviet Union and the other Soviet bloc states, is meagre. The researcher who is used to the study of politics in the West may experience both frustration and exasperation, when confronted with this reality.

One way of circumventing the feeling of frustration and exasperation is to free one's mind of methodological prejudices of what is and is not proper in the study of contemporary history. Instead one must ask oneself whether research has actually been carried out in an area confronted with a similar problem of source material and whether this research has been successful.

One then realises that methodological inspiration should be drawn from archeology, which knows how to reconstruct a meaningful whole from accidentally preserved fragments of material culture, and, more specifically, from historical research on the European Middle Ages, with its tradition, anchored in source criticism, of exacting information about political realities from scattered, preserved written documents, as well as from documents not directly emanating from the political process *sensu stricto*, e.g. annals and legends.

The archeologist-cum-medievalist approach to Soviet studies has been used consciously by the Danish historian Niels Erik Rosenfeldt, who has published two books on the political power centre of Stalin's Soviet Union. Rosenfeldt's results are important for the reasoning in my study, as they reveal the political structure of Stalinism, i.e., the concept that will be used here to denote political structure in the USSR and the Central European states. I will present Rosenfeldt's conclusions as well as the methods he has used, as both aspects are relevant for my own study.

An important point in Rosenfeldt's work is that he does not assume that the centre of political power is described as such in the primary sources available. This is akin to my notion that no direct statements about political power, legitimacy or political stability can be found in what is commonly regarded as primary sources, i.e., the remnants of official political life. In both cases, Rosenfeldt's and mine, the very object of investigation will have to be reached with the help of other types of evidence.

The interesting point of departure in Rosenfeldt's studies is not his observation that Stalin ruled the Soviet Union in an autocratic way without formal rules and checks but rather his assessment that to confine oneself to this observation is to imply that Stalin's load of work was literally superhuman. Rosenfeldt therefore starts from the hypothesis that Stalin had at his disposal an unofficial cabinet or a personal chancellery. There must be, Rosenfeldt asserts, a secret organ which was the organisational counterpart to Stalin's political power. Finding this organ, one will obtain an explanation of Stalin's seemingly superhuman influence.

By analysing statements in different contexts by Soviet subjects or ex-subjects, related to Stalin's closest entourage, as well as Party documents and scattered information on the structure of the Party apparatus and on potentially relevant individuals in Soviet books, magazines and newspapers, Rosenfeldt manages to corroborate the hypothesis about the secret organ. He proves that as early as the 1920s a secret department existed within the secretariat of the Communist Party. Within this department was also found to have been in existence, from 1934 on, a special sector. This was the real centre of power, unknown to the contemporaneous world. It fulfilled four important functions: (1) top security organ of the Party, (2) communication centre of the Party, (3) central chancellery of the Party, and (4) Stalin's personal secretariat.

Rosenfeldt interprets his disparate sources with the help of knowledge of the special cultural circumstances, such as the fact that anyone given a portrait with his biography in the Great Soviet Encyclopedia must be an important person (this was the case with Poskrebyshev, leader of the secret chancellery from 1928 until, probably, early 1953). Rosenfeldt also uses the well-known fact of the political purges in the mid-1930s as circumstantial evidence of a secret political centre. The political purge as an instrument was adopted in the Party statutes at the 17th congress of the Party in 1934. The new statute said that the Party, adhering to periodical decisions by the central committee, should systematically purge itself of 'class enemies', 'degenerates' and other 'scum'. The intriguing point in all this, Rosenfeldt underlines, is that the central committee apparently was ordered to purge itself, as the majority of its members had been purged and executed a few years after 1934.

Rosenfeldt came to the conclusion that the actual decisions to purge were not reached in the central committee. He observes that the number of different criteria of whom should be purged, was a reason to establish detailed personal files on everyone of political significance, files at the disposal of the competent organ, i.e., the special sector. Thus it becomes clear how Stalin could rule the Soviet state not through but behind the back of both the Party and its central committee.

Being human, Stalin was of course dependent on his social and political environment. But he managed to take advantage of the social forces and institutions at hand. With the help of close scrutiny of the sources, Rosenfeldt shows that it was the monopoly on information about the cadres along with control over the communication channels that allowed the secret chancellery of Stalin to cement his dictatorial powers and made every resistance pointless. With the help of a similar hypothesis about a secret chancellery or cabinet and analysis of circumstantial evidence of the situation, researchers such as the Polish sociologist and Solidarity aid Jadwiga Staniszkis, the exiled Polish historian of culture Krzysztof Pomian, and Adam Przeworski, a political scientist of Polish origin, have, as we will see, managed to give a credible explanation of General Jaruzelski's rise to power in Poland and his ability to act as dictator.[58]

It should be evident from what has been presented above that the methodological approach to problems of Soviet and East and Central European contemporary history must be functional in the sense that there are no sources neatly defined and at hand a priori. One has to start with the problem and then treat as sources, different kinds of remnants from the societies in question. What constitutes a 'source' thus depends on the kind of questions posed by the researcher.[59] In my case, the task is to try to find and analyse material that relates to the political culture of the Central European populations, material which reflects their attitudes and values and describes their — politically relevant — behaviour.

The choice of sources for this study may thus seem to be eclectic, since there is no archive or other limited deposit of information that has been systematically and thoroughly examined. The collection of material has been made with the view to the possibility of analysing the interrelated concepts of political stability/instability — legitimation — political culture. In principle, the amount of potentially relevant source material is almost infinite. The search for material has been brought to a halt when what has been analysed is sufficient to allow answers to the overriding questions of the study and rejection of alternative explanations of the events. The sources fall into three categories: (1) remnants — texts and observed and described behaviour — from the respective societies, (2) analyses carried out by researchers from the countries in question, living inside or outside them, the texts being both drawn for factual information of a descriptive nature and interpreted as signs of the respective national political culture, and (3) descriptions and analyses by Western scholars — here one also finds summaries of works belonging to my category 2 and data belonging to category 1.

The representativeness of individual statements and assessments in specific sources may always be questioned. The only possible criterion is to use circumstantial reasoning, i.e., to evaluate the material on the basis of pre-understanding of a general nature of the societies in question and of knowledge of the political, social or cultural status and significance of the individual quoted or referred to in the specific case. To help the reader understand the epistemological conditions, the sources will be characterised with respect to nationality. I am using the method of active interpretation which means that I am trying to see the Central European societies in question — above all the Polish and the Hungarian — from inside. The method should help to denote values that cannot be mapped with survey analyses or opinion polls. It is the quality, the intentional depth of the emanations that count, not their empirical quantity or frequency — but it does not represent an active moulding of source material of the sociological intervention kind, i.e., participation of the researcher in the political conflict being studied.[60]

Of course my use of earlier research does not imply that I have been out 'to seek confirmation for (my) opinions from other published authors'.[61] I regard the results and conclusions of others as findings to be used together with evidence from primary sources. I find it not only natural but also necessary to take advantage of the work of others, as my aim is not to find previously unknown empirial facts but to give a certain interpretation and to take part in the ever ongoing dialogue of historical and social research.[62]

By 'Central Europe' I mean today's Czechoslovakia, Hungary and Poland.[63] Austria is left out of the analysis because she does not belong to the Soviet bloc. The GDR is left out of the analysis, for three reasons. Firstly, Germany did not belong to the common tradition presented above. Secondly, the GDR cannot be said to have shown signs of political instability nor of having challenged the Soviet Union. The strikes and demonstrations in Berlin on 17 June 1953, were not followed by any profound changes either in the short, or in the long run. Thirdly, Germany was not originally perceived of by Stalin and his successors as part of the zone directly bordering on the Soviet Union, but as part of Germany and, hence, of 'the German question'. The GDR has been practically occupied by Soviet troops all the time from 1945 on. The problem of Soviet security has remained the prerogative of the Soviet leaders. The question of legitimacy for the GDR regime has not and need not be raised. However, the regimes of Czechoslovakia, Hungary and Poland, have presented a different state of affairs. Their behaviour and that of their subjects constitute the Central European security question for the USSR.

As Poland has proved to be the major permanent source of political instability in the Soviet bloc, the analysis of this country will form the core of the study. Poland's experience will be compared with that of Hungary after 1956. In 1956, Hungary challenged the Soviet supremacy more seriously than Poland, but thereafter the country has been politically stable. It stands to reason that a comparison of these two countries is fundamental for anyone aiming to understand the possibilities of and hindrances to political stability in the Soviet bloc.[64]

Poland's and Hungary's experiences will be compared with those of Czechoslovakia. The reason is that developments in Czechoslovakia in 1968 proved to be the third major challenge to the Soviet supremacy in the area. It was of an outspoken peaceful kind, obviously centred around the problem of regime legitimation. As the Czechoslovak attempt and its failure have been thoroughly analysed from the perspective of 'political culture' in previous research, my own analysis of this case will be brief and serve as an introduction to the scrutiny of Poland and Hungary.

After presenting the historical background to the study, i.e., the effects of de-Stalinisation, attention is directed towards a discussion of Czechoslovakia's 1968 experience.

The central part of the study is the rather detailed analysis of relevant characteristics in the development of Poland and Hungary, respectively. The respective analyses do not have an identical pattern but are instead structured on the specific processes and events that are salient for the questions of political stability and legitimation in the two countries.

The results of the previous analyses are brought together in a special chapter on Central Europe as a whole. The focus of interest is then switched to the Soviet Union and to the question of how her traditions as well as her experiences under the different challenges have affected the Soviet leaders' concept of security policy and of the relative importance of different foreign policy means.

The final chapter presents the conclusions to be drawn from the study.

Notes

1   Cf. the titles of Ascherson 1981 and Staniszkis 1982a.
2   Johnson 1982, p. v.
3   For the breakdown aspect, see Gerner and Hedlund 1982, Nuti 1982.
4   Pravda, 12 June 1981.
5   Bialer 1981, p. 522.
6   Larrabee 1981/2, p. 39, Summerscale 1982, p. 32.
7   Valenta 1981, p. 50 f.
8   Simes 1982, p. 55.
9   Andelman 1981–82, p. 90.
10 Lange 1981, p. 336 f.
11 Uschakow 1982, p. 31. See also Reddaway 1982, p. VIII.
12 Lüders 1981, p. 95.
13 Pravda, 12 June 1981.
14 *Poland. The State of the Republic 1981,* p. 102 ff., 114 (quotation). See also p. 96 ff.
15 Heller 1982a, p. 46.
16 Handel 1981, p. 127.
17 See Johnson et al. 1980, Jones 1980, p. 556 f., Kaplan 1982, p. 211 ff., Rositzke 1982, p. 142 ff.
18 Marer 1974, p. 144. See also Zimmerman 1978, p. 604 ff., Zimmerman 1981, p. 91.
19 Mlynár 1983a, p. 9 ff.
20 Arvidsson and Fogelklou 1983, p. 26. Rotschild 1977, p. 49 stresses that legitimacy is not a binary but an incremental quality.
21 Gitelman 1970, p. 242.
22 Heller 1982a, p. 49. Cf. Rotschild 1977, p. 42.
23 Rigby 1982, p. 7 stresses this point.
24 Weber 1958, p. 78 f.
25 Cf. Horowitz 1977, p. 23.
26 Rigby 1982, p. 10.
27 Heller 1982a, p. 51. Cf. Krisch 1982, p. 113, who uses the GDR as example.
28 Markus 1982, p. 88 f.
29 Åslund 1983. See also Gerner and Hedlund 1983.
30 Mlynár 1983a. For a summary of the thesis, see Mlynár 1983b.
31 Kaplan 1983, p. 39.
32 Cf. Rigby 1982, p. 17, Pye 1965, p. 8. Friedrich 1972, p. 114 stresses that 'legitimacy' and 'authority' should be kept apart analytically.
33 Cf. Terry and Korbonski 1980, p. 377.

34 See White 1979, p. 6, Pye 1965, p. 8, Hough 1977, p. 225, Paul 1976, p. 4. My understanding is the same as Gitelman 1970, p. 247, i.e. that the concept 'can indicate probabilities in group attitudes and behaviour'.
35 Tucker 1973.
36 Brown and Gray 1977, Paul 1979, White 1979. Cf. also Rupnik 1981.
37 Brown 1977, p. 9 f.
38 White 1979, p. 1 f., 5. (White is quoting Azrael 1970).
39 Pye 1965, p. 15.
40 Skilling 1977, p. 258.
41 Skilling 1977, p. 258 f.
42 Paul 1976, p. 4.
43 Friedrich 1972, p. 114 f., 17, 33.
44 Dittmer 1983, p. 20 ff.
45 Mojsiewicz 1983, p. 11. To denote what I have labelled 'political culture', researchers may also use instead terms as 'ethos' (see Sicinski (ed.) 1983) or 'national consciousness'.
46 I have discussed the question of the Russian heritage in today's Soviet Union at length in Gerner 1980a. For a general introduction to the problem, see Treadgold 1973. For a treatment of the problem of the lack of constitutionalism, see Raeff 1982. The works directly referred to in the text are: Besançon 1980, p. 121 f., Halperin 1978, p. 189, MacKenzie and Curran 1977, p. 79. For a discussion of the expansionism of Russia, see Barghoorn 1965.
47 Cf. Heller 1982a, p. 59 ff., Borcke 1981, p. 4 ff., Tucker 1977, p. XVII. See also Tumarkin 1983 for the Lenin cult as a Russian phenomenon!
48 Meyer, 1983, p. 6, Heller 1982a, p. 46, White et al. 1982, p. 43 ff.
49 Györffy 1970, p. 55 f.
50 Cf. Elster's 1976 discussion of the problem of 'hysteresis' and his definition of culture as the constantly repeated memory of the past. White et al. 1982, p. 53 note 'the retrospective glamour' of things past as an active factor behind recent political behaviour in, e.g., Czechoslovakia. Jönsson 1984, p. 33 notes that such perceptions can be the basis of projections into the future also.
51 Paul 1976, p. 8.
52 MacCannell and MacCannell 1982, p. 11.
53 MacCannell and MacCannell 1982, p. 58, 65, Eco 1975, p. 15 all stress this point. Shapiro 1980, p. 2, highlights that in political science this means that the researcher's attention is shifted from the intentions of the actor studied to 'the linguistic context within which it (the text) is produced'. The research therefore becomes an attempt 'to map the political culture of the writer'. Shapiro also underlines

that 'interpretative approaches share with explanatory (causally oriented) approaches to understanding human conduct the goal of searching for truth' (contextually defined).

54 Heiskanen 1983, p. 4 ff.
55 Berndtson 1983, p. 10 f.
56 Rigby 1982, p. 11. On the 'dual structure', see also Mlynár, 1983b, p. 10 f.
57 Paul 1976, p. 6.
58 Rosenfeldt 1978, Rosenfeldt 1980, Pomian 1982, Staniszkis 1982a, Przeworski 1982.
59 For an elaboration of the argument, see Tägil et al. 1977, p. 22 f. See also Nilsson 1973.
60 Touraine et al. 1983 demonstrate that 'the sociological intervention method' requires a whole team of researchers.
61 The quotation is from Jancar 1983, who criticises a colleague for such illegitimate practice.
62 Lindon 1982b, p. 337 f. indicates that there is still a research gap to be filled regarding 'comparative East European studies'.
63 Kundera 1984 includes Austria as well. But as this country does not belong to the Soviet bloc, I am leaving it out from the analysis.
64 Cf. Terry and Korbonski 1980.

2 De-Stalinisation in Central Europe and the Prague Spring

After Stalin

It is obvious that the regimes established with the help of the Soviet Army, the CPSU, and the Soviet security forces in Central Europe after the war, and consolidated in 1948–53, lacked political legitimacy. The regimes in Czechoslovakia, Hungary, and Poland were not firmly anchored in the national political cultures as they were imposed from the outside and basically were an extension of Soviet-Russian political culture. This was practically true already at the time of the establishment of communist rule. It became entirely true during the period of the anti-Tito campaign and the purges in the Central European countries in the early 1950s, when the vassals became completely 'Stalinised'.

If Stalinist rule imposed conformity and strengthened the similarity between the different regimes and political systems, the attempts at de-Stalinisation revealed diversities and differences between the constituent parts of the empire.

Thus it was not just a coincidence that de-Stalinisation had its first profound effects in Poland and Hungary in 1956. In the area between the Russian and the German empires, these Central European nations had a long history as states, as independent actors in European politics. They had regained full independence after the First World War. Stalin's new order was perceived there as subjugation under Russian rule, as an aberration. De-Stalinisation was understood as a promise of a return to normality, to a national policy, based on national traditions. The new regimes that were erected with Soviet help and under Soviet supervision in the period 1944–48, had completely lacked popular support.[1]

When Khrushchev and the CPSU seemed prepared to do away with the politically repressive Stalinist rule in the USSR, neither the populations nor what was left of leading 'national' communists in Poland and Hungary would accept the rule of the Stalinist Bierut and Rákosi regimes any more. Bierut died shortly after Khrushchev's de-Stalinisation speech, and Rákosi was removed. But this was only a beginning. In Poland in the summer of 1956, social upheavals against economic hardships assumed the character of a political challenge to the PUWP. Order was restored, but not without changes in the Party leadership. Gomulka, who had a reputation of being a 'national' communist and who had suffered political persecution and been imprisoned under Bierut, was appointed the new Party leader. After some hesitation, the Soviet leaders accepted the change.

In Hungary, there had been reshuffles in the Party leadership already some time before the Khrushchev speech. In late October, 1956, the newly reinstated Prime Minister Imre Nagy was carried away by the popular upheaval against Soviet rule. He endorsed demands for the introduction of a multiparty system and Hungarian neutrality in international affairs. This was too much for the Soviet leaders, who finally let the Soviet Army crush the insurrection. Nagy himself was finally captured by the Russians and eventually put to death.

What happened in Poland and Hungary in 1956 showed that the Soviet leaders would not tolerate any loosening of either the military security system as such or of the communist monopoly of political power in the individual vassal states. But developments which the Soviet leaders accepted in the two countries in the following years also showed that Khrushchev and the CPSU accepted deviations from the Stalinist model in the economic, social and cultural spheres. The net flow of economic resources from the vassals to the seigneur was stopped and even reversed.[2] This was paralleled by a change in the professed Soviet view of the nature of East-West relations. The thesis on the historical inevitability of an all-out war between capitalism and socialism was replaced by the notion of peaceful coexistence between states with different economic, social and political systems. This new doctrine, in turn, affected the conditions for political life in Stalin's European empire.

Under Stalin, uniformity, homogeneity and close Soviet control had been the norm in Soviet policy towards the vassal states. The subsequent development meant that different national traditions received some leeway. The security system established by Stalin proved to consist of three geopolitical elements: Germany, the Balkans, and Central Europe.

From the outset, the German question was the main problem in East-West relations. It continued to be a major problem when the successor states, the Federal Republic of Germany, FRG, and the German Democratic Republic, GDR, had been shaped. The GDR maintained its special, close relationship with the USSR after Stalin's death. The precarious international legal position of the regime and its inability to invoke any unambiguous national tradition made it completely dependent on Soviet political support and Soviet troops. No serious challenge to the original Stalinist conception of the nature of the relationship between vassal and seigneur could be said to have existed during either the 1950s or in the 1960s and 1970s. This central pillar of the Soviet security system has remained firm.

Stalin did not succeed with his attempt to dethrone Tito and incorporate Yugoslavia into his empire. But as it soon was evident that Yugoslavia led a foreign policy which also stressed independence from the West — Tito was, together with India's Nehru and Egypt's Nasser, one of the inaugurators of the association of nonaligned states in the 1950s — the Balkans, an area of strifes and perturbations for more than a hundred years, became a comparatively quiet and stable front in the East-West confrontation in Europe. As far as the elements of the Soviet security system were concerned, Bulgaria still followed the Soviet line closely. Romania pursued a more independent foreign and defence policy, and the regime appealed to Romanian nationalism, which, of course, had an anti-Russian flavour. But this offered no threat to Soviet security, since the country was (is) safely located between the USSR itself, Bulgaria, Hungary and nonaligned Yugoslavia and since the Communist Party remained basically Stalinist and did not pose any ideological threat to neighbouring Soviet Ukraine and Moldavia.

If there was a weak point in the security system left by Stalin, it was to be found in Central Europe. Developments in Poland, Hungary and Czechoslovakia made manifest a conflict between rulers and ruled which had remained latent under high Stalinism. The most obvious manifestations of the conflict were the upheavals in 1956 and 1980 and the reform movement in 1968. They had their roots in discontent with the existing order.

The processes in the respective states were different, both with regard to scope and with regard to setting in time and more long-term patterns. For the whole period 1956 to 1968, however, i.e., the period between the Polish October/the Hungarian revolt, and the end of the Prague spring, it can be said that the regimes of Gomulka, Kádár, and Dubcek showed signs of trying to rule with the help of appeals to national traditions in culture and promises of economic wellbeing and social welfare. It was intended that the lack of legitimacy should be removed with the help of the 'protector' and 'economic compensation' devices. As the change in policy was tied to the names of the Party leaders, one may speak of tendencies of trying to use their charisma as well.

In Poland Gomulka seemed to inaugurate a change of policy after 1956. The collectivisation of agriculture was discontinued and even reversed. Workers' councils were allowed to operate in mills and mines. Science and cultural life became less controlled and more diversified. Marshal Rokossovskii was dismissed as Minister of Defence and sent back home to the Soviet Union, and the Soviet government recalled its ambassador, who before 1956 had acted more or less as a general governor of Poland, and posted an 'ordinary' ambassador in Warsaw.[3] However, the rigid planned economy and the priority for heavy industry remained intact.

In Hungary, the Communist Party was reconstructed after its breakdown in October–November 1956[4]. A savage repression, which made it clear to the Hungarians that there was no alternative to Communist rule and Kádár, was followed, after some years, by a marked liberalisation of public life under the motto 'who is not against us is with us'. Soviet troops remained stationed in the country, but a general amnesty in 1963 marked a gradual shift away from the Stalinist model.

Czechoslovakia had her share of post-Stalin unrest in the form of workers' protests against material hardships in Plzen in 1953. The old Stalinist regime managed to handle this situation and remained in power until 1968. It was far from popular, but the standard of living was higher than in Hungary and Poland. This, and the fact that popular discontent, if it existed, was not automatically fuelled by anti-Russian sentiments of the same intensity as in Poland or Hungary, helped make the situation less explosive after Khrushchev's de-Stalinisation campaign. On the other hand, Stalinism continued to prevail in both economy and in cultural life well into the mid-sixties.

Czechoslovakia thus differed from Poland and Hungary both with respect to the point of time for and the manner of the challenge against the system set up by Stalin. In any case what happened in Hungary in 1956, in Czecholsovakia in 1968 and in Poland in 1980–81 apparently went beyond the limits of tolerance of the Soviet leaders, while the development in Hungary *after* 1956 has been tolerated and is obviously regarded in Moscow to be in accordance with Soviet interests.

After 1956: Some general remarks

The 1956 crisis is not treated as a problem but as a point of departure in this study. The reason is, of course, that the outcome of the upheaval in Poland showed that it was possible for the peoples of the vassal countries to exert influence on the political leadership. The whole Soviet system in Central Europe thus became potentially dynamic, especially as it was impossible to know in advance how much would be tolerated, by the Soviet leaders, of national diversification. It was evident to everyone that the vassal states were still pawns in the East-West game. However, what was not so evident, in the post-1956 era of peaceful coexistence, was where this game ceased to be relevant, i.e., how high the 'pawn-percentage' or share of absolute subordination to Soviet wishes really was. This had to be tested empirically. Developments in Czechoslovakia in 1968, in Poland in 1980–81, and in Hungary all the time since 1956, but especially since 1968, have been tests of this kind. As regards Hungary, it still continues in the mid-1980s. The problems then that pertain to the question of stability of the Soviet security system in Central Europe, are why the development in Czechoslovakia in 1968 was not tolerated, why the recurrent challenges in Poland were tolerated for twenty-five years, i.e., up to 13 December 1981, and why the Hungarian devolution of the Soviet model has been tolerated by the leaders in the Kremlin.

The specific events constituting the tests in the three countries will be discussed separately. Poland provides a focal point of the analysis, since the enduring challenge to the Soviet system in Poland must be said to be the most serious one and since she is the largest and thus potentially most dangerous vassal. Furthermore, of specific historic concern for every Russian leader, Soviet or non-Soviet, Poland acts as the traditional gate to Russia for the enemies — the Poles themselves in the early 17th century, the Swedes in the early 18th century, the French in the early 19th century, and the Germans in 1914 and 1941.

As regards Czechoslovakia the problem, from our perspective, is the year 1968. The test was limited in time and the outcome was unambiguous. It draws its main importance from being a case of comparison, both with Poland and with Hungary.

Hungary, in turn, is something of a red herring. One might argue that she should be left out of this investigation, as she evidently has not after 1956 been treated and probably has not been perceived as a serious challenge by the Soviet leaders: they have not intervened, neither directly nor by proxy. This objection is beside the point. For all practical purposes, what the Hungarians have been doing is not that dissimilar from what the Czechs and Slovaks were not allowed to continue. There may be crucial differences, of course. But if so, these should be pin-pointed as they may, perhaps, give us the clues to what promotes and alternatively undermines political stability in seemingly similar processes.

What is presented here are not narrative descriptions and general analyses of the political history of communist Czechoslovakia, Poland, and Hungary. These are available elsewhere.[5] The emphasis is placed on interpretation of the events and processes of relevance to the questions of political stability, legitimacy and political culture, and, hence, to the problem of Soviet security.

The formal institutions of political life in these communist states are not here treated 'per se'. The reason is that these institutions are strictly subordinated to the central apparatus of the Communist Party. When the national parliaments show signs of acting independently, as in Czechoslovakia in 1968 and in Poland in 1981, this is a symptom of crisis in the power structure and not an expression of its normal functioning.[6] The official political system, imported from the USSR is, in practice, a monoparty one. Furthermore, the principle of democratic centralism makes it strictly hierarchical and top-heavy. All organisations in society — trade unions, women's organisations, etc. — are functioning, ideally, as 'transmission belts' from top to bottom. The 'ideal type' of the communist state thus is one where the population is atomised, with the family as the primary group immediately facing the anonymous but all-mighty party-state power machine. The consequence is a gigantic political vacuum. There is no place for interest articulation and aggregation from below. Under genuine Stalinism, the vacuum is compensated for by state terror. Although the communist leaders do not dream of sharing power with their subjects, the significant reduction of terror must be replaced by other means in order to keep the population quiet. Difficulties of finding some substitute for terror must be seen as a general cause behind the crises in and after 1956 in the Soviet empire. And this is exactly where legitimation and attachment to historical political culture come into the picture.

A concomitant feature of the vacuum phenomenon is the lawlessness or illegality of Stalinist rule. Constitutions and laws are violated by the authorities at will.[7] Consequently, there is not much point in describing the formal legal system of the countries under analysis. When this comes into the picture, when people start to bother about it, this is already a sign of crisis in the relationship between the rulers and the ruled. Thus a potential for instability was revealed in Central Europe once Stalinist terror was slackened. The general precondition for political crises that have occurred has been well described by Archie Brown:

> In the absence of competitive politics, autonomous interest groups, and freedom for political protest, and in the presence of political censorship of the mass media, there is no reliable way of telling the Party leadership 'what the public will not stand'.[8]

When the public in communist states attempts to act by itself it can be either in the form of a spontaneous and not premeditated reaction to what is experienced as unbearable hardships: riots, strikes and demonstrations. Or it can be an organised and planned reaction: subterranean groups and societies, manifests and action programmes. In both cases, the actors' perception of the past is important. Behaviour tends to adapt to forms already tried or experienced in the past, either by the actors themselves or by their ancestors. Society has a memory. This memory is highly selective, however, and continuously remoulded by ongoing experience. The point is that when utopias and ideological blueprints of the future are hopelessly discredited by the actions and policies of the communist rulers, the peoples have sought inspiration and guidance in the past — that it is an idealised and even romanticised past seems likely, but this does not affect the validity of the assertion. People can be mobilised even with the help of pure myths and historical symbols.[9] The political vacuum is destroyed when the regime is openly challenged. But before this happens, the challenge is prepared in the ideological sphere. It is in this context that historical symbols and myths become significant.

When Stalinism, i.e., totalitarian control of all aspects of societal life with the help of both supervision and oppression in combination with complete subservience to the Soviet leaders, is challenged, the challenge of course may be of different kinds. It may come from the circles of the national communist leaders themselves, or from oppositional domestic groups, or from individuals from both categories, acting simultaneously or even in coordination. When Stalinism was going to be reformed, politics came to life again. The national political cultures became relevant. While Czechoslovakia in the mid-sixties was not the first example, it was very evident that it really was a matter of conflicting political cultures. Thus it is advisable to start the analysis with this example.

Czechoslovakia's challenge

For two reasons, the establishment of communist rule in Czechoslovakia in 1948 did not represent the clear-cut imposition of an a priori suspect system.

Although Czechoslovakia had been a multiparty, parliamentary republic during the interwar period and again from 1945 onwards, communism, and Stalinist communism at that, had rather strong domestic roots. Immediately after the war, the CPCS got support from roughly 35 per cent of the electorate. The Party had become Stalinised already in 1929. It adhered to the principle of democratic centralism and subordination to the CPSU. While the dominant Czechoslovak political culture was pluralist and imbued with democratic values of the European kind, there was a strong political subculture which was Stalinist. Furthermore, the popular belief in the viability of the old political system, parliamentary democracy, had become weakened by the fact that the First Republic had not been able to defend itself against Nazi Germany.[10]

Politically, the Czechs had been the dominating nation in the First Republic. They had a tradition of looking to the Russians as their big brother, as an asset in the struggle against German domination both before and after 1918. The first postwar years after 1945 saw an upsurge of pan-Slavist, pro-Soviet sentiments not only among communists. After all, this was a rather logical effect of recent experiences, i.e., ruthless German occupation followed by liberation of the country by the Soviet army. Soviet Russian and communist influence in political and cultural life was not whole-heartedly resisted by the political class. According to Czechoslovak sources, the population at large was not given, during the first postwar years, a realistic view of how things really were in Stalin's USSR. Although the definite communist take-over of power in 1948 resembled a coup, the ideological ground had already been prepared.[11] The exiled Czech historian Jacques Rupnik has summarised the four main traits of this voluntary preparation for Stalinism:

1 Benes's encouragement of 'a complete integration of Czechoslovakia into the Soviet sphere of influence' already in 1943–45;
2 The reduction of the scope for political democracy carried out by Benes and the communists immediately after 1945 through the banishment of the two largest political parties of the interwar period, the Czech Agrarian Party and the Slovak National Party, and by ruling that the remaining parties in the so called National Front had no right of going into opposition;
3 'The neutralisation of the works' council movement and the formation of a single trade union operating on the principle of "democractic centralism" ';
4 The expulsion of three million Sudeten Germans from Czechoslovakia according to the principle of 'collective guilt'. Thereby six hundred years of 'conflictual Czech-German coexistence' came to an end, and Czechoslovakia followed in the footsteps of Hitler's Germany and Stalin's Russia, which had also practised 'transfers' of this kind. Moreover, a precedent was set for the expulsion of any group from society on economic, religious and political grounds.

Rupnik labels all this 'the national and peaceful round to Stalinism'.[12]

Communist rule soon became utterly repressive. Firstly noncommunist politicians were mercilessly persecuted, and then there was a purge of communists accused of 'Titoism', 'cosmopolitism', 'Zionism' and 'bourgeois nationalism' as well. The economy and culture life became restructured according to the Soviet Stalinist pattern. Czechoslovakia became not only a vassal but also — *mutatis mutandis* — a fully fledged copy of the Stalinist system in its most repressive form. Stalinism reigned so supreme that it took Soviet influence to soften it a trifle, i.e., in connection with Khrushchev's de-Stalinisation campaigns in 1956 and 1961.[13]

Around 1963, the Czechoslovak economy began to run out of steam. The Stalinist model had become increasingly ineffective and, for the first time after the war, national income actually declined. As the terror had slackened, intellectuals were given some opportunity to analyse and criticise the shortcomings. Economics, sociology, and historical research were revived. A half-hearted rehabilitation of some of the victims of the Stalinist terror took place. Not only the bulk of the population but also many communists seemed to resent the existing order.[14] The Prague spring of 1968 was notable not least for the role played by the cultural intelligentsia in preparing the ground for the reform movement. Among Marxists, Karel Kosík and Radovan Richta were leading figures. The former stressed the humanistic aspect of Marxism, the teaching that socialism should end man's alienation, and the latter the scientistic aspect, the belief that a developed industrial society needed creative, thinking, and innovative citizens. Both views were compatible with the democratic and liberal national tradition.[15] The seasoned Stalinist Antonin Novotny remained in power, but 'the Novotny regime increasingly came to symbolise everything that was wrong with Czechoslovakia'.[16] The regime, which had portrayed itself as the one and only purveyor of welfare and prosperity, had failed. The burden of responsibility for the deterioration of the quality of life in Czechoslovakia was now cast upon it.

The Communist Party of Czechoslovakia rose to the occasion in early 1968, when Novotny was replaced as Party leader by Aleksander Dubcek. The new Party line, which was outlined in a so-called action programme in April, 1968, aimed at breaking up economic stagnation with the help of the introduction of a kind of socialist market economy, greater independence for individual enterprises and workers' councils in them. Censorship was practically abandoned. Science and the arts, which had already shown signs of vitality, were allowed to blossom. Soon the liberalisation process gained its own momentum. The philosopher Ivan Sviták put his finger on the sore point with his demand for democracy, not just 'democratisation'.[17]

In the course of the Prague spring, the traditional political pluralist culture of Czechoslovakia proved itself to be still alive. It had not been exterminated, far from it. It had not even just hibernated. It had become invigorated.

Public opinion polls regarding 'the relationship of Czechs and Slovaks to their history' were carried out in 1968. Comparisons with similar polls in 1946, i.e., before the establishment of communist rule, showed that the population's attitude to the First Republic was more positive in 1968 than in 1946. Now 39 per cent regarded the First Republic as the best period in Czechoslovak history — in 1946 the figure was 8 per cent. Now 81 per cent regarded the first president, Masaryk, as the greatest Czechoslovak leader ever — in 1946 the figure was 74 per cent.[18]

The 'rehabilitation' of the First Republic can most probably be explained with the help of an interceding variable between 1946 and 1968, i.e., the experience of Stalinism, the exposure to communist rule.[19] In comparison, the interwar period was seen in another light than in 1946, when it was perceived as the immediate background to the national catastrophe in 1938–39. The performance of the regime in the consumer commodity field had been so poor also that the prewar period was seen as better.

It is important to note that public opinion polls in 1968 also showed that an overwhelming majority of the respondents was firmly in favour of socialism and supported the reform policy of the Communist Party.[20] However, this was a support for democratic, even pluralist socialism. There were indications of a revival of noncommunist political parties, not least the Social Democractic Party.[21] What seemed to be the net result of twenty years' confrontation between traditional Czechoslovak political culture and the communist subculture, was that the latter became increasingly influenced by the former, and not the other way round,[22] as 'should' have been the case, according to communist doctrine. Communist Party leader Dubcek tried to express what had happened with the famous (for orthodox communists: infamous) words that one would create 'a socialism with a human face'.[23] It can be taken for granted that Dubcek and his supporters were thinking in the category *pars pro toto*: if the face became human, the whole body would as well.

Although the Dubcek regime assured that Czechoslovokia would remain a loyal member of WTO, it was obvious that the question of Czechoslovakia's position vis-à-vis the USSR within the pact was not above discussion.[24]

Although it was not questioned that Czechoslovakia would remain an active member of the CMEA, it was evident that the new economic policy would entail extended trade with the capitalist West and not least with the Federal Republic of Germany. Last but not least, while it was understood that the Czechoslovak communists would continue to preach Marxism-Leninism, there was no possibility of hiding the fact that Marxist-Leninist dogmas were disappearing from the Czechoslovak historical and social sciences. Soviet influence was on the decline in every respect.

The Czechoslovak reformist leaders and Dubcek personally tried to get support for their policy from the socialist neighbours Poland and Hungary. Gomulka was firmly against any reforms, however, and Kádár, who was actually embarking on a reform programme himself, preferred to keep a very low profile. No support from these quarters, then. Apart from this, the Dubcek regime did not try to strengthen its position against the USSR by diplomatic activity in the world arena. [25] Czechoslovakia had to face the USSR virtually alone.

In 1968, the German question was not definitely settled. Willy Brandt's Ostpolitik and Bonn's treaties with Poland and the USSR were still things of the future. Czechoslovakia, with her lengthy boundary with the Federal Republic of Germany, was a frontier state, a bulwark of the Warsaw pact.

When the Soviet leaders wanted to show their discontent with Dubcek's policies, one method was to let Soviet media publish fabricated 'news' of a planned West German aggression, 'documented' by 'findings' of West German arms 'hidden' in Czechoslovakia. A British scholar, Peter Summerscale, argues that a passus of friendliness towards the FRG in the CPCS Action Programme may have worried the Soviet leaders. But we cannot know if they really were that sensitive or only using 'the German threat' as a bogey.[26] An alleged 'German connection' thus was invoked to discredit Dubcek in the eyes of the Soviet subjects. But why? Why was the stamp of traitor fixed to the Czechoslovak leader?

With the abolition of political censorship and the revitalisation of noncommunist political life in Czechoslovakia, the monopoly of power of the Communist Party, and, perhaps, the principle of democratic centralism in it, were jeopardised. The freely voiced demands for complete rehabilitation of all the victims of the Stalinist terror and the appointment of a committee — the so called Piller committee — to investigate the whole phenomenon, threatened to undermine the very foundations for Czechoslovak reverence for and, in the long run, loyalty to Soviet wishes. It was no secret that the investigations would prove the deep involvement of the USSR in the Stalinist repression in Czechoslovakia at the time of the purges and show trials in the early 1950s. The CPSU would be portrayed as a major villain.[27]

As there were no violent uprisings and no popular mass movement challenging Soviet aspirations in Czechoslovakia, the Soviet leaders were not forced to take swift physical action immediately. With the help of verbal abuse and threats and ominous exercises with WTO armies around and even inside Czechoslovakia in the summer of 1968,[28] they tried to cajole the Dubcek group into submission and make it dismantle the reform programme. When Dubcek and his men refused to obey and instead prepared to broaden their support in the Party by convoking an extraordinary Party congress, the Soviet leaders found it necessary to take firmer action. On the night of 21 August 1968, Czechoslovakia was invaded by Soviet, Bulgarian, East German, Hungarian, and Polish armies. As has been underlined by Fred H. Eidlin, an American political scientist who happened to be there at the event, it was a 'strange "occupation"' as well as a 'strange "resistance"'. The occupiers were acting as if they seriously believed that they were supporting the 'legitimate institutions' of the Czechoslovak state. The occupied continued to give their support to the actual functionaries of these very same institutions. Thus 'it is clear that Soviet policy aimed at securing the voluntary cooperation of individuals holding legitimate functions and commanding indigenous political bases'. The Soviet action was not an ordinary occupation but rather 'the ultimate form of political pressure'.[29] It turned out that the 'occupation' was not the end of the reform regime. It was only the beginning of the end. So called normalisation was not completed until Dubcek, under increasing Soviet pressure on the Czechoslovak CP, was sacked and replaced by Gustav Husák in April, 1969. The rationale behind the official Soviet line was formulated in the Soviet *Pravda* on 26 September 1968. In an article by a certain Professor S. Kovalev, it was stated that:

> Communists in fraternal countries of course cannot tolerate that the socialist states remain passive, referring to an abstract notion of sovereignty, once they learn that there is a risk that antisocialism is reborn in the country. . . . When the counter-revolutionary elements in Czechoslovakia attacked the foundations of socialism, they undermined the bases of independence and sovereignty of the country. A formal attachment to the nation's right to self-determination would in the concrete circumstances in Czechoslovakia have meant freedom to 'self-determination', not for the toiling masses but for their enemies . . . .[30]

This became known in the West as the Brezhnev doctrine.

During Husák's rule, the whole reform programme was scrapped, with one exception. Czechoslovakia became a federated republic, with Slovakia gaining a certain autonomy from Prague. The age-old pattern of Czech dominance over the Slovaks was broken. But in the main there was a return to Stalinist policies. As the habit of executing political adversaries was not revived, one may speak of 'a Stalinism with a human mask'. Politically, economically, culturally and ritually, Czechoslovakia was completely subordinated to the USSR. Husák repeated the words of the late Stalinist party boss Gottwald 'with the USSR for ever', adding that this was 'the life credo of all our toiling masses'.[31]

One consequence of the invasion in August 1968 and the following normalisation of Czechoslovakia, was that almost every trace of pro-Russian sentiments, belief in 'socialism' as something good for the people, and in Marxism, disappeared. The atmosphere was one of 'gloom, withdrawal, and alienation'. The difference between Czechoslovak national traditions and political culture, on the one hand, and communism and Soviet ways, on the other, became more obvious than ever before. At the end of the 1970s, the abyss separating the imposed political system from the dominant (though suppressed) political culture was deeper than at any time after 1945.[32] The Communist regime in Czechoslovakia lacked any kind of voluntary support: 'No end was yet in sight to the legitimacy crisis'.[33] On top of this political liability, this potential threat to stability, came the failure of the 'economic compensation' trick. The Czechoslovak economy became dependent on Soviet subsidies in different forms, and in spite of this, an economic crisis of the same seriousness as the one which triggered the reform movement in 1968 was mounting in the early 1980s.[34]

The solution chosen to the problem of democratisation in Czechoslovakia perhaps was the best one possible in the short run for the USSR, given the circumstances. But as Czechoslovakia became a liability and a burden, it was not an ideal solution.

Political stability was resurrected in Czechoslovakia with the help of oppression and not through legitimation of the regime. The 1970s were characterised by political apathy. Several hundred thousand members of reformist persuasion left the Communist Party. The best and the brightest were ostracised from economic and cultural life. A secret poll carried out in Czechoslovakia by the oppositionist 'Listy' group in 1980 witnessed about the apathy. As one respondent, an ordinary teacher, put it:

> The only thing which truly brings us together (including, probably, president Husák himself) is our antipathy for the USSR and the Red Army stationed here. And this is a battle cry that cannot be used publicly.[35]

Eidlin observes that 'political stalemate' remained the central problem in Czechoslovakia.[36] This kind of political stability ought really to be termed 'immobility'.

Eidlin has shown that the Soviet leaders could not un-make what had happened in Czechoslovakia during January–August 1968. The Czechoslovak population had, through the revitalisation of the traditional national political culture, become 'premobilised' to react to the invasion by withdrawing all support from the Husák regime.[37] But at the same time, the reasons of the Czechsolovak defeat in 1968–69 are also to be found in tradition. In the Czech journal *Reporter*, renowned for reformism in 1968, Milan Jungmann wrote on 16 October 1968, that Czechoslovakia, although it had a great culture, had 'no policy whatsoever of its own', and on 30 January 1969, Jiri Hanak observed that the feeling that 'we are small and weak' had proved to be a rationalisation for defeatist attitudes. Otto Ulc, an exiled Czech political scientist quoting these examples, adds that after the establishment of the Husák regime, all attempts by the people to try to influence policies were considered illegitimate by the rulers, and treated accordingly:

> It remains a gargantuan task to generate devotion and ideological commitment in a people equipped with the memory of recent events and with cognizance of the transient nature of whatever values are accepted at any given time. For example, the series of transformations that Dubcek went through in August, 1968 is well remembered: on August 3 he was embraced and kissed by Brezhnev in Bratislava; on August 21 he was arrested in Prague; on August 22 he was denounced in *Pravda* as a rightist opportunist; on August 26 he was a signatory of the Moscow

Protocol. While aware of their own political impotence, the Czecholovaks are also aware of the weakness of the system.

Developments in Czechoslovakia after 1968 have not seen a return to a pluralist political culture. The reformist Charta 77 movement has been ruthlessly suppressed and has not managed to gain any substantial following among the population. The Party leaders have shown no sign of trying to legitimate their rule. Rather they have called for what Ulc labels 'national amnesia' and endorsed as praiseworthy the denigration of national sovereignty by signing, in 1970, a treaty of friendship with the Soviet Union that, according to the Czechoslovak Foreign Minister Jan Nemec, included a principle that implied that 'the entry of allied armies in 1968 was completely legal and in accordance with international agreements concluded at the highest level'.[38]

We need not speculate about discussions in the Soviet Politbureau prior to the decision to invade Czechoslovakia in 1968, to be able to conclude, with Jiri Valenta, that 'Soviet responses to such developments are neither automatic nor foreclosed'[39] and, with Eidlin, that the consequences of the action were largely unintended and that Soviet policy in situations as complicated as this one is neither 'successful, prescient, rational, coherent' nor 'consistent'.[40] The Soviet 'solution' to the security problem in Czechoslovakia in 1968 has not been unambiguously advantageous to Soviet interests. A potentially disloyal vassal country with an economy which cannot sustain growth by its own means, is a fragile foundation for Soviet security.

Czechoslovak-Soviet relations were originally much better than any other Soviet-Central European relation. Immediately after the war, Czechoslovak leaders expressed their feeling of sympathy for and community with the Slavic state the Soviet Union, 'the victorious Slavic Great Power in the East'. This was true not the least of the Czechoslovak communist leaders, who took over the rule of the country in 1948.[41]

However, the pan-Slavism and Russophilism which had been 'enormously strengthened' during the Second World War, disappeared as a consequence of the Soviet-led invasion of Czechoslovakia in 1968. A survey carried out in October, 1968, showed that Czechs and Slovaks considered Austrians and Germans, and Poles and Yugoslavs, respectively, to be closer to themselves than the Russians.[42] The action of the Soviet and other WTO troops in August, 1968, is treated in an official Soviet handbook on Soviet foreign policy under the heading 'The USSR Strengthens Solidarity Among Socialist Countries'. This indicates that the Soviet decision makers are interested in maintaining a facade of legitimacy for their military occupation. The majority of Czechs and Slovaks, who, according to polls, supported the policy of the Dubcek regime[43] are dismissed, in the Soviet book, as 'internal counter-revolutionary elements'.[44]

The evidence of the Czechoslovak polls in 1968, on the one hand, and the Soviet description of events, on the other, confirm that Skilling is correct in his assessment of Dubcek's plight in the period between the invasion and the date of his dismissal (April 1969): 'In fact Dubcek was attempting the impossible — to satisfy both the people and the Russians'.[45] It seems likely that the Soviet leaders can regain the sympathy and confidence of the peoples of Czechoslovakia only if they withdraw their troops and support for the Husák regime, allowing Czechoslovakia to decide her policies herself. As long as this is utopian, Czechoslovakia will remain profoundly alienated — that is the people, not the communist rulers — from almost everything that the Soviet Union stands for. In times of crisis, this must be regarded as a liability rather than an asset for Soviet security concerns: Czechoslovakia needs to be policed at all times, because the Soviet leaders cannot feel confident that the majority of the Czechoslovak people supports its own regime.

Notes

1 Cf. Molnár 1978, p. 133, Lamentowicz 1983, passim.
2 Zimmerman 1978.
3 Lidert 1982, p. 42.
4 Molnár 1978, p. 48 ff.
5 See e.g., Suda 1980, Skilling 1976, Paul 1979, Simon and Kanet, ed. 1981, Woodall, ed. 1982, Kovrig 1979, Toma and Volgyes 1977, Molnár 1978.
6 Cf. Terry and Korbonski 1979, p. 387. Ruane 1982, p. 36 notes that when the crisis hit Poland in 1980, the Diet (the Sejm) had not 'worked' for 25 years.
7 See Ruane 1982, p. 85.
8 Brown 1979, p. 167.
9 For an analysis of this phenomenon in the USSR, see Lane 1981. Cf Brown 1979, p. 168, Goldstücker 1982.
10 Skilling 1977, p. 264, Rupnik 1982, p. 305 ff.
11 Müller 1977, 114 ff., 133 ff., Skilling 1977, p. 264 ff., Brown and Wightman 1977, p. 172, Kovály and Kohák 1976, p. 40, 155 f. Taborsky 1981, p. 232 f. shows that Benes, the President, also trusted the good will of the communists.
12 Rupnik 1982, p. 314 f.
13 Brown and Wightman 1977, p. 188.
14 Skilling 1976, p. 57, 91 ff.
15 See Golan 1976.
16 Eidlin 1980, p. 196.
17 Skilling 1976, p. 357 ff.

18   Brown and Wightman 1977, p. 164 ff., Brown 1979, p. 154 f. See also Ulc 1974, p. 8 f., 35.
19   Brown 1979, p. 154 f.
20   Brown and Wightman 1977, p. 174, Skilling 1976, p. 199 f.
21   Suda 1980, p. 333 f., Müller 1977, p. 281, Skilling 1976, p. 527 ff., 546 ff., Ulc 1974, p. 59 ff.
22   Brown and Wightman 1977, p. 159.
23   See Skilling 1976, p. 209 ff. for Dubcek's 'democratic' speeches in March and April, 1968.
24   Müller 1977, p. 270 ff., 390, Golan 1971, p. 312 ff., Skilling 1976, p. 629 f.
25   Müller 1977, p. 244 f., 261.
26   Golan 1971, p. 327, Summerscale 1982, p. 43.
27   Skilling 1976, p. 836 ff., Kaplan 1982, p. 277 ff.
28   Müller 1977, 270 ff., Valenta 1979, p. 42 ff.
29   Eidlin 1980, p. 207, 244 (first quotation), Ulc 1974, p. 144 (second quotation).
30   Quoted from Liess 1972, p. 124. See also Skilling 1976, p. 729.
31   Koleznikov 1980, p. 89.
32   Ulc 1974, p. 144, Brown and Wightman 1977, p. 190.
33   Suda 1980, p. 374.
34   Kusin 1982, p. 24 ff., Swartz 1982.
35   Telos 1981, p. 157. See also Ulc 1974, p. 144 ff.
36   Eidlin 1980, p. VI.
37   Eidlin 1980, p. 31 f.
38   Ulc 1974, p. 142 ff.
39   Valenta 1979, p. 162.
40   Eidlin 1980, p. 31, VII.
41   Müller 1977, p. 114 ff., 133, 151.
42   Brown and Wightman 1977, p. 172, 182 ff.
43   Skilling 1976, p. 552 ff.
44   Soviet Foreign Policy 1981, p. 323, 327.
45   Skilling 1976, p. 819.

3 The troublesome Poland

Between Germany and Russia

The social upheaval and political activities in Poland in 1980–81 have been called 'the self-limiting revolution' by active participants as well as informed observers.[1]

The spokesmen of the opposition in Poland kept asserting that the activities directed against the government and the ruling Communist Party were not political but trade unionist, and, above all, that there was no questioning of established Polish foreign policy. In practice, the opposition could not help spilling over into the area of political opposition, since the struggle concerned the management of the Polish economy, the power over allocation of resources, which is ultimately a question of political power. Once the monopoly of political power of the Party was called into question, Poland's relations with the USSR also became a matter of discussion.

What happened in Poland in 1980–81 was the culmination of a crisis that had resurged from time to time after 1956. The immediate background to the outburst in 1980 was the result of events in the summer of 1976. In June that year the authorities suddenly decided to increase food prices. This was met by workers in Radom and in the Ursus tractor factory outside Warsaw with strikes and demonstrations. This unrest was countered and subdued by police force, but the decision to increase prices

41

was withdrawn. The regime had shown itself to be both brutal and politically weak.

Violent confrontations between the communist rulers and different groups of the people had taken place before in postwar Poland. Both in 1956 and in 1970 workers had gone on strike and compelled the Party to change leaders, while in 1968 students demonstrated in Warsaw. What was new in 1976 was the reaction after the event. For the first time, oppositional workers and dissident intellectuals joined forces and began to cooperate systematically. Some intellectuals organised special committees for 'social self-defence' and 'defence of workers' — KSS and KOR. Some workers, notably in the Baltic area, began to organise independent, clandestine free labour unions. There were personal links between the different movements.[2] An alternative society emerged, a little along the lines of the occupation years, with 'flying universities', journals, and a publishing house, 'NOWA'.[3] One turned against official lies regarding contemporary conditions in Poland as well as against the communist falsification of history. The history of Poland and her international political situation began to be discussed from perspectives that had been made taboo by the rulers.[4] The two aspects proved to be interrelated, as a nonfalsified picture of Poland's recent history must place the USSR in a far from flattering light.

The development after 1976 thus was not just a strictly internal Polish economic, social, cultural and political crisis. As the crisis matured, oppositional Poles were forced, by the logic of the situation, to introduce into public (though nonofficial) discussion the question of Poland's subordination to the USSR, and the relevance of this subordination for the accumulating problems. In this context, Polish traditions, Polish history and Polish political culture became increasingly salient. As early as May, 1979, the DiP group had reached the following conclusions:

> . . . the state of public consciousness is just as real a fact as the existence of social classes. People's acts, opinions and aspirations are equally produced by the content of the consciousness.
>
> The source of the public consciousness in Poland today lies in the nineteenth century (particularly its second half) and in the first half of the twentieth century. Modern political thought emerged during this period; timetables were set and choices made that are often relevant to this day.
>
> This brings us to the most important and at the same time most difficult problems with which we have yet to deal: constructive proposals or ways to heal the Republic. It is the conviction of our respondents that the most important points at issue here are our national sovereignty, the existing state of international

relations, and external conditions that impinge on us.

. . . public opinion in Poland, in the view of our respondents, sees a deep contradiction between the interests of Poland and the present configuration of international relations, between the interests of the outside world and our national interests.[5]

The views recorded by DiP were the views of intellectuals placed high up in the social hierarchy and with access to information about the conditions in Poland. The quotations above can be regarded as expressing what informed Poles knew and thought, but could not state publicly at that time, i.e., that the political thinking of the Poles is influenced by perceptions of Polish history, and that the experience of internal crisis is linked to the historical question of Polish independence and sovereignty.

To be able to interpret the meaning of the political public debate and of certain public acts in Poland in 1976–81, the investigator, as well as the reader of this study, must have his (her) own picture of Polish history to which to refer. It is therefore necessary to carry out a brief survey of modern Polish political history.

The Polish nation is situated, on the east-west axis, between Germans and East Slavs — the latter dominated by the Russians. Whenever Prussia or Germany and Russia or the USSR have been strong, the Poles have had great difficulties in defending their national independence. It is significant that Polish state sovereignty was reborn in 1918, when both Germany and Russia were temporarily weakened, and that sovereignty ceased once these countries had regained strength and joined forces in 1939. The first three partitions of Poland took place in the late 18th century, with Austria taking part, in addition to Prussia and Russia, in the first and the third.

The Dual Monarchy Austria-Hungary was dissolved after its defeat in the First World War in 1918. It was succeeded by the national states Austria, Hungary, and Czechoslovakia, with the remaining parts of the old empire going to Italy, Romania, Yugoslavia, and Poland, respectively.

When Poland was resurrected, the reborn state found herself in conflict regarding her boundaries not only with Germany and Soviet Russia, but also with Czechoslovakia — over the Duchy of Teschen — and Lithuania — over Vilna and the surrounding district.[6] To find a viable solution for Poland was not easy, especially as political groups in Poland in 1918 held different opinions regarding which foreign policy line should be chosen.

There were three currents of thought in Poland in 1918 concerning the territorial location and status of the state. Russian-orientated communists asserted that the national state belonged to the feudal and bourgeois past and that the Poles should join the East Slavs in a proletarian dictatorship, which would soon, after the spread of the revolution, include the Germans as well. This line was not supported by many Poles, however, as was to be proved during the Polish-Soviet war in 1920.[7]

The other two streams of thought were not geared towards utopia but anchored in Polish history. The 'Jagellonian' idea consciously referred to the tradition of the Polish-Lithuanian union and aimed at resurrecting the frontiers of 1772 (i.e., before the first partition) and creating a federative state, with Lithuanians and Ukrainians (Belorussians were hardly considered as a nation in their own right) subordinated to the Poles. Poland would, in this conception, be the Great Power of East Central Europe, barring Russia and Bolshevism from any contact with Germany. This line was pursued by the first Head of State and Commander-in-Chief, Pilsudski, who had made his political career in the Polish Socialist Party (PPS) and his military career as the leader of the Polish Legion, which fought the Russians on the German side until Pilsudski came into conflict with the Germans over the future Polish state. As a result he spent the final stages of the World War in a German prison. His reputation as a Polish patriot was unblemished.

What may be labelled the 'Piastian' conception referred to the oldest Polish state from the tenth century, which was situated more to the West and included what later became German East Prussia, Posen, and Silesia. According to this conception the whole Duchy of Teschen, as an old Piastian land, should belong to Poland. Politicians in favour of this line were also in favour of an ethnically and culturally-religiously homogenous Polish, Roman-Catholic state; during the partition this had been combined with a pro-Russian (pre-October, 1917!) stance, epitomized by the National Democrats under Dmowski.[8]

While the Polish boundary with Germany was delimitated according to the decisions of the Paris peace conference in 1919, the Poles under Pilsudski did not accept the so called 'Curzon line' in the east, which would have left the major part of Western Ukraine (with Lvov) and Belorussia in Russian hands. The outcome of the war with Soviet Russia in 1920 meant that the border line was drawn further to the east, giving Lvov to Poland. Vilna was conquered by the Poles and thus the new Lithuanian republic had to content itself with Kovno as capital. As a result of a decision by the victors of the World War in 1920, Teschen was divided between Poland and Czechoslovakia at the very time when Poland's situation was especially precarious, as the Soviet Red Army was approaching Warsaw.

The Polish republic, although ethnically and culturally heterogenous, did not become a federation along 'Jagellonian' lines. The Polish dominance was clear. Nationalism was fuelled not only by tensions with Ukranians, Germans, and Jews in Poland, but also by the enduring conflicts with Czechoslovakia over Teschen — the Polish authorities never became reconciled with Czechoslovakia's retention of the better part of the former Duchy — and with Lithuania over the Vilna district.[9]

Although the boundary question seemed to be settled in late 1920,

Poland's position still left much to be desired. Relations with all the neighbouring states had been soured and the country was politically split. Important questions remained to be solved: which economic policy should be chosen, how should division of power between the executive and the legislative be arranged, how should relations be with regard to the national minorities? In 1930 there were 4.8 million Ukrainians, 2.7 million Jews, 1.5 million Belorussians, 700,000 Germans, 80,000 Lithuanians and Russians each, and 30,000 Czechs, (the Poles themselves amounted to 22 million).[10] In 1921 the political right and centre, with leaders as Dmowski, and Witos, respectively, were able to get a constitution passed in the Diet *(Sejm)* which made Poland a centralised state that gave little power to the Head of State and made the government responsible to the *Sejm.* An obvious immediate reason behind this choice of policy was to try to keep Pilsudski out of power by making the office of Head of State politically unattractive.

The new Polish state was ridden by high unemployment, rural poverty, and inflation. The economy was difficult to manage not least because of the fact that the respective parts of the partitioned country had been integrated into Germany, Russia, and Austria. Reintegration into the new Polish state proved difficult. Politically, the country was split up between more than 60 parties, half of whom were represented in the *Sejm.* Government crises succeeded one another. The bureaucrats retained their habits of corruption, while the people at large continued to regard the authorities as an alien evil that should be cheated whenever possible. This was also a part of the heritage from the partition period.

In foreign policy, there were problems with Weimar Germany, which refused to recognise the settlement of the frontier question as final (although Germany's government accepted her boundaries to the west in Locarno in 1925). To the east was the USSR, deprived of parts of the Ukraine and Belorussia. In 1922 Germany and the USSR began to cooperate closely in economic and military affairs (the Rapallo agreement), and in April, 1926, these two states signed a pact of nonaggression and neutrality. At this time, Poland and Germany competed for permanent representation in the Council of the League of Nations.

In the spring of 1926 demonstrations against unemployment turned into upheavals that were violently crushed by the government. The left was kept out of a new government, led by Witos, which was appointed on 10 May. At this juncture, Pilsudski chose to re-enter the scene. On the 12 May he marched on Warsaw with loyal troops. These had been concentrated close to the capital by General Zeligowski (an associate of Pilsudski and the man who was in charge of the occupation of Vilna back in 1920), who had been Minister of Defence prior to 10 May. Pilsudski's declared aim was to make the President, Wojciechowski, dismiss the Witos goverment, which, Pilsudski argued, was leading the country to catastrophe by undermining the authority of the armed forces and thus jeopardising the external security. The President, however, refused to yield, which led to an armed struggle. The government was defended by troops commanded by officers who were adversaries of Pilsudski, i.e., professional officers who had, before 1918, served in the Imperial and Royal Austrian Army. The government most probably could have suppressed the revolt, had it been reinforced with loyal troops, especially from the western areas, where Pilsudski was not very popular. The railroad workers, however, who were organised in a union under the influence of the PPS, blocked the transport of loyalist troops to Warsaw. On the evening of 14 May, the government troops capitulated to Pilsudski. The speaker of the *Sejm* became provisional president. He appointed a new government with Pilsudski as Minister of Defence. Parts of the political centre, and the whole left, including the Communist Party, supported Pisudski's coup and the new government (although the communists were soon ordered by the Comintern to withdraw their support).

After 1926 the government became more independent of the *Sejm*, particularly in relation to the formulation of foreign policy. Pilsudski had himself elected President, just to demonstrate that he had the confidence of the people. Once elected, he resigned from the post and was succeeded by Moscicki, a man of no political importance. Pilsudski contented himself with the posts Minister of Defence and Commander-in-Chief, which he kept until his death in 1935. For two periods, he was Premier as well. He was bestowed with the honorary title 'Father of the Fatherland'.

Pilsudski's new government was to stand above the political parties. It would 'sanitize' politics and labelled its own policy *sanacja*. The administration became increasingly filled with military men. The former legionaries, i.e., the old followers of Pilsudski, revolutionaries turned officers, advanced at the expense of the former Austrian officers and those who had resisted the coup in 1926. In 1932 the legionaries definitely took over foreign policy, when Colonel Beck was appointed Foreign Minister.[11]

Pilsudski and Beck tried to improve relations with Germany. In January 1934, a pact of nonaggression was concluded with Hitler's Germany. (A similar pact was concluded with the Soviet Union in 1932.) During the later 1930s, Beck tried to have Poland lead an independent foreign policy as an East Central European Great Power, but in the wake of the German advancement. This was especially evident regarding the policy towards Czechoslovakia. During the Sudeten crisis in 1938, the Polish government kept demanding that the Polish minority in Czechoslovak Teschen should have the same national rights as were given to the Sudeten Germans.

Poland's quarrel with Czechoslovakia in the interwar period, and especially from 1934 onwards, was about some 100,000 people in a small area. It was this very question, however, which turned out to make impossible any co-operation, under French influence, between Poland

and Czechoslovakia against Germany. Polish propaganda portrayed the Czechs as pro-Russian pan-Slavists who formed a potential bridge to Europe for the Bolsheviks. Furthermore, Czechoslovakia was perceived of as a barrier between Poland and her 'natural' ally, Hungary. One can safely say that Poland's bad relations with Czechoslovakia paved the way for Hitler's irredentist policy, the ultimate victim of which was to be Poland.[12]

The outcome of the Second World War and the incorporation of Poland into the Soviet empire, severed Poland's contacts with Europe and the European culture of which the Poles had been an integrated part. Then came de-Stalinisation and October 1956. This affected Polish foreign relations as well. On 18 November 1956, a common Soviet-Polish declaration was signed, which was meant to signify a change in the relations between the two parties. 'The union and the fraternal bonds' should become 'broadened and confirmed and be developed on the basis of complete equality . . . sovereignty and non-interference in internal affairs.'[13]

According to the November declaration, Poland should be allowed to build socialism in a national way, without slavishly copying the USSR. According to a semi-official Polish commentary on the 25th anniversary of the declaration, in 1981, the ruling communists had not, before 1956, 'sufficiently observed the fact that they were at the head of historical states with definite cultural traditions and aspirations for an autonomous life and sovereignty'. The same source said that in 1956 it had also become evident that the relations between socialist states were traditional interstate relations, a fact to which attention had not been paid before 1956. One took care to note, however, that Party relations and ideological bonds remained intimate.[14] The point is that after 1956, the 'special relations' with the USSR were specifically tied to Party, and not state, institutions. It became possible, at least theoretically, to pose the question if it was necessary for Poland to regard the Soviet state as her protector. The 'Al Capone relationship' of course remained in force, but it concerned the Party and not necessarily the state and thus might not be eternal. Anyhow, this kind of reasoning surfaced twenty years later during the struggle over the new constitution in 1975–76 (see later comment). The possibility of a rebirth of politics in Poland could be discerned, once the nature of the relationship had become redefined by the rulers (if this was mere lip service, it gave in any case a licence to think otherwise).

Another threat to the USSR in its role as Poland's protector and seigneur came in 1970, immediately before the December uprising on the Baltic coast, with the signing of the treaty between Poland and the Federal Republic of Germany. This meant the de facto recognition by Bonn of Poland's western boundary. After that it was no longer credible to depict the Federal Republic as a revanchist threat to Poland. The Polish opposition took notice of this change.[15]

An eventual re-orientation of the foreign policy of Poland could naturally not be openly discussed under 'normal' political circumstances. Such a discussion could come into the open only when the Party began to lose its grip on society after 1976 and when its legitimacy as ruler began to be openly questioned.

The failures of Gomulka and Gierek

The period after 1956 in Poland can, in retrospect, be seen as a period, when the ruling communists tried to get some kind of support from their subjects, i.e., a certain legitimacy. The Gomulka regime apparently at least got some popular support in its early years, as collectivisation of agriculture was stopped and reversed, as workers' councils were allowed in factories and mines, as cultural life was allowed to flower a little, and as Cardinal Wyszynski was set free and the Catholic Church allowed to operate more freely in order for instance to give schoolchildren religious education.

The liberties of the Church soon became restricted, however, cultural life restrained, and the workers' councils reduced to powerlessness. Material welfare still left very much to be desired. The Gomulka regime continued to adhere to the canons of the command economy. The legitimation devices 'protection of national culture' and 'economic compensation' did not work. But terror had slackened. Hence the stage was set for a new act in the Polish drama.

The first outbreak of discontent came in the cultural sphere. In Warsaw. in March 1968, the drama 'Dziady' (the Fathers) by Poland's 19th century national poet Mickiewicz, was withdrawn from the repertoire of one of the capital theatres at the request of the Soviet ambassador to Poland: the piece is about Russian oppression of Poland in the early 19th century. Students took to the streets to demonstrate their misgivings about this act of political censorship of a national classic. The demonstration was put down by force, and a violent 'anti-Zionist' campaign followed, as some of the student leaders happened to be of Jewish origin (more about the significance of anti-Semitism in Polish politics later). One could speak of a general clamp-down on cultural life in Poland.[16]

In mid-December, 1970, the government suddenly announced that food prices were to be increased significantly. Workers in the Baltic ports reacted by demonstrating in the streets and going on strike. Troops were called out and a number of workers — how many was never disclosed — were shot to death. The workers' upheaval was quelled.[17]

As a consequence of the riots in December, 1970, Gomulka had to resign as Party leader. He was succeeded by Gierek, the Party boss of Silesia.

The Gierek regime withdrew the price increases and tried to establish a *modus vivendi* with its subjects. The first concern was to try to solve the food problem. The state increased its payments for both meat and cereals to the farmers. The farmers' financial situation was also improved by lowering land taxes and by investment programmes.

Obligatory delivery quotas were abolished, and many farmers were also given formal rights of property to the land which they tilled (about 80 per cent of agricultural lands in Poland was — and is — cultivated by private farmers). The results of the new policy seemed promising. From 1970 to 1973, production of cereals increased by 20 per cent, and that of meat by 28 per cent.

Exports increased as well. The prospects looked bright for an economic modernisation of Poland, for a transition from 'extensive' to 'intensive' growth, i.e., for an increase in production by enhanced productivity and not only by putting more resources into the production apparatus.

In order for the new economic development strategy to succeed, it was necessary to increase imports of technologically advanced equipment from the capitalist West and to buy licences for new technology. The whole programme was to be financed with the help of Western credits, which were to be repaid with the help of increased exports to the West, once the new strategy had begun to bear fruit. The development of the economy was swift. In 1971–75 total investments increased by 18.4 per cent annually and industrial investments by 21.9 per cent. The change in consumption levels was as rapid, with nominal personal income increasing by 10.1 per cent in 1971 and 17 per cent in 1974. Price increases were insignificant during the same period.

According to the plan, investments would increase by 42 per cent between 1971–75, as compared to 1966–70. The actual outcome was 90 per cent. Real incomes were planned to increase by 39 per cent — the actual figure was 69 per cent. Not only real wages, but also pensions and other transferations were significantly raised.[18]

The increases in resource use were covered by imports. This seemed to be no problem in the early years. Around 1975, however, the economy began to show signs of disharmony and lack of balance between imports and exports. It soon became clear that the new economic strategy was heading for disaster. What reasons can be found for this failure?

Some of the factors impeding further growth in Poland were beyond the decision-makers' control, i.e., bad weather and the oil price increase and the economic recession in the capitalist countries. However, others were the consequences of decisions taken and the ways in which the economic system operated in Poland. The forced investment programme was not matched by an adequate institutional framework. The heavy bureaucracy remained firmly seated at every level and plans continued to be rigid. Branch ministries and different kinds of lobby groups — local Party leaderships, for example — managed to hang on to the investment programme. The spread of investments became very broad, and expensive imported goods were distributed throughout the whole economy instead of being concentrated to the important growth sectors. Equipment was imported for projects that were not part of the original plans and which had not, consequently, obtained the necessary domestic resources allocated to them. Consequently, a substantial proportion of the imports was wasted, i.e., lost in investment programmes that were never completed.

At the same time, the increase in the standard of consumption for wage earners in Poland also hampered potential exports, as it was of course easier for producers to sell at home than abroad. The planned gradual increase in exports to the West, which was considered to be the means by which funds would be raised to pay for the credits, turned into a relative decline. The gap between the planned and the actual export figures quickly widened.[19]

As before, the economic troubles expressed themselves in the shape of a food crisis. In 1974, relative prices began to work against agriculture, and production declined. There was bad weather as well. In order to save their cattle, the farmers increased production of fodder at the cost of commercial crops. In spite of this, part of the cattle stock had to be slaughtered with the result that meat production soon fell.

In 1976 the situation was precarious and the regime tried to restrain consumption by introducing the price increases which triggered the strikes and demonstrations in June. The price rise was cancelled. The economy continued to deteriorate. From 1976 on, the regime tried to counter the spectre of rising foreign debts by curbing imports and by encouraging export oriented industries. Both devices failed. The reduction in imports hit industry hard by depriving it of certain goods necessary for the planned expansion.

The encouragement of the export sector and the space for increased household consumption made industry concentrate on delivering goods directly for export or consumption. The foreign trade agencies became stocked with products that could not be sold, the lack of domestically produced investment goods became increasingly acute, and the amount of unfinished projects grew. The shortage of resources thus entailed waste of resources![20]

According to the programme initiated by Gierek, an initial deficit in the balance of trade would result from the creation of the new industrial structure. Increased exports would subsequently help to pay for the credits and debts, and eventually exports would surpass imports in value. The whole strategy failed.

Exports did not grow sufficiently, partly because of factors outside

Polish control. As far as imports were concerned, however, the regime must take the brunt of the responsibility. It used the tactics of trying to 'please' certain groups in society to avoid expressions of discontent and imported consumption goods that could be bought by the well-paid: i.e. apart from the Party officials, a few groups of workers, miners for example, police, military officers and some intellectuals.[21]

At the same time as the economy was deteriorating, the Gierek regime tried to tighten its control over the population. The youth and student organisations were brought under a common organisation under Party surveillance. Private farmers were discriminated against in comparison with the state farms in the allocation of credits and machinery. There was no sign of political 'liberalisation' then, although Poland had become opened up to Western contacts and influences as a consequence of the economic development strategy.

In the early 1970s, the course chosen by the Polish leaders appeared to be a viable alternative to the reform movement ushered in by the Czechoslovak leaders in their country in 1968, and which had proved to be unacceptable to the Soviet leaders. No economic decentralisation, no freedom of opinion, no political pluralism but import of capital and technology from the West seemed to work, i.e., to keep the population quiet and, maybe, even content, without jeopardising either Soviet influence or the Soviet sense of security. But once the economic policy failed, nothing was left for the regime to rely on. The politics of *divide et impera*, i.e., of treating different key groups differently within a segmentalised structure — the Party 'consulting' workers, 'having a dialogue' with the Church and 'discussing' with some intellectuals — were not enough. The 'feudalisation' of authority structures, noted by Polish social scientists, only increased the divisions in the society.[22]

The hierarchical and segmentalised structure of society in combination with the privilege system served to further alienate the majority of the Polish population from the state and to atomise society. DiP's first report in 1979 presented the ugly picture of an utterly corrupt social system with pockets, or rather large patches, of poverty. Medical care was nominally free but in practice reserved for those who could afford to pay substantially, the housing situation, especially for young couples with little money, was catastrophic, and alcoholism was rampant. People seemed to be apathetic.[23]

The situation was aggravated further by the malfunctioning, or rather nonfunctioning, of political life. There was no place for interest articulation and aggregation from below. Information was not allowed to circulate freely. This was true not only regarding the economy but also concerning the whole social system. The rulers were isolated from the people and were not able to perceive the tense atmosphere. The workers were unable to work properly in the state enterprises but tried to take care of the needs of the family by moonlighting, working in the black economy. Sociological surveys, which the rulers either did not read or simply ignored — there was after all no change of policy — showed that the Poles in general felt affection only for the family and for the abstract notion of the nation, but for nothing in between. The state and the society were alien factors to be avoided. Belief in the official state ideology, Marxism, was very weak.[24]

At the same time, the sociological investigations showed that the new, young working class that was being shaped in Gierek's Poland, placed a high value on equality and freedom of information. Its members were fairly well educated and could compare the miserable conditions and the system of privileges in Poland with the conditions for workers in the Western European welfare states. However, they lacked the means to express their misgivings. The labour unions were part of the established power structure and served only as 'transmission belts' for the Party. Even language served to alienate the workers from the state. The official language was replete with lies and absurdities that were impossible to believe in and to use for expressing grievances.[25]

The workers were barred also from communication with the authorities because of a linguistic barrier of another kind. Their way of conceptualising their experiences, their code, was not adapted to political discourse. Although they were rather well educated, their traditional language restricted their political thinking to concrete phenomena. Policy was viewed merely as a question of morality and considered exclusively as a matter of good and evil. This restricted code was both a counterpart to and was reinforced by communist political culture. The result was political mutism. Polish social scientists and intellectuals belonging to or associated with KOR, on the other hand, had command of a wider linguistic code and possessed a political language which was possible to use against the rulers. During the strikes in August 1980, such intellectuals won the confidence of the workers because of the fact that their criticism of the official lies was perceived by the workers as morally right, as the truth. Once this had happened, however, the intellectuals could 'translate' the more fundamentalist, morally defined and person oriented demands of the workers into more pragmatic, matter of fact arguments which the representatives of the Party could not evade discussing.[26]

A further consequence of the growing alienation of the population from the regime was that the political vacuum had a counterpart in what may be labelled as an ideological vacuum. The void had to be filled by something. It is in this context the role of the Catholic Church gains importance. Nationalism, traditions and culture also enter the scene.

The Catholic Church and Polish tradition

The Catholic Church had become partly rehabilitated in 1956. It was soon repressed again and was involved in a bitter struggle with the Party over how to celebrate the Catholic Polish state's milennium in 1966. There was also a difference of opinion with regard to relations with West Germany at this time, the Church being in favour of reconciliation at last, while the Party tried to uphold the image of (West) Germany as Poland's archenemy.[27]

Under Gierek, and especially after June 1976, the Regime tried to utilise the Church to compensate for its own lack of legitimacy. Wyszynski was courted. On his 75th birthday, 3 August 1976, the Premier Jaroszewicz sent him a bunch of flowers in red and white, Poland's national colours.[28]

The common sense explanation of the important role of the Church in Poland is to point to the fact that it was the only national institution which could give to the Poles a sense of community and common fate during the time of the partition. But this explanation is not sufficient to explain the Church's influence over workers and intellectuals alike in today's Poland. The workers' movements in partitioned Poland were often anticlerical, and during the interwar years the Church was part of the political establishment, while the workers were not. Many intellectuals had become secularised. In the main, it was only the nationalist political right which insisted that one could not be a true Pole without being a Catholic as well.

Under the German occupation, the Church regained its old role as a uniting factor, however. Secularisation came to a halt. The difference between being a Pole and being a Catholic lost its significance in the course of the war. Firstly the Orthodox and Uniate Ukrainians and Belorussians were incorporated into the USSR. Then the overwhelming majority of the Jews were murdered by the Nazis. Finally the Germans in former East Prussia and the provinces of Posen and Silesia fled or were driven away. Poland became ethnically and religiously homogenous.[29]

However, this was not the whole story of the re-emergence of the Church in Poland. Under Stalinist rule after 1948, the Party leaders behaved as an oppressive, ruling elite while the Catholic priests were both severely persecuted by the communists and led a humble life among ordinary people. The servants of the Church gained in popular respect as dismay and despair about the communists spread among the people, peasants and workers alike.[30]

When Gierek attempted to pose as the caretaker of Catholic Poland — among other things, he paid a visit to the Pope in Rome in 1977 — the Church acquired even more authority without the regime, apparently, benefitting at all. When Cardinal Wojtyla was elected Pope in 1978, the impact of the Church became even greater. The Pope's first visit to his old country in June 1979 became an enormous demonstration for the Church and, implicitly, against communism in general and the regime in

Poland in particular. It is well known that the authorities tried to play down the significance of what happened, among other things by refusing to allow the state-controlled television to show any picture of the immense crowds that had gathered in Warsaw and at other places to pay homage to the Pope. The irresistibility of the emotions of national pride for the Polish Pope was even manifested by state officials. For example, the speaker of Radio Warsaw exclaimed to his nationwide audience, when commenting on the Pope's open-air mass in Warsaw: 'Ladies and gentlemen, now the whole world is listening to our Polish Pope'.[31] Probably practically every adult Pole at this moment remembered, with national pride, the well known lines by one of the great Polish poets of the 19th century, Julius Slowacki:

> Among the quarrelling, the Lord struck
> On a mighty bell;
> Lo, for a Slav Pope
> He provided the throne...
> He shall spread love, as today the Powers
> Spread weapons...

This was written in 1848, the year of national upheavals and *Völkerfrühling* in Central Europe. Its enduring message was hardly lost on the Poles one hundred and thirty one years later.[32]

When the Catholic Church became pre-eminent in the minds of the Poles — a Lutheran Polish priest even spoke of Catholic fanaticism[33] — national feelings were enhanced as well. The mixture of Catholic religious and national symbols in the public life of the Solidarity (Solidarnosc) movement made this quite obvious. Let us turn to the more specific role played by national symbols and tradition in the 'selflimiting' revolution, let us look closer at the cultural environment in which Solidarity was born, in order to throw light on it as a potential political organisation with its roots in Poland's noncommunist, traditional political culture.

The Solidarity movement and Polish tradition

The very name 'Solidarity' was obviously chosen because it had no special communist connotation but reminded one of Christian and national traditions and went beyond class divisions: all patriots could be covered by it.

An opinion poll, which was taken secretly — and not according to strict sampling methods — after the establishment of Solidarity and at a point in time when the Party, i.e., the ruling Communist Party, seemed to be in disarray, showed that a mere three per cent would have voted for the Communists in the event of free elections. Thirty four per cent would have voted for Christian Democrats, 27 for a Socialist, and 19 for a Liberal Party.[34] The accuracy of the numbers may be questioned, but scarcely their general tendency.

This was the climate of political opinion in the Poland of 1980, after 35 years of communist rule. Solidarity did not fit into the official system at all but superseded it instead and became the haven for a revitalised traditional political culture. So let us examine this alternative political system from inside.

Just before the first national congress of Solidarity in the early autumn of 1981, one of the movement's papers, 'Wiadomosci Dnia', published an analysis called 'Solidarity from within'. The author was a professor of sociology at the university of Warsaw who was also a member of Solidarity's committee of specialists, Jacek Kurczewski.

According to Kurczewski, the stated purpose of those who initiated the movement had been to create only local, autonomous trade unions within the framework of a loose federation. It came as a surprise to those who had organized the triggering strikes in Gdansk in August 1980 that Solidarity soon became a real union. The basic principle was preserved, however, i.e., that the organisation should be according to work place, and not to industrial branch. Thus at every workplace and in every geographical region one had a united front against the employer, i.e., the combined state and Party apparatus. Of course there was a wide range of differences of attitudes and interests among Solidarity members. The basic contradiction, which made these differences seem to be of secondary importance, however, was between the working people and what Kurczewski chose to call 'the ruling class'.

Solidarity had, according to Kurczewski's data, about 9 million members in August 1981. The greatest support was to be found in the age group 20 – 29 years and in towns with more than 20,000 inhabitants. In the central region Mazovia, where Warsaw is situated, 66 per cent of the workers and 46 per cent of the intellectuals, who were Solidarity members, declared themselves to be believing Catholics. Thirteen per cent of each category belonged to the Communist Party.

It is evident from Kurczewski's investigations that Solidarity was not a trade union in the technical, restricted sense of the word. Instead it functioned as a substitute for the link that had been missing between the private world of the individuals and the state. The once atomised citizens had changed into political subjects, who were filling the political vacuum with an interest organisation of their own making. With Kurczewski's words, Solidarity members 'were showing a high degree of public activity which had to be preserved'. The impression that there was a real need on the part of the people to fill a vacuum, is strengthened by Kurczewski's finding that 70 per cent of the Mazovian Solidarity members had not before been members of *any* political, social, or cultural organisation.[35]

Krzysztof Pomian has rightly underlined the fact that Poland's past became 're-actualised' with Solidarity. The workers who had been killed by the regime's bullets in 1956 and 1970 were now at last rescued from oblivion by the erection of monuments to their memory in Poznan and Gdansk. At the one and only Solidarity congress in 1981 a resolution was passed that demanded that history education at all levels should be purged of falsifications, lies, and omissions. It was not a coincidence, Pomian maintains, that the organisational structure of Solidarity was patterned on the ancient territorial division of the country, the one which existed until Gierek 'reformed' the province system in 1975. Solidarity took up an old Polish word for province, *Ziemia* and named the main regions according to tradition Mazovia, Great Poland and Little Poland. It was no coincidence either that KOR named its paper for the workers *Robotnik* (*The Worker*). This was the name of the paper, founded by Pilsudski, of the Socialist Party, PPS, from 1892 until the dissolution of the Party (its enforced merger with the Communist Party) in 1948. The message was clear: Poland had a genuine national socialist, and democratic, tradition to revive.[36]

Hence the emergence of Solidarity was not only the people's answer to the economic failure of the communist regime, an expression of the fact that the 'economic compensation' strategy had failed. It was also a proof of the fact that the regime had met with disaster in its pretension to act as the 'protector' of national culture. Let us examine how this came about, i.e., how the regime tried to use national traditions and how this back-fired, once KOR and Solidarity were there to reap the fruits.

In its endeavours to act as the benign guardian of the national heritage of the Poles, the Gierek regime actively encouraged interest in Poland's past. In retrospect it can be confidently stated that the attempt received a response beyond all expectations. As the regime could not do the trick with 'economic compensation' it turned out that the posture as 'protector' was not a valid substitute.

When the regime failed in its attempt to take care of the material interests of its subjects, and as the privileged Poles at the top devoted themselves to conspicuous consumption, the effect of this reawakening of the past was that the bulk of the population started to regard the Church and the oppositional small groups of intellectuals — e.g. KOR — as the legitimate representatives of the cultural heritage of the Polish nation. We will look closer at this inversion process as it illuminates the hazards, for a Communist regime, in trying to rule with terror slackened and without a good economic record. Thus what happened in Poland from June 1976 up to 13 December 1981, is of interest as a possible precedent for other vassal regimes of the Soviet empire that try to make political capital out of national traditions.

When the Communist Party through the mouth of the Head of State and professional historian Henryk Jablonski assured the Poles, in September 1979, that they were entitled to be proud of their martial past, their old warriors and the *szlachta*, the opposition distributed leaflets with information on the fate of the Polish officers captured by the Russians in 1939 and refound in a mass grave in Katyn in Belorussia in 1943. On the 40th anniversary of the Soviet attack on Poland (which took place on 17 September 1939) KOR 'published' a document reminding Poles of the following facts:

1 the Nazi-Soviet pact of 23 August 1939, which led to the fourth partition of Poland;
2 the Soviet attack on Poland on 17 September 1939, an aggression which violated the Soviet-Polish pact of 1932 as well as the peace treaty of Riga in 1923;
3 the fact that in 1939–1941 more than one and half million Poles were deported to the USSR, where 600,000 of them perished; and
4 Katyn.

'About all these events, official Poland had kept silent', an ex-Hungarian historian, Ferenc Fejtö, commented.[37]

When the Party, adhering to one of the first decisions by Gierek in 1971 and with the help of fund raising from the population, had the old royal castle in Warsaw rebuilt from the ruins, and decided to move the romantic historical paintings of the 19th century Polish painter Jan Matejko from the National Gallery to the castle, with the motivation that the pictures would make a stronger impression there, the well known writer Tadeusz Konwicki published, in the publishing house NOWA, which was illegal, a novel called 'The Minor Apocalypse'. Among other things, the book dealt with the Sovietisation of Polish culture and the deterioration of the historical sites of Poland.[38]

However, what was probably of decisive importance for the complete shift in popular reverence from the Party and to the organised opposition, was that the Party, without comprehending the fact or its consequences, allowed the nation to say farewell to the established communist, Soviet-influenced cultural varnish in ritual life as well.

Five of Poland's eight national holidays had remained ecclesiastical, and all ceremonies that marked the life cycle of the individual were still in the hands of the Church. This in itself was a kind of vaccination against communist ritual life.[39] But apart from this, the Church and the political opposition managed to take over non-ecclesiastical national celebrations as well. The non-, or rather anti-, Party interpretation of these turned into a kind of historical education for the new generation, which became initiated into the national community not on the premises of the Party but on those of the Church and the opposition.

According to orthodox communist history, it was the October revolution in Russia in 1917 that was the 'real' cause of Poland's independence. This event occurred on 7 November, according to the Gregorian calendar. The date is the major official festival in the Soviet Union and its vassal states, including Poland.

The Bolsheviks could apparently never reconcile themselves with the fact that the resurrected Polish state slipped out of their hands and that they could not bring it under their own domination in 1920: Molotov, the Soviet Foreign Minister from May 1939, called the Polish republic 'the monstrous bastard of the Peace of Versailles' and Stalin mocked 'pardon the expression, a state'. The British historian Norman Davies, quoting these and other expressions in the same vein in his history of Poland, himself is closer to the facts with the following observations:

> The Polish republic came into being in November 1918 by a process which theologians might call parthenogenesis. It created itself in the void left by the collapse of three partitioning powers. Despite Molotov's assertion, it was not created by the Peace of Versailles, which merely confirmed what already existed and whose territorial provisions were limited to defining the frontier with Germany alone . . . It owed its procreation to no one, not even the Poles themselves, who, fighting with distinction in all the combatant armies, had been constrained to neutralize each other as a political force.[40]

Obviously, it is impossible to fix a definite date. In the interwar years, however, the '11th of November' was celebrated as the state's birthday. On this day Pilsudski, who had arrived in Warsaw the day before after being released from the German prison (in Magdeburg), began acting as provisional Head of State and Commander-in-Chief of the Polish republic.

The postwar communist rulers were thus faced with two solemn dates to celebrate in November. During Stalinism there was no hesitation; the Poles had to celebrate the anniversary of the Great Socialist October Revolution in Russia and not the emergence of the bourgeois creation which called itself the Polish republic. Later, however, when the regime was trying to appear in a more patriotic light, a more ingenious solution was found: 'the 7th of November' was transformed into Poland's day of resurrection by a cunning interpretation of history. On this day, in 1918, the socialist Daszynski had formed a provisional government in Lublin in Eastern Poland. Although Daszynski subordinated himself almost immediately to Pilsudski, it seemed very convenient to the rulers of Poland to celebrate the 50th anniversary of the resurrection of the Polish republic on 7 November 1968. The thesis that 7 November 1918, was the day of rebirth was also upheld ten years later, in 1978, by the Communist Party's ideological organ *Nowe Drogi*.[41]

In 1978, however, the Gierek regime was already faced with the mounting economic crisis. Faced with the failure of the 'economic compensation' device, the Party sought almost desperately to play its other card, that of being 'protector' of the Polish nation. The subjects were allowed to celebrate the 11th of November. Far from bowing her head in humility and reverence, however, a main protagonist on the national scene, the Church, responded by issuing, through Cardinal Wojtyla, a pastoral letter, demanding 'the creation of conditions that would enable the people to feel that they were the masters of their country'. In Warsaw a mass was celebrated in memory of all those who had given their lives for the freedom of Poland. In one of the capital's churches a bust of Pilsudski was set up. [42]

Pilsudski came to symbolise the 11th of November. From the very beginning his person, or rather the myth surrounding it, also became a symbol for Solidarity. In his first public appearance as the movement's leader, Lech Walesa had a portrait of the late 'Father of the Fatherland' behind him on the wall.[43] In 1981, the three elements Solidarity, Pilsudski, and the 11th of November, merged completely. All over the country, Solidarity celebrated the date with masses, demonstrations and public speeches. One of the speeches was held at Pilsudski's tomb in the crypt of the cathedral in the Wawel castle in Cracow. The weekly *Tygodnik Solidarnosc* featured a facsimile of Pilsduski's decree from 1918 about the resurrection of the Republic, and a photo of his sarcophagus, covered by flowers and surrounded by verterans, on its front page.[44]

Pilsudski, his foreign policy, and his coup, became once again a figure of political relevance: the more Poland's subordination to the USSR became questioned, the more Pilsudski's deeds were praised. Moreover, the more the Communist Party apparatus gave way to the military, the more people were forced to think of Pilsudski's precedent, i.e., of the military in the role as saviour of the nation. However, in 1981 the role of the military was quite different.

Once reawakened, the Pilsudski myth in its turn influenced public opinion in People's Poland. The Pilsudski cult gave new life to an irredentist dream which had never died: Pilsudski's corpse is in the sarcophagus in the cathedral of the Wawel Castle, but his heart lies in his mother's grave in Vilna in Lithuania, now part of the Soviet Union.

The 11th of November, 1981, became the day of a veritable orgy in national, noncommunist, anti-Russian symbols. In Poznan, Solidarity held a rally at the Mickiewicz square, and in Warsaw the movement put wreaths at the Tomb of the Unknown Soldier — explicitly also to the victims of Katyn. The speaker, from Solidarity's Mazovian branch, declared that one celebrated the anniversary confident that Solidarity would be the guarantor of a new resurrection of a truly free and sovereign Poland.

In Gdansk, the anniversary celebration was organised by the Club of the '3rd of May'.[45] Thus a link was forged with the other 'holy' date in modern Polish history. In interwar Poland, this day was being celebrated as the second national festival. Its history goes back to the 18th century. Solidarity had dug deeply into Polish history in order to underline its legitimacy.

The first partition of Poland took place in 1772. Trying to avert the menace of a second one, the *Sejm* and the king, Stanislaw August, passed a new constitution for Poland on 3 May 1791. The *liberum veto*,which had made the central government so weak, was abolished, and political rights were broadened beyond the *szlachta* class. The obvious aim was to forestall further Russian interference in Polish affairs. Some members of the nobility, who feared for their privileges and who hoped for Russian support against Prussia, formed a confederation, at Targowica, however, and asked Catherine II for help against Warsaw. The Russians delivered their 'fraternal aid' — but in co-operation with the Prussians. Poland was doomed. The partition, with Austria joining once again, was completed in 1795/96. For patriotic Poles, the word 'Targowica' became equivalent to treason.

As has been remarked above, the 3rd of May was celebrated as a national festival after 1918. The strong official commitment to the day can be illustrated by a minor cause célèbre in the mid-1930s: Czechoslovakia's ambassador to Poland was to pay a visit to Moscow. He chose the beginning of May for the visit and took part in the May-day celebrations in Moscow. He was not back in Warsaw in time for the 3rd May festival. The Polish government informed the Czechoslovakian government that it regarded what had happened as a deliberate insult.[46]

During the first 35 postwar years, the 3rd of May was not officially celebrated. Instead, May-day, the day of the Communist Party, was used as an occasion for allowing people to pay homage to the leaders in the Soviet Russian way.

However, public demonstrations on 1st May were perceived and resented by many Poles as demonstrations for the Russian masters. Their thoughts were instead directed towards 3rd May, an association which was made easier by the fact that buildings and streets were cleared of flags and flowers immediately after the 1st with a swiftness, which was rather atypical of Polish habits. The reason, of course, was that nothing should make 3rd May appear to be something special.[47]

Hence up to 1981, the celebration of the 1st of May was associated in the mind of many Poles with the noncelebration of the 3rd of May. In 1981, the Solidarity leadership declared that the movement's members were of course free to take part, if they wished, in the May-day demonstrations. However, the movement also announced its intention to celebrate 3rd May. Even in the state controlled Polish radio, attention was paid to the celebration of 3rd May by a special programme on its historical importance. In the radio broadcast it was declared that Solidarity was the contemporary embodiment of the progressive tradition in Polish history, which had found an early expression in the constitution of 1791.[48] Solidarity had become the incarnation of Polish political traditions.

Although Polish communists during the war had expressed the opinion, with the words of A. Lampe, that 'Our May 3rd is not any contradiction to, but a national complement to the May 1st Festival, which has international importance and belongs to the whole world',[49] subsequent history made the celebrations in 1981 an act of at least veiled anti-Russianism, directed not only against the Russia of Catherine II but also against the USSR of Brezhnev, who, as everybody knew, did not look upon Solidarity with friendly eyes.

In the last instance, the Solidarity movement's use of national symbols in combination with the revision of history which it entailed, cast doubt on the justness of official Polish relations with the USSR.

Attitudes towards the Soviet Union

It is evident that the popular demonstrations on national holidays were perceived by many Poles as acts of protests against the power of the USSR over Poland. On 11 November 1980, i.e., the day after the registration of Solidarity as a legalised union, anti-Soviet slogans were heard in abundance.[50] Negative attitudes towards the Russians and the Soviet Union must be said to be part of traditional Polish political culture and, consequently, of increasing political importance once this culture became revitalised. Although it is impossible to chart these attitudes in any concise manner, because of the nature of the sources, they obviously cannot be excluded from our analysis.

An opinion poll in the autumn of 1980 showed that a mere two percent of the people who were asked their opinions about the USSR answered that they regarded it a 'friendly country'. According to a survey investigation carried out by Polish sociologists at the same time, 49.6 per cent of the respondents regarded the Soviet Union as the worst threat to Polish independence.[51] That these findings were representative of Polish attitudes generally, is corroborated by the conclusions reached by the very well informed contributors to the first DiP report:

> The dislike, to put it mildly, for the Soviet Union has assumed, in broad segments of our society, an almost pathological character. How many times have we been shocked to see the hostile reaction of crowds to Soviet athletes at sporting events. Yet the decision-makers in our country, even when they

recognize such phenomena, draw entirely wrong conclusions from them. They still think that they can talk the nation into having the right attitude and shape its consciousness by excising some trends and facts in history and by carefully retouching the past. In this way the schizophrenic character of our society is created, full of bitterness toward a country and nation with which we actually ought to be developing relations based on the principles of good neighborliness and friendly coexistence.[52]

In the autumn of 1981, a former member of the PUWP, the old journalist Józef Kusmierek, showed the connection between on the one hand, Soviet and Polish communist hypocrisy, and, on the other hand, the popular Polish attitude towards the USSR. This he did in an open letter, which he directed to Leonid Zamyatin, head of the CPSU CC:s Department for International Information. The background was that at a press conference in Moscow, Zamyatin had condemned the attempt at democratisation in Poland after August 1980.

Kusmierek frankly declared that the enforced subordination to Moscow had given 'People's Poland' a ruling class which was the result of 'negative selection'. He argued that those in power were criminals. The nation at large was avid for revenge and was hoping that the Russians would soon face another Tsushima (the defeat suffered by the Russian Navy at the hands of the Japanese at Tsushima in 1905 triggered the revolution in 1905, which, in turn, came to be seen, in retrospect, as the beginning of the fall of the Tsarist Russian empire: Poles obviously think in historical terms).

According to Kusmierek, Soviet propaganda was to blame for this unfriendly Polish attitude. As the official slogans about 'cooperation' and 'community of interests' between Poland and the USSR rested on political lies and falsifications of history, the way was effectively blocked for a genuine, amicable alliance between the Polish and Russian peoples. The experience of two hundred years of strained relations could not be wiped out with the help of idealising declarations. The permanent flattering of the USSR and all things Soviet in the official propaganda was not only built upon false premises. It was also humiliating for the Poles and thus served to fuel hatred of the Russians. No nation could stand being perpetually reminded that everything which it had achieved, its life, society, state boundaries and place in the world, was the result exclusively of the magnanimity, self-sacrifice and good will of another nation.[53]

Kusmierek's grievances should be compared to offical Soviet statements on the same subject at that time. On 17 September 1981, i.e., the anniversary of the Soviet attack on Poland in 1939, the CC of the CPSU and the Council of Ministers of the USSR addressed a letter to their Polish counterparts, complaining about the 'reckless campaign against the Soviet Union' in Poland. Seen in the context of Polish attitudes, documented in the opinion poll and the survey referred to above and by DiP and Kusmierek, the Soviet arguments could not but further deepen the animosity of the Poles:

> The history of the relations between our two countries is being blatantly falsified... The Soviet people, who have made great sacrifices to liberate Poland from the fascist subjugation and who have helped and now are helping your country altruistically, has the full moral right to demand that an end should be put to the anti-Soviet insults in the People's Republic of Poland.[54]

The Soviet statement implies that the sovereignty of Poland is limited, since the Russians demand that the Polish rulers should act according to Russian will. The statement further contains a postfactum falsification of history of exactly the kind which both DiP and Kusmierek had denoted as being especially harmful. The 'sacrifices' by the Soviet Union in World War II were of course being made, not for the sake of the Poles, but in order to defeat the Germans. Kusmierek put his finger on the correct point raising the relevant question as to what would have been the fate of Poland, if Hitler had kept his part of the bargain with Stalin, which included the fourth partition of Poland, and had not attacked the USSR in 1941.[55] Concerning the same question, the renowned Polish philosopher in exile, Leszek Kolakowski, has brought attention to the fact that Stalin was prepared to let Poland be dissolved in 1939.[56]

As is clear from the arguments quoted above, relations with Germany are, so to speak, the other side of the Polish-Russian/Soviet ones. The original reason behind the establishment of the South-East and Central European empire of the USSR was to help safeguard the Russians from any possible threat from Germany. Seen from a Polish perspective, the nature of her relations to (West) Germany should affect her relations to the USSR as well. The agreement with Bonn in late 1970 eroded the very foundations, at least theoretically, for Poland's subordination to the USSR, i.e., the USSR in its capacity as the power which could, and would, defend the western frontier of Poland against (West) German revanchism and revisionism. The potential significance of Bonn's *Ostpolitik* in fact was touched upon in the Polish press.[57] Leading representatives of the PUWP such as Wojna and Rakowski underlined that Poland was no nullity in European politics but the 'second greatest' socialist state in Europe.[58]

The Party itself raised the question of the nature of Poland's relationship with the USSR by bringing it into the new constitution, which was being drafted in late 1975. Besides the explicit inscription of the leading role of the PUWP into the consitution, the Party also wanted to insert that 'unshakeable fraternal bonds' existed between Poland and the Soviet Union and the other socialist states.[59] This might be interpreted as 'a corollary to the policy of détente': a similar phrase had already been adopted in the new constitution of the GDR. The rationale behind these acts is most probably the one which has been underlined by the (West) German economist Renate Demus:

> The USSR wants assurance that detente stays in the economic arena, and so the national communist administrations made political concessions in order to have a free hand in economics to use East-West relations to increase their standards of living, which were necessary for growth and legitimation. And finally it makes clear to the people what detente cannot be.[60]

In the Polish case, however, the insertion of the friendship phrase into the constitution rather served to highlight the basic illegitimacy of the regime. 'Economic compensation' could obviously not be utilised by the regime to counter a lack of credibility as 'protector'. Accordingly, the reaction in Poland to the suggested new obligation in the constitution was vehement. Twelve Polish lawyers, who were members of the Polish Academy of Sciences, sent a letter to the CC of the PUWP, stating that a clause of the suggested kind would mean an unacceptable restriction on Polish state sovereignty. There were other letters as well. According to the estimate of a Polish intellectual, KOR member Adam Zagajewski, at least 40,000 Poles signed protests in the same vein.[61]

The Party did not publish the criticism voiced against the draft, but the phrase about the USSR was slightly diluted. The article in question was worded in the following way in the constitution of 10 February 1976:

> In its political decisions the Polish People's Republic: . . . 2) is committed to the noble traditions of solidarity with forces of liberty and progress, consolidations of friendship and co-operation with the USSR and other socialist states.[62]

The entire 'constitution affair' was not settled by this minimal retreat by the Party. The strong reactions seemed to, in the words of an outside observer, 'bring into question the implicit assumption that there was a basic agreement among the Poles on the country's international position and its fundamental foreign policy aims'.[63] This conclusion is borne out by the attitude revealed by leading intellectuals in Poland after the adoption of the new constitution.

In April 1976, the grand old man of Polish economics, the nonagenarian Edward Lipinski, sent an open letter to the Party secretary Gierek (the letter was only published in the West). Lipinski made clear the connection between Poland's international situation and the changes in the constitution, criticizing the foundations of both:

No one doubts that the alliance with the Soviet Union has become a political necessity... We would like to be good neighbors and form relations based on mutual trust. That is impossible until Polish policy toward the Soviet Union is purged of all traces of servility. That will not be feasible until the Soviet Union has the courage to openly admit the 'errors' she has committed against Poland. In the present circumstances, imposing a love of the Soviet state on us and introducing it into our constitution, demonstrates a total incomprehension of human psychology...[64]

It should be noted that it was in the wake of the conflict over the new constitution that small oppositional groups began to mushroom in Poland. Although conventional wisdom would say that it was the economic crisis and the ill-advised decision to raise food prices in June 1976, that triggered the revolutionary development in Poland, and although some researchers in the West tend to adhere to this explanation,[65] the evidence suggests that the two dimensions, the economic and the national-cultural one, were intimately related to each other and helped each other achieve what could be called a 'synergetic effect' i.e., the net result of the two phenomena being greater than their mere addition would have suggested. Nationalism was fuelled by economic discontent and vice versa. The best summary of the complex process taking place in Poland in 1976 that I have found, is one by the American political scientist Richard K. Herrmann. In a special study of 'contemporary Polish perceptions' he has made the following, very accurate observation:

As the debate on the causes of Poland's economic problems continued, some intellectuals moved directly to a discussion of Poland's political order and the country's international position. The intellectuals attempting to channel general economic dissatisfaction into political pressure identified the fundamental cause of Poland's economic plight as its nonliberal, non-democratic political order and lack of state independence with respect to the Soviety Union. Therefore, in the discussion on the 'roots' of Poland's economic dilemma, very basic foreign policy issues were introduced . . .[66]

One of the respondents in the first DiP report voiced the opinion that the 'friendship clause' in the constitution contributed to the economic misbehaviour in Poland, as it worked as a 'dull, dark and ubiquitous factor paralysing the will'.[67] And in the second report from DiP — which was signed on 3 May 1980, i.e., the anniversary of the constitution of 1791 — the character of the relations with the USSR was once again discussed. On this occasion there was even a hint that the intimate alliance with the

USSR was not only superfluous but a potential danger to Poland. Although veiled, the allusion to the USSR's war in Afghanistan, which had started in late 1979 and showed no signs of being a quick and costless affair, is clear in the following excerpt from the second DiP report:

> Participants in the poll who addressed the problem generally recognized that in the foreseeable future, Poland will continue to be part of the existing political, economic, and military structures, the existing system of alliances: the Warsaw Pact and the Council for Mutual Economic Assistance. Many, however, also pointed out that the state of Polish-Soviet relations is cause for vital concern among the public, including a deep sense of the unequal nature of these relations. . . . Recent international events have also elicited public concern lest, considering the country's unequal relations with its strongest ally, it be drawn without any prior consultation or approval into events, which, given its general conditions, could have catastrophic consequences.[68]

Viewed against this background, an assertion by a Polish political scientist in an official Polish publication, must be considered as a symptom of cynicism on behalf of the rulers, or, if this is ruled out, hypocrisy, since an article on that subject was hardly a private matter in early 1980 Poland. Thus a certain W. J. Szczepanski expressed the official creed:

> In the daily practice of Polish foreign policy a permanent mechanism was created many years ago which allowed broad use to be made of the achievements of science in the formulation of aims and the taking of decisions in the fields of foreign relations. For years this mechanism has been functioning rather more efficiently than in other spheres of socio-economic life . . . It would appear that these direct links between theory and practice are . . . an important determinant making possible the taking of correct decisions in Polish foreign policy and encouraging growing activity by Polish diplomats abroad.[69]

One may safely assume that Poles in general did not hold the foreign policy of the regime in such high esteem. If it had been so, it would not have been necessary to stress, in the Programme adopted by Solidarity at its congress, on 7 October 1981, that the foreign relations would have to be created on fresh grounds. In the programme, it is first stated that one must take into consideration and accept the balance of power erected in Europe after the Second World War, and that Solidarity has no intention of working towards the dissolution of this system. It is then added, however, that the existing alliance system would become more, not less, stable, given the following condition:

> Our nation, which is inspired by a deep affection to dignity, patriotism, and tradition, can become a valuable partner only if she can take on her obligations voluntarily and consciously.[70]

The Russians chose to retaliate against the Poles with the assertion, published in the Moscow *Pravda* on 13 October 1981, that the 'conspiracy in Gdansk' (i.e., Solidarity's congress) had demanded that Poland left the CMEA and the WTO and that the international agreements and obligations of Poland were annulled.[71] Already before this, the Soviet leaders had brought the Polish constitution into the discussion, in the letter of 17 September quoted above. In this warning to the Polish Party and government, the latter were reminded of the fact, as the Russians saw it, that friendship and co-operation with the USSR had been written into the Polish constitution. In other words, the constitution was interpreted as stating a 'foreign policy Servitute' towards the USSR.[72] Hence the implication of what was said in the *Pravda* on 13 October was that discussion and implicit questioning of the official foreign policy of People's Poland among the Poles was anticonstitutional, i.e., illegal. However, during the whole period after 1976, the Poles refused to obey this commandment.

One underground organisation that 'surfaced' after the 'constitution conflict' in 1975–76, was the so called PPN, the Polish Association for Independence. Its actual membership remained unknown to all but those directly involved through the whole period 1976–81.[73] This did not stop it from publishing, illegally, of course, both its programme and a number of other materials. It is impossible to say how representative the views put forward here really were. On the other hand, it is clear from the almost open public discussion in Poland in 1980–81, when these arguments were treated as self-evident truths by the Solidarity movement, that they belonged to the core rather than to the fringe of Polish tradition and the revived political culture. In its programme from May 1976, PPN stated as its political goals, Polish sovereignty, democracy, and freedom in cultural life, in science, and in journalism. The programme also declared that all the treaties that had been enforced upon Poland lacked validity in the eyes of Poles. Hence the demand was raised for an independent Polish foreign policy, based on the Polish national interests.[74]

A statement made by PPN in 1978 is of general interest in the context of this study, as it observed that Poland was situated, not between Russia and Germany, but between the imperialist Soviet Union, i.e., a Russia which had occupied the Ukraine and Belorussia, and a Western Europe that was integrating and overcoming old nationalist conflicts. Once Poland's western frontier became definitely secure, and once a reunited Germany was integrated into a united (Western) Europe, Poland would not need any Russian protection whatsoever. The document asserted that many Poles accepted the alliance with the USSR only because they remembered the German atrocities during the occupation. But the Federal Republic now had, in contrast to the GDR and the USSR, admitted its guilt toward Poland for crimes carried out during the war. It was said in this PPN document that especially young Poles were not aware of the fact that not only the territory of present-day West Germany housed those guilty of crimes against the Poles.

It is obvious that emancipation from Russian dominance was just one side of the coin for PPN. The other side would have inscribed on it: 'Back to Europe!'. This is the only reasonable interpretation of PPN:s 'pro-German' stance, i.e., its argument that it was only the Soviet Union and communists that were dependent on the USSR that had anything to gain from the continued partition of Germany. The western territories taken from Germany to Poland after the war in accordance with the Soviet scheme, were very valuable, PPN remarked. A lasting relationship of good neighbourness between Poles and Germans could never be built, however, if the parties had to base their relations on Soviet guarantees. PPN voiced the opinion that a free Poland and a free and reunited Germany would not be bothered by any frontier questions, as they would both become integrated into Europe to such a degree that the state boundaries would lose their former significance. Poland had nothing to gain from the closedness enforced upon Europe up to the Elbe and the Danube by the 'backward police-Russia'.[75]

Although the respondents to the DiP questionnaires were anonymous as well, the background of the whole enterprise should assure us that the opinions reflected in its reports must be representative of more than just a few members of the Polish intellectual elite. Thus it is interesting to note that the second DiP-report underlined the necessity of Western connections as strongly as did PPN a few years before:

> The aspiration to maintain a policy of openness, stimulated by international détente, is, we think, not only a desire of the respondents of the survey, where the point recurs several times, but equally a reflection of the attitude of the whole society. This attitude stems not only from cultural ties and traditions, but also from the feeling, deeply rooted in the hearts and minds of the citizens, that they have the right to freedom of movement. Important economic considerations also favour such a policy: Poland is dependent of Western raw materials, spare parts, and food, as well as Western credit, and it will remain so for a long time to come. The breaking off or even weakening of relations with the West would threaten the country, quite simply, with economic paralysis.[76]

The wording is more careful politically in the DiP than in the PPN statement, but the gist of the argument is the same: Poland should become integrated into Europe, into the Western world to which her citizens really belong.

The Church and a prominent catholic intellectual also touched the question of Poland's foreign relations, albeit in a rather ambiguous way. In the pastoral letter of 11 November 1978, mentioned above, the bishops were telling the people that it was entitled to learn the truth about its own history and that the 'alienated property' of the nation should be returned: 'The nation which had suffered injustice should have its land given back to it and its rights restored'. A (West) German researcher has interpreted the phrase just quoted as saying that the territories taken from Poland by the USSR in 1939 should be returned.[77] The statement may gain a different status, however, if it is put into a different context of arguments.

The well known Polish catholic publicist Stefan Kisielewski in an article, which could not be published officially in Poland, argued that the Poles had to recognise geopolitical and international political realities. Reconciliation with Russia, the USSR, was a must. Kisielewski's suggested solution was not to withdraw Poland from Russian tutelage, but to make this protection less harmful to Poland. The trick was to remove the Polish communists from the commanding posts in Poland. Once this was accomplished, Poles and Russians would be able to reach a *modus vivendi* based on mutual respect and trust. This would amount to 'giving the land back to the nation'. As an exiled Polish intellectual has underlined, Kisielewski's conception is reminiscent of the pro-Russian line of the National Democrats prior to 1917: their goal was to acquire greater Polish autonomy within the confines of the Russian empire.[78]

The only catch in Kisielewski's nostalgic/utopian argument is that events themselves must be said to have compromised beyond repair the whole idea of a voluntary and happy Polish subordination to Russia. Poland has become ethnically homogenous, almost totally catholic, and placed under Russian protection. But it is a *communist* Russia or as has been aptly summarized by Pomian in a stinging comment:

> After being in power thirty-five years, the communists have carried out the ancient, insane dream of the Nationalist extreme right, acquiring at the same time the basic confidence of Moscow as the executor of her orders.[79]

What happened on 13 December 1981, and in the following period, seems to have confirmed Pomian's interpretation of the nature of the relationship between Russia and Poland, as mediated through the Polish communists (in military uniforms — so there is one novelty, after all). Developments have been running in the opposite direction from what both DiP, the Catholic Church and PPN, and Kisielewski, would have wished.

As Wojciech Jaruzelski went to Moscow to pay homage to Leonid Brezhnev at the turn of February and March 1982, the exchange of words between the two revealed that it was a matter of the vassal coming to his seigneur. Brezhnev declared:

> We helped socialist Poland and we shall continue helping it. These are not just words. There is no doubt that both our countries will benefit by the plans we made for economic co-operation. I want to express profound satisfaction with the fact that the entire course of our negotiations is marked by an identity of views and an identical understanding of current and coming tasks.

Jaruzelski replied:

> The relations which unite Poland with its great neighbor are of paramount importance for our people and our party. The Soviet armed forces, directed by the party and the Soviet government together with the armies of the Warsaw Treaty member states, are the principal guarantee of peace in Europe and thus the guarantee of security and territorial integrity of our country and of the inviolability of its just and unchangeable borders. . . We want again to cordially thank for this assistance the Soviet people, the leadership of the Party and the Government as well as you, Comrade Leonid Ilyich Brezhnev, personally.[80]

The reports from the encounter in the Kremlin of Moscow do not say how the two protagonists behaved during the encounter. The scene must have been the opposite, so to speak, of Matejko's famous painting, familiar to all Poles, 'Hold Pruski', on which the Prussian Duke swears allegiance to the Polish King. It stands to reason that the majority of the Poles see in Jaruzelski, not a follower of another leader in military uniform, Pilsudski, but a 20th century heir to the men from Targowica.[81]

One should note that there is in Jaruzelski's address to Brezhnev, a kind of refutation of the arguments put forward by PPN and DiP. Jaruzelski chose to stress that the USSR is protecting Poland's western border. Every true patriot should rejoice. There was a decisive difference, however, between this outcome and the one recommended by Kisielewski: Jaruzelski was the leader of the Communist Party of Poland. He stood out not as the man who was defending the dignity and national pride of the Poles, but as the obedient tool of the Russian rulers. In his person, he incarnated the real limitations on Polish sovereignty.

It is evident that popular Polish feelings for the Russian rulers and the USSR are cool and negative. Thus article six of the Polish constitution of 1976 is an attempt to square the circle in its assessment that Poland is committed to 'consolidation of friendship and co-operation with the USSR'.[82] Friendship in the sense of sympathetic popular feelings remains to be established at all while the co-operation in question is, so far, nothing more than a relationship based on Soviet power.

All this said it is important to note, however, that the Poles are divided in their attitudes to the Russians/the USSR. Richard K. Herrmann, who has assessed Polish attitudes by means of analysis of the content of Polish publications, has reached the following results regarding Polish attitudes towards the USSR and the Federal Republic of Germany (the present heir to the other traditional Polish adversary, Prussia/Germany):

> For 'conservative communists', 'the Soviet Union is perceived as presenting a tremendous opportunity', and as a state 'upon which Poland is wholly dependent for security and prosperity'. The FRG is seen as a threat;
> For reform communists the USSR is perceived as presenting an opportunity, but significantly less so than in the conservative communist opinion, and as a state upon which the security and prosperity of Poland depend. The FRG is seen as a threat, although less so than in the conservative communist view;
> In the view of noncommunist catholics, 'the Soviet Union is perceived as a highly threatening state which is not only overwhelmingly more powerful but largely in control of Polish politics'. The FRG is viewed 'as a very slight threat;
> In the view of democratic socialists, 'the Soviet Union is perceived as a highly threatening state with an overwhelming capability advantage' although less the latter than in the catholic view. The FRG is perceived 'as presenting a very slight opportunity as an implicit ally'.[83]

Although the former two categories are those that decide the politics of Poland, Herrmann's findings should be compared with a clandestine Polish poll in the autumn of 1980, which showed that three per cent supported the Communists, 34 per cent the Christian Democrats, 27 per cent the Socialists (Social Democrats), and 19 the Liberals, had there been such parties.[84] The validity of the poll is uncertain, but it gives one reason to believe that most Poles view the USSR as a 'highly threatening state'. This assertion is strongly corroborated by the result of the Survey Research 'Poles 80', carried out by the Institute of Philosophy and Sociology of the Polish Academy of Sciences in December 1980. The survey, which was based on a representative quota sample of 2500 adults, showed, among other things, that 49.6 per cent regarded the Soviet Union as the worst threat to the independence of Poland. Thirteen per cent regarded 'socialist countries, the Council for Mutual Economic Aid, neighbours, friends' as the greatest threat, and 10.7 per cent the Federal Republic of Germany.[85]

Upon this ground, Soviet security is built in Poland.

In spite of sixteen months of self-limiting revolution, the key posts apparently had continued to be controlled by people who were impeccably loyal to the Russians. The democratic elections to the extraordinary Party congress in July 1881 obviously had not affected the real decision making centre in the country. The core of power, something resembling Stalin's secret chancellery, remained intact in Poland.[86]

The question of power

Thus the eventual outcome of the events in Poland after 1976 on 13 December 1981, showed that the Russians were still able to safeguard their interests and to keep the security system intact. Mass terror had been already abandoned at the time of Stalin's death as the ruling class in the Soviet Union began to be consolidated. This consolidation process was completed under Brezhnev.[87] A certain support could be acquired for the regime in Russia proper just because it was Russian and could take advantage of Russian tradition and nationalism.[88]

In Poland, however, although Gomulka and Gierek might be said to have been each allowed a honeymoon with their subjects in the wake of the fall of their immediate predecessors, the communists could never gain political legitimacy. Ultimately, the 'economic compensation' also failed beyond repair. By late 1981 almost every Pole knew that if economic welfare would ever come, it would be in spite of, and not thanks to, communist rule. As my discussion above has indicated, the 'protector of the nation' device turned into an argument against the regime as a consequence of the constitution struggle and of the intimate relationship between this dimension and the economic one.

In the earlier cases of challenge to their rule, the Russians had resorted to the *ultima ratio regis*, (the inscription on an old gun in Wawel Castle) i.e., Soviet and WTO troops, in Hungary in 1956 and in Czechoslovakia in 1968, respectively,

It is not necessary to hypothesise that the Soviet leaders master-minded the whole process leading to Jaruzelski's action on 13 December 1981, in order to be able to assert that the action itself was a proof of their ability to adapt to changing situations. The act surely benefitted the Soviet leaders, and not the Polish people. But how was the trick done this time?

Lenin once observed that a revolutionary situation is at hand when those 'at the bottom' do not want to go on living as before, at the same time as those 'at the top' are unable to rule in their accustomed way, and a general crisis is hitting both parts.[89]

Lenin's observation points to an opaque detail in the Polish self-limiting revolution. What did the ruling Communist Party do? The revolution was indeed a movement from below. Its leaders kept repeating that they knew that it was out of the question to think of dethroning the Party, as such an attempt, if it showed signs of being successful, would trigger a Soviet invasion. At the same time, however, the PUWP, in spite of the fact that it continued to rule, at least nominally, and had congresses both in February 1980, and in July 1981, and changed leaders repeatedly, seemed to lack coherence and will. It seemed less an actor, more a barrier to change.

As late as January 1980, the then Premier and Politbureau member Babiuch wrote in *Nowe Drogi* that the Party was looking forward to the pending congress 'confident that it has satisfactorily fulfilled its duty towards the working class and the nation'.[90] This statement was made in a situation when DiP had already presented its first, alarming report that the country was heading for catastrophe and when the official statistics, though not public yet, but certainly known to the rulers, were showing that the gross national income was beginning to decrease.[91] Seven months after the reassuring declaration by the Premier, in the Polish August of 1980, the Polish 'working class and the nation' rose against their self-righteous masters.

The whole Western world could, in a bewildered state, follow what happened in Poland in August 1980. The prominent Polish film director Andrzej Wajda, who in 'The Man of Marble' (shot in 1976 and issued in 1977) had depicted the Bierut and Gomulka regimes and their crimes and decline, caught the moment and made 'The Man of Iron'. It was a work by a creative artist but at the same time a kind of sociological analysis containing documentary sequences, which were not cut in after the event, but were part of the script. (Some scenes were filmed at the real negotiations in Gdansk in August 1980.) In this film the centre of political power in the country emerges as a black box, dim, opaque and always referred to by the film actors with the word 'them'. The expression epitomises the fundamental split between 'us' and 'them' which is typical of all the Soviet vassal states. But it also points to the remarkable anonymity in the exercise of power and of the repressive organs. An American political scientist of Polish background, Adam Przeworski, has used 'The Man of Iron' as his starting point for a thought-provoking analysis of the relations of power in communist Poland.

Przeworski notes that the communist rulers have never acquired any genuine authority or legitimacy in Poland. Decisions are reached somewhere in the dark — at the time of Przeworski's article, nobody knew, for example, who decided about the firing squads to be used against the workers in Gdansk in 1970,[92] or at how the different decisions in 1980–81 were arrived:

> Yet throughout this turmoil someone was deciding which newspaper will get how much print, that Radio Free Europe

broadcasts should be jammed, that police should forcibly enter a building in Bydgoszcz, that some people should not get their passports. Who they are is unclear, but they must be those nameless men of power shown by Wajda . . . these inner cores of power provided the continuity of the Polish regime during the turmoil of the past year. The shadow cabinet of party bureaucrats, the Department of the CC, continued to exercise their functions. . . . when the institutions of the old regime become dismantled and the old leaders depart, these inner cores of power gain complete autonomy.

Przeworski's conclusion is that the split at the top visible to all — a Babiuch and a Pienkowski being replaced one after the other as Premiers, Gierek and then Kania being sacked as Party bosses without any ceremonies — strengthened the powers of the invisible men in the state and Party apparatuses. The Party made concessions. Nothing was really changed.[93]

Pomian also underlines the fact that it is impossible to learn how decisions are reached within the power structure in Poland. Individual Party members are isolated from each other, they do not know either. Viewed from within or viewed from without, power remains opaque. Pomian notes that 'the true power-holders prefer to remain in the shadow'.[94]

Discussing the problems of analysing the relative independence of Poland vis-à-vis the USSR, an American political scientist, Andrzej Korbonski, who has studied Polish politics for decades, maintains that the main difficulty is 'that we lack reliable information regarding the whole question of decision-making in a country such as Poland and are forced to rely largely on impressions, intuition, and informed guesses'.[95]

The Polish sociologist Jadwiga Staniszkis, who wrote the first major sociological and political analysis of the self-limiting revolution and also took part in it as a Solidarity counsellor, has pointed to the necessity, when discussing the question of power, of not treating the Party as a unitary actor. Analysing the events at Bydgoszcz in March 1981, when local Solidarity functionaries were beaten by the police, with the result that the conflict between the Party leadership and Solidarity became aggravated, she starts by asking the question: what was the purpose? The confrontation, 'which was provoked by the police and mysterious individuals who remained behind the curtains', served to compromise the state apparatus, as its local representatives appeared to be the major villians of the affair. But the local Party members also lost their credibility in the eyes of the Solidarity members. The whole conflict in Poland now became increasingly polarised.[96]

Staniszkis's analysis of the Bydgoszcz incident makes it appear as part of a conscious policy, of somebody's strategy. Pomian has noted that the affair, which lingered on as Solidarity threatened to release a general strike if those who were responsible for the repressive acts were not found, was accompanied by a veritable campaign in the state controlled Polish press; not solely about the Bydgoszcz incident, but also about the on-going, continuing big military exercise 'Soyus-81' of the WTO, taking place around Poland and in Polish waters. Pomian thus hints at a possible Soviet connection behind the provocations in Bydgoszcz. There was neither a general strike nor a WTO invasion of Poland, but the conflict remained. From this time on the relations between Solidarity and the Party leadership deteriorated steadily.[97] In retrospect, it seems likely that Jaruzelski was setting out for a final showdown.

The suspicion that there was always a centre of power behind the curtains gains credibility as one tries to follow the development of the visible political life in Poland in 1980–81.

During the eight months between August 1980, when Solidarity began to challenge the rulers, and March 1981, when, as we have seen, Jaruzelski probably set the course towards a decisive battle, half of the local Party leaders in Poland were replaced. At the extraordinary Party congress in July 1981, only 18 of the previous 146 members of the Central Committee became re-elected.[98] It appeared as if some form of democratisation was taking place in Party life, which would have generally favourable consequences for political relations in Poland. However, things were not that simple.

Both at the beginning and at the end of the period of self-limiting revolution in Poland, representatives of the Party apparatus indicated that there was something fictional in the visible exercise of power by the Party. At the CC plenum in August 1980, i.e., at the beginning of the events, Olszowski, an experienced Party leader who had just been reco-opted on to the Politbureau, remarked that the Party had neglected the vital needs of the country. A remarkable statement from a leading Party member! Olszowski's description of the way the Party had acted is of direct relevance for our discussion of the power question:

> The theatrical nature of the activity of the Party and of the social organisations must be done away with, as well as the rigging in advance of congresses, conferences, and meetings . . .
> The theatricality of public life and the manipulation of state institutions such as the Diet and the National Council make these institutions lose the significance ascribed to them by the constitution, as well as their reputation.[99]

And when the end was approaching, in November 1981, one of the two main Warsaw papers, the *Zycie Warszawy* observed that the Party was bleeding to death from wounds inflicted upon it by its own superiors. In the eyes of the public, the Party was a monstrosity.[100]

The official Party line was that those who were visible to the public were responsible for the shortcomings. At the CC plenum in December 1980, the enthroned Party leader Gierek was criticised for having 'encouraged intrigues and exchanged genuine democracy for appearances'. The Central Committee, the Politbureau, and the Secretariat, had become absorbed by minor questions. The decisions about the crucial problems had been taken outside these organs. 'Comrade Gierek' was also responsible for serious mistakes concerning cadre policy at the centre.[101]

The natural question is to ask: who did the 'rigging' (Olszowski's assertion), who inflicted the wounds on the Party (*Zycie Warszawy*)? It is of interest to note that when Jaruzelski, who had been appointed Premier in February 1981, was also appointed Party secretary on 18 October, this was an evident violation of the decision of the extraordinary Party congress in July that nobody should hold the top posts in the government and in the Party at one and the same time. It is also of interest to note that the introduction of a 'state of war' on 13 December 1981, was a violation of the Polish constitution. The legislative prerogative of the Diet was usurped: as it was in session, it should, according to the constitution, have approved Jaruzelski's action in advance. Hence, the Military Council, which became the new ruling organ in Poland, was not a result of the proclamation of a 'state of war'. On the contrary, the proclamation was a consequence of 'the extra-constitutional initiative' of this previously formed 'extra-constitutional organ'.[102]

It is obvious that there was not any correspondence between the rules of the constitution and the actual way of making political decisions, i.e., a lack of correspondence between formal and real power in Poland. The strains on the system in 1980–81 showed that it had retained some basic similarities with Stalin's original Soviet political system.

As the Danish historian Niels-Erik Rosenfeldt has been able to demonstrate in the two excellent investigations referred to in the introduction to this study, the foundations of the Stalinist system are that certain key persons are in a position that allows them to manipulate all the social forces and institutions at play in any concrete situation. The strategy can work because of excessive secrecy in the administration, which effectively stops anyone outside the centre from obtaining an overview, and because of the fact that the centre can play the different administrative organs against each other — courts, the security police, the army and the civic administration — by purposely keeping them uninformed about the limits of their competence; hence they will compete with one another and become susceptible to manipulation from the centre.[103]

After Stalin, and outside the USSR, however, it was no easy task to try to establish complete manipulation within the vassal states. As a result of the slackening of terror and greater leeway for domestic forces in the politics of the vassal countries, the Kremlin could not count on the different organs never trying to join forces and thus slip out of control. Something of the kind apparently was under way in Czechoslovakia in 1968.

The retreat of the Polish communists when confronted with Solidarity, was most probably both a surprise and an annoyance to the Soviet leaders. If the Party had been doing its job well, if the security organs had, if the courts had ... the revolution would have been impossible. The diffusion of competence in this case obviously had resulted in inactivity and not in double checks from above. The puzzle was solved by the creation of a new organ by individuals who were still 100 per cent loyal to the Soviet leaders. It is very telling that Jaruzelski could ignore the decision of the PUWP:s extraordinary congress and the Polish constitution without being criticised by the Soviet leaders for having violated 'party discipline' or 'socialist legality'. Instead they approved of his actions. The creation of the Military Council in Poland signified that the old Stalinist power machinery had been adapted successfully to new circumstances. We will return to the question why the military was chosen, but let us first take a closer look at the specific local environment, i.e., the Polish scene.

While it is evident that political power was not exerted according to the Party statutes and the constitution, it is clear that a model suitable for the analysis of the development of political life in socialist Poland cannot be directly derived from political science theories concerning the functioning of contemporary multiparty systems either.[104]

Erik-Michael Bader, correspondent of the *Frankfurter Allgemeine Zeitung* in Warsaw until the autumn of 1981, has made an analysis of what happened in Poland which is theoretically explicit at the same time as it avoids the fallacy of treating Poland as just another variety of a general contemporary pattern. Bader takes his model from history.

Bader looks upon the creation and the court registration, i.e., legalisation, of Solidarity as the beginning of a new political system. The trouble was that this could not be openly admitted by the actors, as it contradicted the sacrosanct Leninist principles of the leading role of the Party and democratic centralism. Theoretically, however, Solidarity was playing the same role as that played by the parliaments in Western Europe at the transition from absolute to parliamentary monarchy. With the establishment of parliamentarism, Solidarity's role would have been that of the political opposition in Parliament.

However, this theoretical development outlined by Bader had no operational consequences. The Party may have forfeited all moral right to rule because of its mismanagement of the economy. Politically, it was impossible to remove by pressure from below. After the agreement with Solidarity on 31 August 1980, the Party was faced with the task of having to attempt to play three roles simultaneously: it had to play the role of the defeated party, which is utilising the fall from power to renovate itself, the role of the party coming to power with a coherent programme, and, finally, the role of the old ruling party, which continues to rule because it deserves it and has the confidence of the people.[105] The Party could not play any of these roles, however. Solidarity might, but was not allowed to.

The perspective from the vantage point of the seemingly impotent but obviously obstinate Party, was shown in article in *Nowe Drogi* in September 1981, i.e., at the time of Solidarity's congress. The title was 'The trade unions — partners or adversaries?'. The counterpart to the unions was, it should be understood, 'the Party and the state'.

The author of the article in *Nowe Drogi*, a certain W. Rogowski, expressed his indignation at the fact that Solidarity was treating the socialist state as if it was a capitalist employer which had to be forced into concessions. Rogowski admitted that the 'success propaganda' of the regime had been exaggerated. This was no excuse, however, for the present 'perfidious black fiasco propaganda' of Solidarity. Solidarity was showing animosity towards the Party and the state institutions. It was time for the movement to make up its mind concerning its role in the future:

> trade union — or sociopolitical movement or even a political party?
> scrutinizer of the state and the economy — or decision maker and leader?
> supporter of a genuine development of the socialist system, of state and social property — or adversary to all this?
> recognition of the leading role of the Marxist-Leninist Party — or support for bourgeois political pluralism?
> for the socialist allies of Poland — or against them or without them?

Rogowski stressed that it was the alternatives first mentioned in each case which were acceptable to the Party. Solidarity had to liquidate the extremist forces within its ranks, those who were inimical towards the Party and real socialism.[106]

When the 'state of war' was proclaimed, Solidarity was 'suspended'. Then the independent trade union lingered in limbo, trying to find an answer to the rhetorical question posed by the Party organ *Trybuna Ludu*: independent from whom and from what?[107] At last the Jaruzelski regime gave the answer and declared Solidarity illegal. This was a logical outcome. Solidarity had tried to check the Party from below, thus jeopardising the Soviet grip on Poland. Jaruzelski checked it from above, or from within, from behind the scene.

The arguments put forward by Rogowski as well as the actions carried out by the Jaruzelski regime, should be compared with an analysis of the roots of the malfunctioning of Poland, presented by Solidarity's Centre for Social and Trade Union Problems in February 1981:

1 The dominating features of the system are lack of democratic mechanisms of decision-making, lack of responsibility for the decisions taken, and neglect of the necessity to change personnel in the executive organs. The society is kept outside decision making. The decisions are being made by different parts of the bureaucracy.

2 The bureaucratic way of ruling makes it impossible to correct mistakes. Often it is even impossible to speak about the consequences of the decisions, because of the censorship, of secrecy, and of the resistance against every attempt of independent analysis and evaluation.

3 The bureaucratic system laid over the state and the economy has resulted in the emergence of a closed group of rulers out of control of the ruled ones. The bureaucratic apparatus is counter-attacking every attempt at changes that would possibly undermine its own position, material benefits, and power.

4 The structure just depicted has made impossible any salvation from the crisis. The existing political system in Poland has not been able to, and has not had the strength to, cure itself.

The conclusion of this analysis was that no economic reform would be successful if it was not combined with a profound reform of the system of government, the socio-political system in Poland.[108]

This description by Solidarity of the working of the political system in Poland is similar to the description of the Stalinist system by Rosenfeldt. In both cases, one notices the importance of secrecy and lack of transparency from the outside for the functioning of the system (as seen from the point of view of the ruler).[109]

Those active within this system naturally become moulded by it. They accept as a natural thing that there must be a central agent behind everything, every movement in the society, that there must be a central power which controls all institutions and organisations of society, from the Military High Command to the smallest nursery. They apparently believe that this is politics, what politics must and should be. Consequently, they cannot imagine that the adversaries of this system can arrive at their conclusions independently and from different starting points, without being united in a conspiracy. They cannot believe that there are people who are seriously aiming at erecting a truly pluralist political system, where no one will be allowed to put his foot on the neck of somebody else. They are permeated by the conspiracy and power for power's sake mentality. This belief in conspiracy is combined with a Manichean world-view with its roots in the Eastern Christendom, Russian (Greek) Orthodoxy. In this perspective, every conscious act by a human being must be either for or against you. The answer to the question 'who is behind' is to be found in an analysis of 'who benefits'. Fellow men and women are viewed as mere tools, for your own side, the good one, or for the other, the evil one.[110] Last but not least, Stalinist political thought takes it for granted that the centre of political power must not be subject to public control.

Political anti-semitism

The Stalinist political culture which has been imposed upon Poland and which the majority of Poles tried to get rid of in 1980–81, can be illuminated by an indirect method, by an analysis of how the local proponents of this political culture view their adversaries, or, rather, the adversaries of their Soviet masters.

Because of the history of Poland, the combination of a strong but suppressed nationalism and anti-semitism, which had been developed during the partition period and also in the interwar years, it was close at hand for those serving the powers to regard the Jews as the enemies, as the 'counter-conspirators', as it were. Seen from a communist perspective, an obvious advantage with ascribing to Jews the role of arch enemy, is that Jews are to be found everywhere in the world and hence may be described as organisers of a global conspiracy against communism. It should be noted that according to communist logic, a Jew who is treated as a good communist, if he is a communist, is not a real Jew, while the communist Jew turning out to be unworthy thereby has proved himself to be, a Jew.

The usefulness of a conspiracy theory is not limited to the fact that one can rally the people behind the rulers by depicting a threat which is, allegedly, out to destroy both categories. The other side of the coin is that such a theory can be used for the eliciting of scape-goats, for finding the culprits for defects in the society which cannot be negated; 'scape-goating', as we know, is a trade mark of communist politics. The responsibility for conditions for which a single individual really cannot be held responsible but which are the result of the policies of the communist leadership *in corpore*, cannot be accepted by the Party. A conspiracy has to be found, or at least shown to the people.

In the following, we will see how the official Stalinist political culture imposed upon Poland is enriched by conspiracy theory and anti-semitism. The ability of the rulers to handle these phenomena has most likely been of importance for temporary political stabilisation in the country, being an attempt at acquiring legitimation by blaming scape-goats. It is necessary first briefly to outline the history of the Jews in Poland, to be able to demonstrate the political relevance of anti-semitism in the country.

The Jews arrived in Poland in the Middle Ages. Here they found a haven from the persecutions in Western Europe at the time of the crusades. The ruling nobility of Poland welcomed the diligent Jews because they would fill the empty space, economically, between the nobility and the peasants. The Jews became merchants, artisans, shopkeepers and manufacturing workers. The majority were very poor and lived in closed settlements called *staedtl*. They spoke Yiddish. They were not assimilated.

When Poland was partitioned, the majority of the Jews became subjects of the Russian empire. As was the case with the other non-Russian nationalities, they became the object of suppression and persecution. At the turn of the 19th and the 20th centuries, the regime allowed pogroms to be carried out.

The ideological currents of 19th century Europe, nationalism and socialism, exerted a strong influence on many minorities in Russia, Poles and Jews among them. Jewish as well as Polish nationalism was to be found to the left as well as to the right on the ideological scale. In both nations there were also socialist internationalists.

When Poland was resurrected in 1918, the socialists of internationalist leanings gathered in the new Communist Party (an amalgamation of the old SDKPiL and PPS-Left), which became a member of Comintern. The relative percentage of people who were not ethnic Poles was high in the Polish Communist Party. Many were Jews.

In the 1930s, the communists in Poland became persecuted by the *Sanacja* regime. In the nationalistic climate of the time, anti-semitism flourished in Poland. Many Jewish communists went to Stalin's Soviet Union. The better part of these perished during the purges. In 1938 Stalin had Comintern dissolve the Polish Communist Party.[111]

Ninety per cent of the Polish Jews or close to three million people were murdered by the Nazis. About 300,000 survived, mainly those who had been living in the areas conquered by the USSR in 1939 and who had been evacuated to Soviet Central Asia when the Germans came in 1941.

A considerable proportion of the Polish communists (the new Party was created in 1943), who with Soviet help took power in Poland after the war and in the course of the Stalinisation of Poland in 1948–49, were of Jewish origin. This was not very strange, since communism was despised by most ethnic Poles just because it was so Russian. There were few volunteers. Conversely, the same communism was regarded by many Jews as a means of putting an end once and for all to national discrimination. In communism the ethnic Pole saw Russia, while the Jew saw socialist ideals. Of course the Jews did not numerically dominate the new Party formed under Russian surveillance in Poland: in late 1948 the old PPS was forced to amalgamate with the Communist Party (the 1943 edition). The result was the PUWP. However, many of the leaders were of Jewish origin, though they did not lead a Jewish life religiously or culturally. And they were, of course, fierce anit-Zionists. All the same . . .

Today it has been a long time since Jews were prominent in the Polish

Communist Party. The anti-Zionist campaign in 1968 made most of the remaining Jews leave Poland. How this happened is well known and need not be retold here. What is of interest is that anti-semitism still seemed to be virulent in the early 1980s, drawing its inspiration partly from the communist conspiracy theory, partly from a special interpretation of the history outlined above.

The logic of contemporary active Polish anti-semitism, as it appeared in 1980–81, is simple: all that is wrong in Poland, all evils, are the effects of Jewish conspiracies. Stalinist terror in 1948–56 was of Jewish making, the student demonstrations in 1968 were directed by the Jews, and it was the Jews who, masking themselves in the garments of the KOR, took control of Solidarity and the strike movement in 1980.

There is no need to use the words 'Jews' or 'Jewish' to suggest Jewish responsibility for all the hardships of the Poles. And after all, communists should not be caught red-handed abusing certain nationalities. It is sufficient to write about 'Zionism', 'cosmopolitism' and 'people who have changed their second name' (i.e., from Jewish-sounding ones to genuinely Polish ones). The trick consists in leading the reader to the conclusion that it is the depicted culprit's being a Jew which is at the heart of the matter.

In 1980–81 the method mentioned above was primarily used by the nationalist movement Grunwald, a so called patriotic organisation which could act so freely that it must have been at least accepted, if not endorsed, by the rulers. On 13 December 1981, Solidarity was 'suspended', and in 1982 it was declared illegal. Grunwald did not meet with a similar fate. What is more: its arguments, as they can be re-constructed from a book which appeared in Warsaw in 1981, could be found also in the state-controlled mass media after 13 December 1981.

The book from 1981 was issued under the pen-name Ida Martowa and bore the title *March 1968 — an attempted coup d'état which failed.* The starting point of the book was a description of the present situation and the organisation KOR. KOR was declared to be an ideological and political parasite, trying to use a real workers' mutiny for its own ends. These ends had already been revealed in March 1968. Martowa asserted that the student demonstrations in Warsaw in that year had been spontaneous. They were a Zionist-Trotskyist attempt designed to lead to a coup d'état. The actions had been prepared well in advance and aimed at resurrecting Stalinism in Poland.

The thesis stating that the March events in 1968 were part of a Zionist conspiracy is not new. It was sustained by the Gomulka regime at the time. What is interesting is that Martowa combines March 1968, both with KOR and with the Stalinist rule in Poland in 1948–56. Martowa asserts that 'the Polish road to socialism' was shelved in 1948, when Jakub Berman was running the security police. Berman co-operated with his Soviet colleague Beriya, and this was no coincidence:

Beriya and Berman were united by many things. Both supervised and in practice directed the work of the state security services in the USSR and Poland, both came from rich bourgeois Jewish families, and both were prominent actors in the Zionist movement.

According to Martowa, Beriya and Berman took part in a conspiracy against the Soviet and Polish Communist Parties and states. After making this assertion, the author goes on to describe developments in Poland. A summary of the description will be given here as it is of wider significance.

Berman and the other Jews in the Party leadership deliberately educated a 'caste' which would inherit power from themselves. Concepts such as 'the nation', 'the Fatherland' and 'patriotism' were dismissed with the argument that they were expressions of rightist nationalist deviation. Jewish 'commandos' took over the old Polish nationalist boy scouts' movement. Later, these commandos from 'the caste of Stalinist rulers' would take over the leadership of the students and inaugurate the demonstrations ('provocations') in 1968. The leading names were Jacek Kuron, Karol Modzelewski, and Adam Michnik, i.e., those who were also the central persons in KOR. These figures and their friends regarded themselves as the chosen children, the chosen politicians, and the chosen intellectuals. They infiltrated the institutes of sociology, philosophy, economics, history, mathematics, and physics of the University of Warsaw. At the cost of the state, they travelled to the West to establish contacts with the enemies of People's Poland, especially Zionists and Trotskyists. They also co-operated with the dark forces trying to carry out a counter-revolution in Czechoslovakia in 1968.

In 1956, the communist regime in Poland became truly national again, as Gomulka came back to power. The commandos now realised that it was impossible to topple the communist regime either with the help of arms or by parliamentary means. Therefore, they concentrated on inspiring discontent and on infiltrating different institutions. They attacked the principle of the leading role of the Party and propagated pluralism. They did this in order to prepare the ground for the re-establishment of Stalinism. They placed their hopes on the country's youth, who did not know the history of the Stalinist period. Especially the students in Warsaw who were regarded as an important group. Here Adam Michnik was designated to form a group that should become 'the staff and the mind' of the machinations.

The student demonstrations in March, 1968, thus were the result of many years' conspiratorial work. In the years before, Kuron and Modzelewski had been gaoled, being convicted in 1964 for crimes against the state, but the authorities handled the case against these Trotskyites so clumsily that the convicts became heroes in the eyes of the youth. When the two were released in 1967, they quickly regained power over the students and started organising the March provocations. The plans were that first the students, then the workers, and at last the soldiers should be incited to rebel and accomplish a sanguinary 'Polish Budapest'. Although many different groups took part in the conspiracy, it was orchestrated by the Zionists. The Party showed resolve, acted correctly and crushed the insurrection, but the struggle against socialism in Poland was carried on by exiles in Israel, the Netherlands, West Germany, France, Austria, the United States, and Sweden.

In 1980 the Trotskyist-Zionists appeared again on the political scene in Poland, this time in the shape of KOR. The Stalinist caste from which these people came is the one which once had power in Poland, in the politbureau of the Party, in the government, in diplomacy, in foreign trade, in cultural life and in the press, and in the apparatus of terror, i.e., the security service and the courts, which were instruments of terror under Stalinism. Martowa is anxious to underline that today's Polish youth should be taught these facts. The libellous pamphlet ends with a warning that the Trotskyist sons of the old Stalinists now (1981) were trying to destroy Poland, as well as Hungary and Czechoslovakia.[112]

Similar warnings were issued by the Grunwald organisation in November 1981. It asserted that Solidarity was being undermined systematically by a Zionist conspiracy and ran the risk of meeting with the same fate as the Party leadership, 'which is already dominated by the Jews'.[113] (The last assertion indicates that the Grunwald organisation, while tolerated by the Party, expressed the opinion of one special fraction within it.)

Neither Martowa's nor Grunwald's arguments were substantiated by any proof. The analysis of Martowa is confused, to say the least, in its endeavour to bring together Zionism, Trotskyism, and Stalinism to a common denominator: Jewish conspiracy. It would not be of great interest but for one important fact: its lines of thought, interpretation of history, and arguments against KOR, were featured in the Polish official media after 13 December 1981, i.e., when censorship and supervision from above was tight again. Nothing would be printed and broadcast on such a politically sensitive subject without the approval of the regime.

The following excerpts from the Polish media in December 1981, and in the spring of 1982 may seem random and insignificant. They should be interpreted, however, against the background of Martowa's text. Martowa's book may be seen as an expression of individual idiosyncrasies. What is printed in state controlled media is, when the subject is politically sensitive, a part of the official ideology.

In the Polish army daily *Zolnierz Wolnosci* on 13–14 March 1982, a certain Jan Lew — a pseudonym for Eugeniusz Banaszczyk — almost literally repeated the main thesis of Martowa, i.e., that Jewish 'commandos', who had been educated by the Stalinists, had created KOR. Lew added that Gomulka had not managed to purge all the Stalinists in 1956. The latter continued their undermining activities and could successfully block all attempts at reforms. After the fall of Gierek, the commandos came into the open and revealed their true face, which was 'cosmopolitan in the worst sense of the word'.[114] (The Jewish sense, that it.)

On 24–25 April 1982, the central Party daily *Trybuna Ludu* featured a large article by a rather well known publicist, Józef Kossecki, on 'the methods of operation of KSS-KOR'.

Kossecki started by enumerating some of the leaders of KOR, mostly bearing Jewish surnames. Following Martowa's model, he explained that these people had been educated by their parents and at special Trotskyist training courses to become political conspirators. According to Kossecki, the March events in 1968 became a turning point. The 'commandos' drew their lessons from their failure and started to cultivate contacts with the Catholic Church and rightist emigrants such as Leszek Kolakowski (the philosopher is also mentioned in a similar context by Martowa). They created KOR, a professional political organisation, which, Kossecki declared, quickly took over the leadership of Solidarity. The workers, who were politically inexperienced, had no chance to defend themselves, because 'when a professional and an amateur are competing, the professional must dominate'. The KOR activists did not have themselves elected nominal leaders, according to Kossecki, because they feared to lose in free elections, but preferred to operate behind the curtains and manipulate Solidarity's nominal leaders from there.[115]

But why could this conspiracy be so successful? What about Grunwald's assertion that the Jews were manipulating the Party leadership as well? Kossecki had the answer, one answer, to these two questions. In a programme, transmitted by Radio Warsaw only two days after the introduction of the 'state of war' in Poland, i.e., on 15 December 1981, Kossecki said, among other things, the following (quoting, approvingly, a neo-ND leaflet):

'There is no doubt that the Gierek regime could have liquidated KOR in a matter of hours. If it did not do this, it is because it agreed to the existence of KOR. Moreover, there was a discreet collaboration between KOR and Gierek. For instance, a condition of many foreign loans was that KOR be left in peace and Gierek accepted this.
This co-operation has lasted until this day. Among other things, it is KOR in Solidarity which effectively blocks demands that the Gierek leadership account for their policies and that food exports and new loans be proscribed!' I continue quoting: 'Some of its (KOR's) maturer members are responsible for the terror of Stalin's time, when thousands of the best Polish

patriots were murdered.' And so on and so forth. 'The younger ones, as they themselves declare, had until 1968 been supporters of so called Trotskyism. Several instances of the practical realisation of Trotskyist doctrine show that they continue to be Trotskyists.' Well, I do not know if the Trotskyists would agree exactly with this wording, but this is a separate problem...[116]

Although Kossecki was quoting a leaflet of a non-communist, nationalist organisation (we recall that the original, prewar ND was the party of Roman Dmowski, the so called *Endecja*), the only point where he took care to voice an objection was about whether the policy of KOR had 'practically realised' any 'Trotskyist doctrine'. He did not object to the absurd allegation that KOR should have got support from Western bankers. As Charles Levinson has shown, it was exactly the belief in the non-existence of disturbing opposition and ensuing threats to the political stability that originally attracted Western capital and made it give loans and credits to Poland and other communist states.[117]

The political anti-semitism in a Poland that has scarcely any Jews, is a perverted version of the 'protector of national culture' legitimation device. The rulers are not trying to show that they are protecting the nation against the actual threat, i.e., the demands of the CPSU. They invent a fictitious menace instead. The use of political anti-semitism is an indication that the rulers have doubts about the legitimacy of their regime. The conspiracy thesis also mirrors their own conception of politics.

The background to and the breakdown of the 'self-limiting' revolution: a summary

Taking into consideration what had happened to Czechoslovakia in 1968–69, every politically conscious Pole would understand that economic decentralisation and pluralisation of political and cultural life at one and the same time would not be tolerated by the Soviet leaders, who would not hesitate to use any means necessary to quench a similar development. On the other hand, exactly at the time of the Czechoslovak events, the Gomulka regime was heading for a major confrontation with its alleged supporters, the manual workers. The communist leaders evidently came to the conclusion that what threatened to destabilise the social and political system in Poland, and by implication also Soviet security, was material discontent on the part of the workers. The solution, then, apparently would be found in feeding and clothing the workers a little better. This was the background to the economic policies of the Gierek regime.

It is important to note, in the general context of this study, that the Gierek regime tried to solve the problem of menacing destabilisation not with the help of innovative reforms, but through substitutes: imports from the West of capital, technology, and know-how (cf. so-called 'turnkey factories' built in the country by Western firms). The so-called planned economy remained, and with it centralisation of the state economy.

It is also important to note that the Gierek regime did not see any 'liberalisation' of cultural or political life. On the contrary, repression was in some instances rather severe.[118] The mushrooming of opposition groups from 1976 on was not due to any conscious liberalisation policy of the regime. It was a symptom of the Party leadership losing its control of Polish society.

The failure of economic policy, of the attempt to 'build a second Poland', as the Party propaganda said, stimulated the growth of the black economy and the privatisation and atomisation of social life. The attempts by the Party leadership to counteract the general economic stagnation only made conditions worse. Society became increasingly split and segmented as the regime tried to placate certain key groups and enterprises by handing out privileges. Under Gierek Polish society became feudalised, to use Staniszkis's expression.[119] It was not a question of positive decentralisation, however. When local government was reformed in 1975, central control was strengthened: the provinces became forty nine instead of twenty two, which meant that they became smaller and less capable of implementing a policy of their own. At the same time, Party control of local government became more rigid. The whole reform was 'designated toward concentration of the central power'.[120]

From the beginning however, the 1975 administrative reforms did not enhance efficiency. As late as 1980, a Western student of the subject, Jaroslaw Piekalkiewicz, observed:

> At present the local administration is generally in a state of chaos, which normally follows any extensive changes in the administrative structure. This confusion is magnified by a certain variety of territorial divisions in which local government territory does not necessarily correspond to regions of the specialized administration. Also, the new political hierarchy of authority and responsibility was created in which some power holders were demoted while others were promoted. Their mutual relationships as well as their relationship toward the power center must develop new interdependent structures.[121]

What we have just seen described is a structure reminiscent of the Stalinist power system, depicted and analysed by Rosenfeldt. There were two differences between the two phenomena however, that are of major importance: Gierek would not or could not apply the same ruthless terror as Stalin did and thus could not have the subordinates concentrate their competition on just denouncing each other, and Poland was not autarchic and isolated from the outer world. Poland had made herself dependent on the world economy, though she could not adapt to it successfully. Instead of a stable Stalinist structure, the outcome was an unstable shack.

What happened was that the forty nine provinces became increasingly isolated from each other. Faced with the effects of the national economic stagnation, the local leaders tried to close the frontiers of their provinces to stop the 'export' of food and consumption goods in general to the neighbouring provinces. At the same time, they competed with each other in trying to have the central authorities allocate investment resources to them. They were partly successful, which meant that investments were spread out without regard for any national coherence.[122]

Viewed in this perspective, it was logical that the 'self-limiting revolution' in 1980 spilled over from the economic to the political sphere. As the two dimensions were intimately related in government policy, the opposition was forced to take up both issues. The events from August 1980, until 13 December 1981, thus became part of a process where the oppositional forces were trying to modernise the political system. Polish sociologists have called this 'a cultural revolution' or a 'break-through'.[123]

Far from enhancing stability and Soviet security, the policy of the Gierek regime had revealed that the system was still very vulnerable. When 'economic compensation' failed, the 'protection of the nation' trick failed as well. It turned out that it was the Catholic Church and the Solidarity movement, rather than the regime, which had the support of the majority of the population. These actors consciously took up national traditions and national culture, and, by so doing, revitalised Poland's pluralist political culture. It was exactly this re-activation of national traditions and of the non-Stalinist political culture that became a threat to the established political order. This revival, if it was to become established, would not be compatible with the principles of the leading role of the Communist Party and democratic centralism. If the latter were abolished, the Soviet leaders would risk losing their ability to exert direct influence over Poland and her international relations.

One may say that the 'self-limiting revolution' or 'break-through' in Poland was history's revenge on the Soviet leaders and their vassals in the country. What had happened can be summarised accordingly.

The political system imposed upon Poland between 1944 and 1949 entailed the imposition of an alien political culture. A basically Western society, with traditions of ideological and political pluralism, was subjugated under a despotic, monolithic rule. The new holders of power, the communists, never acquired any legitimacy in the Weberian sense. Their power was based on force and threats, and, in the last instance, Soviet power.

The fundamental instability of the new political system in Poland was revealed under the impact of the crisis which hit the whole Soviet empire after Stalin's death and during the de-Stalinisation process. The erosion of the foundations of the system in Poland was thus linked to external events. But these became enforced by domestic events. The leaders tried different ploys to gain legitimacy, or at least the resemblance of it, but it was all in vain.[124]

The malfunctioning of the Polish economy was an important factor behind the manifestations of popular resistance to the regime in 1956, 1970, 1976, and 1980. These manifestations were also triggered, however, by the political effects of de-Stalinisation (1956), the demise of the myth of a West German revanchist threat (1970), the East-West process of détente in Europe, epitomised by the Helsinki agreement in 1975 (1976), and the visit of the Polish pope to his Fatherland in 1979 (1980). All this served to underline, in the minds of the Poles, their distance to the USSR and relatedness to (Western) Europe. Thus the already weak ideological influence of the Communist Party became still weaker, and the traditional Polish political culture re-emerged. The definite turning point came in 1976, when intellectuals and workers, learning their lessons from the defeats of the respective classes in 1968 and in 1970, began to co-operate politically.

The oppositional movement which grew after 1976 in Poland and which resulted in the creation of Solidarity in August 1980, was able to obtain the support of the majority of the Poles because it acquired political legitimacy. It was clearly anchored in tradition, drawing on experiences as distant as the resistance to the Russians and the quest for (relative) democratisation in the 1790s. It came to symbolise the strife for legality in the relations between governors and governed (as distinct from rulers and ruled). It had a charismatic leader, Lech Walesa (a 'son of the people').

The regime could not match the opposition in any of the dimensions of legitimacy. The idea of Solidarity remaining just a trade union was, in this situation, absurd. But as the Party could not abdicate, though it had lost its ability to rule, Poland became a society adrift. Alienation grew between the rulers and the ruled. Did the former have control and would the latter obey? The conflict became increasingly polarised. The age-old distinction between 'we', i.e., the people or the workers, and 'them', i.e., the power holders, became reinforced, with the new 'red bourgeoisie' taking the place of the old gentry. And what had originally been a political subculture in 1976, the KOR movement, and then had gained in importance as a counterculture in the summer of 1980, now finally, in 1981, emerged as the alternative political culture, expressing itself in Solidarity.[125]

After the congress, in the autumn of 1981, there came a change of mood inside Solidarity, where fundamentalist, authoritarian, anti-intellectual and even anti-semitic currents became visible. The frustration from not seeing a way out brought forward the mirror image of the communist political culture among sections of the workers. Communist indoctrination had thus made itself felt in an indirect way, and, ironically, in an increasingly anti-communist atmosphere. The answer of the regime was to shelve ideology and politics altogether. On 13 December 1981, it transformed Poland from a 'party-state' into an 'army-state'.[126] At this juncture, Solidarity can be said to have already declared war on the regime. Meeting in the movement's birthplace on 11 December 1981, the direction of Solidarity decided to propose a referendum in all Poland and let the members answer the following questions:

> Are you prepared to express your non-acceptance of the Jaruzelski government?
> Do you support the idea of the creation of a provisional government and of free elections?
> Do you want Solidarity and the provisional government to guarantee the military interests of the USSR?
> Do you think that the PUWP may still be the instrument of such a guarantee in the name of the whole society?[127]

Of course this Solidarity manifesto was not the cause, not even the immediate or triggering cause, of Jaruzelski's action on 13 December. Such a large operation could not have been arranged overnight. On the contrary, Jaruzelski's rise to power during 1981 ultimately pointed to this solution to the problem.[128] But the manifesto implied that the Polish 'crisis' was possible to solve only if a major upheaval hit the entire Soviet empire.[129]

Discussing the Polish events one should note, finally, that the issue of the need to safeguard Soviet security might be the ultimate reason for the instability. This is not only an effect of the imposition of the disastrous Soviet economic system upon the country. There is another aspect to the problem as well.

The representatives of the Communist Party all the time have kept repeating that profound reforms of any kind are impossible because of 'the geopolitical situation of Poland' or because it would be an insult to the 'socialist friends'. The consequence was, of course, that the Poles began to consider the USSR as the major and decisive barrier to any change, even to nonpolitical change. Consequently, the opposition in Poland became forced, by the logic of the argument itself, to put the question of the nature of the relationship to the Soviet Union on the agenda. This was expressed very explicitly in the 11 December manifesto, but it had come to the fore already earlier, during Solidarity's congress. An appeal was then issued to the workers of the other WTO and CMEA states to start to create independent labour unions of the Solidarity type. The meaning of this could not be anything else than to try to undermine the Soviet hegemony by inciting opposition elsewhere. The gesture had no practical consequences in terms of support for Solidarity, not least because there was not any large, widespread sympathy for the Polish workers in the other vassal states. But it was of symbolical significance. It signalled awareness of the fact that any opposition movement in a country such as Poland would have to gain support from other quarters if it was to be able to retain what it had achieved. As an isolated Polish event, the 'self-limiting revolution' was bound to fail.

The parallel between the appeal by Solidarity and Dubcek's attempts to get support from Gomulka and Kádár for his reform programme in 1968 is obvious. At that time the Czechoslovaks asked for help, now the Poles. Both failed. In both cases, there were hints that the Hungarians were sympathetic but found it better not to come out into the open.

Notes

1 Cf. the titles of the books by Ascherson 1981 and Staniszkis 1982a. Arato 1981–82, p. 36 speaks of Solidarity as 'a revolutionary movement without a revolution', thereby implying a revolutionary logic and at the same time stressing that the obstacles were great.
2 See Lipski 1982a. Lipski was a member of KOR.
3 See Raina 1981 for the organisations formed after 1976.
4 See Gross 1979 for an analysis of the occupation years.
5 *Poland. The State of the Republic 1981*, p. 57 ff., 102.
6 See Gerner 1983 and Gerner 1972 for the origins and development of these conflicts.
7 See Gerner 1972, Westoby and Blick 1982.
8 Cf. Uschakow 1982, p. 35 f. See also, for Pilsudski's as well as Dmowski's programme, Davies 1982, p. 52 ff.
9 Cf. Pistakowski 1939 who states that an agreement with Czechoslovakia in 1931 was never ratified by the Polish government because it would have meant a recognition de jure of the frontier with Czechoslovakia established in 1920. See also Grazynski 1939, reporting on his irredentist activities on behalf of the Poles in Czechoslovakia from the day he became *wojewoda* in Katowice after Pilsudski's coup in 1926.
10 See Davies 1982, p. 406.
11 For a detailed analysis of Pilsudski's coup, see Rotschild 1966. For the whole interwar period, see Polonsky 1972.
12 Cf. Polonsky 1972, p. 506 f.
13 Sprawy Miedzynarodowe 1981, p. 11 f.
14 Sprawy Miedzynarodowe 1981, p. 13.
15 Blazynski 1979, p. 211 ff.
16 Davies 1982, p. 568. On the anti-semitic aspect, see Korey 1978, p. 101.

17 See The Kubiak Report 1982 for the records of what happened in the Baltic ports in 1970, i.e., that General Jaruzelski took part in the decision that the workers should be gunned down.
18 See Fallenbuchl 1980.
19 For figures, see Fallenbuchl 1980.
20 For a more elaborate analysis of the economic slowdown, see Gerner and Hedlund 1982 and Fallenbuchl 1982.
21 Staniszkis 1982b.
22 Staniszkis 1979.
23 *Poland. The State of the Republic 1981*, p. 3 f.
24 See especially Nowak 1980. Cf. Staniszkis 1981, Mink 1981. See also Bates 1982.
25 Cf. Zagajewski 1981, p. 9, 'the contamination of two realities and two languages'; Bauman 1981, p. 51, 'no language for social discourse', Michnik 1981, p. 67, 'most of our society lost its language'; Wojcicki, p. 100 (on the effect of the 1980 revolution), 'the Poles can finally speak the truth'; and Mink 1981, p. 130 (on the public opinion surveys carried out by sociologists in Poland), 'The problem of truth appears as a central social problem in all investigations'. See also Baranczak 1979, p. 48. Korbel Albright 1983, p. 128 underlines the Party's gradual loss of control of the content of the press as a factor that contributed to the fact that society outside the Party could regain a language for political discourse: 'The public began to be in a position to discuss issues that had been debated only in the highest Party circles'.
26 Staniszkis 1982a, p. 122 f., Staniszkis 1983, p. 195 f., Gella 1982.
27 Bingen 1982, p. 155 f., Lipski 1982b.
28 Bromke 1981, p. 8.
29 Pomian 1982, p. 112 ff. Chojecki, the leader of NOWA, also stressed this point in a court declaration, 12 June 1980 (Raina 1981, p. 61).
30 Zagajewski 1981, p. 57 ff.
31 Radio Warsaw, 2 June 1979. Cf. Nowak 1982, p. 12 f.
32 Ascherson 1981, p. 123 and Bingen 1982, p. 149 both quote Slowacki in this context.
33 Czembor 1983.
34 Mushkat 1981, p. 88.
35 Kurczewski 1981.
36 Pomian 1982, p. 200 ff. See also Touraine et al. 1983, p. 185 which observes that the organisation 'brought to life the collective memory of the nation'.
37 Jablonski 1979; Fejtö 1982, p. 25.
38 Lorentz 1978; Konwicki 1981.
39 Pomian 1982, p. 117.

40 Davies 1982, p. 393 f. For the Soviet assessment of Poland in 1920, see Westoby and Blick 1982!
41 Zielinski 1978.
42 Blazynski 1979, p. 355.
43 Singer 1982, p. 233. It is also significant that the workers gave a repair shipyard at the Lenin shipyard in Gdansk the name of Pilsudski: 'Gdansk Stocznia Remontowa im. J. Pilsudskiego'. At least this was the name of the shipyard in question on the unofficial lists of interned people, circulating clandestinely in Poland in early 1982.
44 Tygodnik Solidarnosci, November 20 1981.
45 Tygodnik Solidarnosci, November 20 1981.
46 Papée 1937.
47 Personal information to the author from anonymous Poles.
48 Radio Warsaw, May 3 1981. Cf. Ruane, p. 158 f. See also Libiszowska 1981, p. 128, stressing that the Constitution was the second one in the world of its kind after the American.
49 Quoted in Konstytucja 1981, p. 45 f.
50 Pzreworski 1982, p. 28 f.
51 Mushkat 1981, p. 88. Cf. 'Poles 80' 1982, p. 187.
52 *Poland. The State of the Republic 1981*, p. 105.
53 Kusmierek 1981. For Zamyatin's statement, see Ruane 1982, p. 198 f. Zamyatin spoke on July, 20, and Kusmierek's answer is dated October, 15.
54 The letter is printed in Europa-Archiv, nr 4, 1982.
55 Kusmierek 1981.
56 Kolakowski 1982.
57 Blazynski 1979, p. 211 ff.
58 Blazynski 1979, p. 213 (Ryszard Wojna), *Guardian Weekly* August 31, 1980 (Mieczyslaw Rakowski).
59 Kolankiewiez and Taras 1977, p. 119 f.
60 Demus 1981, p. 109.
61 Blazynski 1979, p. 244 f., Zagajewski 1981, p. 157 f.
62 Quoted from Dabrowa 1982, p. 23.
63 Herrmann 1980, p. 47.
64 Quoted from Blazynski 1979, p. 248.
65 See, e.g., Kolankiewicz and Taras 1977, Demus 1981.
66 Herrmann 1980, p. 57. Blazynski 1979, p. 249 views the struggle over the constitution as 'the turning point' in the contest between the Gierek regime and the oppositionist forces.
67 *Poland. The State of the Republic 1981*, p. 104.
68 *Poland. The State of the Republic 1981*, p. 167 ff.
69 Quoted from Dabrowa 1982, p. 23 f.
70 Quoted from Europa-Archiv 1982:4, p. D 108.

71 *Pravda* 13 October 1981.
72 See *Poland. The State of the Republic 1981*, p. 57, 96 ff. See also Uschakow 1982, p. 34, who puts the letter of 17 September 1981, into this context.
73 Matejko 1982, p. 122 f: 'PPN . . . remains fully clandestine and is known publicly only from its pronouncements'. Cf. Raina 1978, p. 468, note, who asserts that Kuron was not a member.
74 PPN 1978, p. 1 ff. Cf. *Poland. The State of the Republic 1981*, p. 167 ff.
75 PPN 1978, p. 55 ff. (An English translation of the Programme is to be found in Raina 1978, p. 46 ff).
76 *Poland. The State of the Republic 1981*, p. 168.
77 Lidert 1982, p. 64.
78 Lidert 1982, p. 63 f.
79 Pomian 1982, p. 124. See also Davies 1982, p. 551.
80 Quoted from the *New York Times*, 2 March 1982.
81 Michnik 1982, p. 8.
82 Quoted from Dabrowa 1982, p. 23.
83 Herrmann 1980, p. 78 f.
84 Mushkat 1981, p. 88.
85 'Poles 80' 1982, p. 187.
86 Stroebel 1983 points to the fact that the influx of inexperienced people into the Central Committee strengthened the influence of the men behind the scene.
87 This is the gist of analyses carried out by Voslensky 1982 and Zaslavsky 1982.
88 White 1977, p. 29 ff.
89 Quoted from Istoriya i Sotsiologiya 1964, p. 8.
90 Quoted from Rhode 1982, p. 278..
91 The decrease was reported to be 2 per cent in 1979.
92 See The Kubiak Report 1982, where this Secret report of the PUWP commission mentions the whole Politbureau, including Jaruzelski, as responsible for the decision.
93 Przeworski 1982, p. 21 ff.
94 Pomian 1982, p. 48 ff.
95 Korbonski 1980, p. 355.
96 Staniszkis 1982a, p. 88 f.
97 Pomian 1982, p. 159 ff.
98 Lewis 1982, p. 135 ff.
99 Quoted trom Rhode 1982, p. 283.
100 Quoted from *Osteuropa*, No 4, p. A 263.
101 Quoted from Rhode 1982, p. 289.
102 Osadczuk-Korab 1982, p. 263.
103 Rosenfeldt 1978, 1980. See also Gerner 1981.

104 Cf. the ill-judged attempt by Dellenbrant 1982 and the criticism by Mägiste 1983!
105 Bader 1982, p. 219 ff., 227.
106 Rogowski 1981, p. 52 ff, 59 ff.
107 Quoted from the *Frankfurter Allgemeine Zeitung*, 13 May 1982.
108 Radio Free Europe 1981, p. 5 f.
109 For the transparency-opacity problem, see Gerner 1980b.
110 See Gerner 1980a, p. 191 ff. Cf. Elster 1983, p. 10, pointing to this aspect of Marxism.
111 See Baryka 1982 for an analysis of communism in Poland before 1943.
112 Martowa 1981, passim. See also Checinski 1982, p. 256 ff. Checinski notes (p. 260) that 'Grunwald was officially legalized on 28 April 1981 with almost 100,000 members throughout the country'.
113 Lippe and Heese 1982, p. 208, quoting articles in the Warsaw weekly *Polityka*, 24 November and 5 December 1981. It is worth noting that the theme of Zionist conspiracy in Poland was not confined to Polish sources only, but surfaced in official media in the Soviet Union and Czechoslovakia as well (see Ruane 1982, p. 134 and *Literaturnaya Gazeta*, 21 April 1981).
114 Lew 1982.
115 Kossecki 1982.
116 Documents 1982, p. 65.
117 See Levinson 1977.
118 See Kostecki 1982, p. 149 ff.
119 Staniszkis 1982a, p. 205.
120 Piekalkiewiez 1980, p. 188.
121 Piekalkiewiez 1980, p. 188.
122 Staniszkis 1982a, p. 196 f.
123 For the former expression, see Staniszkis 1982a, p. 28, for the latter, Kutylowski 1982, p. 103.
124 Lamentowicz 1983 gives a detailed analysis of the different, successive attempts.
125 Cf. Pietraszek 1983, p. 95 f. and Wyka 1983, p. 122 ff.
126 Cf. Staniszkis 1982a, p. 300. Anti-Semite attitudes among Solidarity activists are documented in Touraine et al. 1983, p. 157.
127 Fetjö 1982, p. 23.
128 Cf. Pomian 1982, p. 225 f.
129 The assertion in Touraine et al. 1983, p. 31 that 'Solidarity was in no sense a revolutionary movement' cannot be upheld in the light of what actually happened.

4 Hungary: from rebellion to compliance

NEM and a 'New international structure'

The Hungarian revolution in 1956 ended in defeat. But the defeat did not mean a return to Stalinism. The Communist Party was reconstructed in December 1956, retaining a mere 12 per cent of the members of the old Party.[1] For a few years, political repression was severe. Thousands of people were imprisoned or executed. The collectivisation of agriculture was brought to a successful end. But terror was soon discontinued. Politically, the significance of the development was that everybody understood that there would be no return to the old ways, neither to the methods of Stalinism nor to the politics of Nagy. Economically, collectivisation actually meant a modernisation of agriculture.[2]

In the first years after 1956, Kádár was not exactly regarded as a hero, but he was at least seen not as the worst, but as the second worst alternative.[3] Almost everybody in Hungary, within the reconstructed Party and outside it, seemed to agree that the country was defeated and had to recognise and adapt to the circumstances, and make the best of them.[4]

A turning point which meant a definitive break with the Stalinist past and an opening up towards a different future, was the general political amnesty issued by the rulers in 1963. People were allowed to work in different positions inside and outside the Party without having to indulge in self-criticism. No attempt was made to take up the sins of the Nagy regime in October 1956, i.e., political pluralism and a re-orientation of foreign policy. But Nagy had not had the time for any action on the economic front. Thus the room for economic reforms was comparatively large. The rulers chose a very pragmatic course. They made it clear to the people that they were interested in compromises of different kinds rather than in dictates. The suggestion was that Hungary would follow the road to socialism not because of any ideological obsession with Marxism, nor because of any need to copy the USSR, but because it would lead to a system which was suitable for Hungary, given the general external restrictions.[5]

In the mid-1960s, Kádár and other leaders had come to the conclusion that something had to be done to the economy, if nonautarchic Hungary was to prosper. Theoretically, the ground for reforms had been prepared by a debate starting already in 1953.[6] In 1964, a Plenum of the Central Committee of the Party adopted a resolution to investigate the possibilities of comprehensive economic reform. The question from now on, was treated as a technical one, and not as a political one (cf. the Czechoslovak 'mistake'!).[7] When the reform, the so called New Economic Mechanism (NEM), came into force on 1 January 1968, it had been preceded 'neither by major political and ideological decisions nor by a wide-ranging theoretical debate'. The whole approach of the decision-makers was empirical rather than theoretical.[8]

The NEM aimed at changing the incentive structure of the economy away from fixed quantitative indicators towards market demand. While the planning authorities retained control over prices of raw materials and continued to set up general indicators, other prices were allowed to be set according to market demands. The idea of 'real' prices is so prominent in the NEM conception that to many experts, it constitutes the core of the whole reform.[9]

There is no need for us to go into the details of the working of the NEM. We will have to concentrate on what is of political importance, i.e., look upon the phenomenon as an example of (successful) 'economic compensation'. In the following I will make only a brief summary of the ups and downs in the Hungarian economy after 1968.

As Hungary's domestic market is comparatively small (the country has 10 million inhabitants) and as part of it remained protected, the allocation functions of prices did not work according to the textbooks. Besides, manual workers in the major industries could not take advantage of the market mechanisms. On the contrary, they were adversely affected by the changing price relations. This was rather awesome for a regime which allegedly was the workers' own.[10] Moreover, Hungary, which is poor in energy resources, was hard hit by the rise in world market prices for oil in 1973. The 'golden years' of annual growth of the national income with seven per cent, came to an end. As a consequence, central control over the economy became strengthened again. Some of the larger enterprises were brought back under direct ministerial rule, and there was a freeze in the move towards more small enterprises. This crisis for NEM was overcome however, in 1977, when the development towards decentralisation was continued.[11] The price reforms were continued as well, with the aim of making the Hungarian currency, the forint, convertible. With the words of the Head of the Hungarian Materials and Prices Office, Béla Csikós-Nagy, 'monetarisation' of the economy was viewed as the best way of not only sustaining, but of accelerating the reform programme.[12]

One of the architects of the NEM, Rezsö Nyers, was removed from his position as Minister of Finance in connection with the halt in the programme in the mid-1970s. He continued to be active in economics however and is, at the present time, Head of the Institute of Economics of the Hungarian Academy of Sciences. What he is doing and saying thus must be regarded as being of political significance. It is of interest, then, that Nyers has pointed to the fact that the NEM is of political importance because it has as one precondition a certain autonomy for Hungary vis-à-vis the USSR and the CMEA. In a speech in 1981, Nyers underlined that the experience of the 1950s had shown that the necessary alliance with the USSR could be 'misused'. According to Nyers, the Kádár regime had therefore decided that Hungary should not try to copy the USSR but be an active member of the CMEA at the same time as she led a policy of 'independent determination of the politico-economic strategy and tactic of the nation'. The point was that reliance on the CMEA must not be excessive, because of certain characteristics of the organisation, i.e., of its non-Hungarian members:

> One of the noteworthy symptoms of the new situation is that the other socialist countries are only slowly switching to the intensive i.e., efficiency-driven development of their economies. Another fact, of great importance to Hungary, is that the motor of socialist cooperation, the Soviet economy, was thrown into lower gear, aiming at external cooperation of a different structure, and this all has a less stimulating effect on the development of the smaller economies. It is likely that this also signals a lasting change, to which Hungary must adjust in the appropriate way.[13]

The 'external cooperation of a different structure' of the USSR that Nyers was referring to must have been, among other things, that after the oil price increases in 1973 and 1979 by the OPEC states, the USSR followed suit by raising the price of Soviet oil exports to the other CMEA states, albeit with a certain time-lag. Moreover, an upper limit was put upon what could be purchased in the 'soft' CMEA currency, transferable rubles: the additional oil, i.e., above the agreements, Hungary had to buy from the USSR on the spot market, at current prices, and it had to be paid for in US dollars. Due to these changes, Hungary's terms of trade deteriorated by twenty per cent between 1973 and 1980. According to a Hungarian source, this equalled a loss of ten per cent of the national income.[14]

Viewed against this background, it is hardly surprising to find that Csikós-Nagy concluded that 'in contrast with earlier ideas, the CMEA countries have to take initiatives separatedly'.[15] The Head of the Institute for World Economy of the Hungarian Academy of Sciences, József Bognár, also underlined (in 1980) that Hungary's further adaption to the world economy was necessary for the very survival of the country, and in September 1982, the then Foreign Minister of Hungary, Frigyes Puja, made the following remarks (in a speech at the Institute of East-West Security Studies in Washington, D.C.):

> In the interest of the country's economic development, economic relations with Western states should be undisturbed and even improved. We wish to attain economic objectives while further strengthening the connection of the Hungarian national economy with the world economy. Hungary's joining the International Monetary Fund and the World Bank is also a manifestation of this intention. With a view to developing the Hungarian national economy we shall also in the future need to make use of outside sources, we are willing to accept foreign participation in carrying out certain investment projects.[16]

But this development is not only of economic significance. Bognár, in an article with the intriguing title 'Global Economic Security and Growth', has stressed that Hungary's adaption to the non-socialist world was not just a matter of concern for the economy. It also entailed 'substantial' changes in the social and cultural structure and in the organisation of science and research in Hungary. The previous stability which had been based on the relative international isolation of the country, was gone. The regime must find new ways of integrating the society. This was due to the fact that society had become more vulnerable, more exposed to dangers and insecurity, when the economy became increasingly integrated into the world economy. Insecurity and economic mistakes or failures might be misused by 'negative power factors' trying to direct society in the wrong direction under the slogan 'law and order'. If the regime put itself in a situation that was economically disastrous, political changes were likely to follow.[17]

It is not unlikely, although the reference is vague, that what Bognár had in mind was not only Hungarian experiences, but also the contemporaneous development towards catastrophe in fraternal Poland. But in spite of the social strains accompanying the economic reforms in Hungary, there has not been any eruption of the Polish kind. This difference may partly be explained by the fact that the Hungarian rulers have kept their subjects informed about pending changes in the economy, not least the price increases on consumption goods, and allowed a fairly open public discussion of the social problems.[18] However, a factor of perhaps greater importance has been that the regime has succeeded in giving the people the impression that rulers and ruled all are in the same predicament and that it is necessary to take up the old Hungarian ways of survival under foreign rule. In the 16th and in the early 17th centuries Hungarian Transylvanian princes co-operated with Ottoman sultans to save what could be saved, and after the defeat at the hands of Vienna in 1849, the Hungarian leaders managed to reach a compromise — the so called Ausgleich in 1867 — which gave to Hungary a high degree of autonomy within the Hapsburg empire.

Nobody can say with assurance, in 1984, that Hungary has succeeded, that NEM has made her practically invulnerable from setbacks and crises. Far from it. Hungary's economic situation is precarious. Her foreign debts are relatively high. The interesting thing, however, is that the social environment has remained comparatively stable and helped to prevent a further deterioration in economic conditions. If one may speak of an evil or negative 'socio-economic spiral' in Poland after 1976, one may speak of a neutral 'socio-economic dynamic equilibrium' in Hungary after 1968. It is clear, however, that Hungarian social scientists, who were allowed to put forward their views in the state controlled media, in the early 1980s showed themselves to be aware of the fact that Hungary was reaching an impasse and that another major, collective effort would be needed, if the gains of the last fifteen years were not to be lost. But in spite of inequalities, the remaining poverty that affected sections of the population and a deplorable housing situation — in spite of all this the Kádár regime must be said to have handled the 'economic compensation' device sufficiently well. However, as indicated above, this mechanism had not worked on its own. Before we return to the legitimacy and stability problems of the Hungarian regime today, let us also examine the 'protection of national culture' mechanism.

The functions of history

The well known 'Kádár formula' 'who is not against us, is with us' can be interpreted as aiming at the creation of a very special kind of legitimacy through 'negative legitimation' for the imposed and despised communist regime in Hungary.[19] The rulers and the ruled should unite in a common struggle for economic prosperity and the preservation of the national culture.

One of Hungary's leading economic historians, Ivan T. Berend, in a book which was published in 1980, underlined that the great difficulties that Hungarian society experienced in trying to adapt to the new situations after 1918 and after 1945 were caused by the lack of structural changes in the economy that would have brought about its integration into the world economy. The same problem had now reappeared. Reviewing the book, a Hungarian critic welcomed these words as hard but necessary. He added that most important of all now was that the whole society obtained a clear and realistic picture of the position and prospects of the Hungarian economy.[20] This may be compared to Bognár's assertion that the economic strategy chosen (in the beginning of the 1980s) meant an end to that social security which was equivalent to rigidity. 'Socio-political risk taking' in the economy must be further increased, however, if Hungary was to become successfully integrated into the world market. National consciousness should, according to Bognár, become still more tied to the understanding of economic criteria:

> I feel that in Hungary public opinion concerning the great national issues is excessively centred on language and literature After such important economic progress economic factors should be felt to a greater degree as part of the national consciousness.

To achieve this shift of attitudes one should, Bognár maintained, remind the nation of the noble achievements of earlier generations of economic reformers in the old Hungary.[21]

One can trace in Bognár's admonition a sense of insecurity that the Hungarians' interest in their culture and history would make them question the success of the 'protection' part of the regime's unwritten 'legitimation contract' with its subjects. Perhaps the Kádár regime is not perceived as a new instance of the 'survival regimes' under the Turkish Sultan and the Hapsburg Emperor? But what then had this dimension looked like during the NEM era?

Bognár's comment on 'language and literature' points to the important role of these in Hungarian society. As the critic Miklós Hernádi wrote at the same time as Bognár made his plea:

> For centuries, literature has been the main vehicle for national and political self-expression in Hungary. . . . the leading writers of Hungary, poets . . . have always been aware of a mission given them by the latent public opinion of the country.[22]

What 'political self-expression' of a latent opinion might look like was indicated by another literary critic, Tamás Tarján, in a review of a Hungarian performance of Peter Weiss's play 'Marat/Sade'. Tarján underlined that the director (János Acs) gave to the mental patients in the play the shape of political prisoners and with help of 'the idiom of associations' referred to concrete events in the modern history of Central Europe, such as the events in Hungary in 1956 and 'the Polish situation which has been becoming more and more acute over the years'.[23] (This was written in 1981.)

Latent public opinion is obviously being evoked by the appeal to a common latent interpretative code among the public: both the director and the critic in the case just mentioned could refer to a history which could safely be assumed to be known and interpreted in a certain way by spectators and readers, respectively. We begin to see how 'negative legitimation' may work in the cultural sphere: the regime need not be credited with anything positive as long as it allows the public to re-experience and express resentments at what went wrong in the past. One can speak of a kind of projection of today's tragic predicament into a likewise tragic history. The present-day experiences become sublimated into just the latest representation of a myth, the myth of continuous defeat and the eternal hope of redemption. We will find some superficial similarities as well as some profound differences in relation to the function of history (and myth) in contemporary Poland.

In communist Hungary, the official holidays are New Year, Easter, and Christmas, and 4 April (the Day of the victory of the Soviet Army over Hungary in the Second World War), 1 May, 20 August (the Day of the constitution — by a happy 'coincidence' also the ancient St. Stephen's Day [more on the significance of St. Stephen below]), and 7 November. An opinion survey carried out by a Hungarian sociologist in 1978 showed that Christmas was considered to be the most popular holiday and the 7 November, i.e., the day of the Russian revolution, the least popular one: it was held in esteem by Communist Party members exclusively. Moreover, two thirds of the respondents considered that the 15 March should be a national holiday. This is the anniversary of the 1848 revolution in Hungary, directed of course against Vienna, but drenched in blood by the troops of the Russian Tsar Nicholas I.[24] The salience of the latter date to many Hungarians is further corroborated by the fact that in the early 1970s, radical leftist students tried to organise 'counter-demonstrations in competition with the official celebrations'.[25] Apparently, both groups have been trying to appropriate the day for their own purposes.

Such counter-demonstrations reportedly were held in 1972 and in 1973. At the latter date, forty one people were arrested and denounced by the authorities as 'irresponsible nationalists'.[26] To assert that they were nationalists begs the question, as the very day chosen was the most 'national' day possible. But as the day symbolised not only 'national independence' but also 'social reform',[27] and as the slogans were such as 'All power to the workers' councils' and 'Down with the bureaucrats',[28] the legitimation relevance in general of the manifestations must have been

102

obvious for the rulers. Of course the Russian part of the suppression of the revolution of 1848–49 will recall experiences of a similar event in 1956. But it is possible to go much further back in history to recall, in the mind of the Hungarian public, 'repetitive situations' that give a certain perspective to today's tribulations.

The Mongol (Tatar) invasion in the 13th century did not only hit Russia and Poland, but Hungary as well. King Béla IV failed in his attempt to unite the Hungarians and defend the country. The Hungarians were defeated by the barbarians from the East. In a monastery annal in 1241 a monk wrote:

> In the said year of the Lord, owing to the Tatar destruction, Hungary ceased to exist.

Commenting on this event in 1980, the literary critic Anna Földes made the following observation, which as will be shown, is of interest to our argument:

> Today, 739 years later, it would be a rather pointless gesture to engage in a detailed refutation of that statement. It is a much more exciting enterprise to examine the figure who was the hero of that national catastrophe and of the ensuing reconstruction, the King who is revered as the second founder of the Hungarian state. Béla IV was not only a descendant of the rulers of the House of Arpád and the son of Endre II (the King of the Golden Bull), he was also the son of Gertrud of Merano. History cast Gertrud as the foreign woman at the Hungarian court, and no one was more hated than this cruel, haughty schemer who acted consistently in the interests of her compatriots and against those of the Hungarians.

The examination of Béla IV, mentioned by Földes, was carried out in a play by Magda Szabó, 'The Boy from Merano', which was staged at the Madách theatre in Budapest in 1980. Commenting on the play, Szabó said that her interest in the subject was awakened because of the fact that she felt that there was a strange repetition, a pattern of recurrent events, in the history of Hungary. Béla was the first Hungarian ruler who had to struggle against popular suspicion of his alleged dependence on a foreign power. And the 1240s marked the first case of the ruling class of the country refusing to recognise the seriousness of the danger, which was threatening Hungary from the East. Although one got information about the approaching Mongols, the necessary measures of defence were not carried out.

When 'The Boy from Merano' was being performed in Budapest in 1980, the spectators were so enthusiastic, according to Földes, that it looked like 'as if people were hoping against hope, perhaps this time the national catastrophe could be prevented'. This was explained by the fact that 'the audience does not stop seeking and feeling the topicality of the play. In the gaps deliberately left in the historical tableau they try to find signs of the present and to the historical questions posed they come up with the replies of the 20th century'.[29]

We can allow ourselves to be still more outspoken that Földes and her compatriots in Budapest in 1980. Looking at Béla IV on the stage and the attempts of the King to try to posture as a uniting figure of the nation in spite of a suspect foreign connection, the audience must have been reflecting on the task of Kádár and Hungary's precarious situation in the present time. One moral is that Hungary did not cease to exist because of the defeat in 1241. And it may be resurrected once again. Here we have got an example of history working as a myth[30], in this case the myth of the necessity of hope in national revival.

The example of King Béla IV and his appearance in a play which was being viewed as of relevance for today, reveals the role of history, or, rather, perceptions of history, as the common frame of reference for reflections upon the actual political situation of the People's Republic of Hungary and of her rulers. The whole problem of history and historical education is the subject of serious discussion in Hungary. Of interest to us are the arguments of a professor of literature in Budapest regarding this matter, not the least because he was referring to the official doctrine of Marxism.

Tibor Klaniczay, in an article published in 1978, defines 'tradition' as 'the passing down of collective experience and values from one generation to the next'. He goes on to say that a new social class, when it takes power, needs new symbols of its own. But once the new power is firmly established, this new class becomes the inheritor of the whole national tradition, the 'progressive' as well as the 'non-progressive':

> In the present consolidated socialism, the Hungarian public will have to heed value as such, apart from whether something happens to be progressive or not. There is a special duty to preserve all of national tradition of great value, turning it into a treasure owned by everybody.

According to Klaniczay, traditions must be used and mobilised to the highest possible degree, if society was to hold together. Thus he expressed sharp criticism of Hungarian school policies. In the teaching of history, Klaniczay asserted, Hungarian history prior to 1800 was not sufficiently heeded. He argued that the position of the humanities should become strengthened in education and that the authorities should pay attention to the educational power of the 'visible past', i.e., take care of historical buildings and monuments. Klaniczay deplored that there was no central long range plan in Hungary envisaging 'research into the national tradition (history, literature, language, art, music, ethnography, etc.)'. The actual shortcomings were serious:

> Historiography plays a most essential part in keeping national traditions awake. But Marxist historiography, in its role of forming human consciousness, has not displayed sufficient effectiveness yet. ... It is especially in school that the dehumanizing of history takes on a tremendous scale, with abstract laws moving into the forefront overshadowing man and culture.

It is of interest in our context that Klaniczay was bothered about the lack of public Hungarian interest in the culture and history of the neighbouring nations, especially the Russians:

> There is ... an illusion shared by many Hungarians of absolute superiority compared with the other nations of Eastern Europe ... Some kind of incomprehensible aversion to publishing books on the cultural heritage of the neighbouring nations, especially Slavs, prevails in Hungary. (Klaniczay goes on to mention neglect of Russian culture only.)

But why is this important for internal relations in Hungary, for the relations between the rulers and the ruled within the country? Though Klaniczay did not approach the problem in such a straightforward manner, the dimension was there when he declared that Hungarians must learn and appreciate the fact that they do have many cherished heroes from history literally in common with the neighbours:

> Miklós Zrínyi (1508–66), who defended the castle of Szigetvár, is a national hero for Hungarians and Croations alike. The historic epic Szigeti Veszedelem (Menace of Sziget, 1646) by his great-grandson, also Miklós Zrínyi, is considered a classic by Hungarians and Croats alike. And what should one say about Péter Beniczky (1606–64), who wrote verse in Hungarian and Slovak, János Kájoni (1629–87), who called himself Valachus but wrote his songs in Hungarian, or the Slovak-speaking Jan Jesensky calling himself a 'nobilis Hungarus' and yet he died a martyr's death for Czech freedom? As part of Hungarian national traditions we respect a number of writers, artists, historical personalities, or artistic relics that are also claimed by other nations. If one considers these facts, then the most delicate of the Hungarian national tradition, the memory of old Hungary, and the cause of the former Hungarian territories and the Hungarian minorities living there will have less touchy difficulties for us.[31]

The heart of the matter is the last sentence of the quotation above: the history, and hence national traditions of Hungary, are not restricted to the territory or population of today's Hungary. When Hungary lost two thirds of her territory and one third of her Hungarian — Magyar — population in 1919 (Treaty of Trianon), this meant that large Hungarian minorities came to live in Romania (Transylvania), Czechoslovakia (Slovakia), and Yugoslavia (Vojvodina). After the Second World War, this status quo was re-established. However, with the words of the HSWP:s Secretary for Culture, György Aczél, even today 'Hungarian intellectuals take a lively interest in questions of the national identity and the national minorities question'.[32] Hungarian historians stress that all Hungarians belong to the same ethos.[33]

Immediately after the Second World War, the question of the Hungarian minorities abroad was most sensitive as regarded relations with Czechoslovakia, as Benes, the President, and his followers wanted to oust all Hungarians in the same manner as was being done with the Sudeten Germans. These plans could not be carried out, however, because of the resistance of the Western powers. Actually, the whole plan was dropped after the communist take over of power in Czechoslovakia in 1948. Slovak historiography has continued to be rather anti-Hungarian, though, and in early 1983 a Hungarian spokesman in Slovakia was accused of anti-state activity and prosecuted. He was adopted as a prisoner of conscience by Amnesty International, i.e., considered to be the victim of political persecution.

The fate of Hungarians in Slovakia is not definitely settled, then, but this question has been less burning than that concerning the biggest Hungarian minority, the one in Romanian Transylvania, which probably is in the order of three million people. The Hungarians are mistreated and discriminated against by the Romanian authorities.[34] The Hungarians of Hungary are especially sensitive in this case, as Transylvania is regarded as the cradle and diamond of Hungarian culture. Hungary's Minister of Culture in the early 1980s, Béla Köpeczi, comes from there. In an interview which was broadcast by the Hungarian Television in 1979, he underlined that Transylvania was especially important to the Hungarians because the area has got so many visible, concrete remnants from its Hungarian past. In distinction to the rest of historical Hungary, Transylvania was not systematically destroyed by the Turks (it retained some kind of semi-autonomy). Those who grew up in this Hungarian 'historiocity' under foreign (i.e., Romanian) rule became inspired by a sense of continuity in history, and of stoicism:

> We were drawn to conclude that, in spite of all historical tribulations we had to try and survive, and the quality of survival was the all important question.

This history itself was a superior grade of history, in the sense that it was a history capable of evoking and handing down values.[35]

Why this special attachment to Transylvania? The answer lies in history, i.e., in the perception of history.

After the second Hungarian national catastrophe (the first being the one in 1241, referred to above), i.e., the defeat at the hands of the Turks at Mohács in 1526, historic Hungary was partitioned into three parts. The Western one, with the capital in Pozsony (Bratislava), came under Hapsburg rule. The central part, with Buda, became subjected to harsh, direct Turkish rule. The Eastern part, however, i.e., Transylvania, managed to acquire a relatively autonomous position under the Turkish Sultan.

During the latter part of the 16th century, Calvinism got a foothold in the Hungarian nobility in Transylvania. At the same time, resistance against the Turks began. The leaders in Transylvania thus had to try to use the Hapsburgs against the Turks without being subjected to the Catholic counter reformation. From this manoeuvring there developed a political style of accomodation to a foreign master which is of considerable interest when one tries to understand political culture in today's Hungary. So let us look at some significant traits of that old Transylvanian–Hungarian history, when the foundations of this Hungarian style were laid.

When the Hapsburgs from Vienna were helping the Hungarians in the latters' 'long war' against the Turks in 1593–1606, they tried to change Transylvania into a Hapsburg province and to carry out counter reformation there. They did not succeed. The Hungarians under Prince István Bocskai fought back in a veritable war. In the treaty of Vienna in 1606, Transylvania had her autonomy as a Turkish province guaranteed and in the same treaty, all protestants in the Hapsburg parts of the country were guaranteed religious freedom.

Bocskai was followed as Prince of Transylvania by Gábor Bethlen, who tried to balance between the Turks and Hapsburg. He supported the rebellion of the Czechs against Hapsburg in 1618 and asked for help from the Turks against Poland, which was allied to the Hapsburgs. He had himself been elected King of Hungary but did not manage to get himself crowned before his defeat at the hands of the Hapsburgs on 8 November 1620, in the battle on the White Mountain. In 1621 Bethlen reached a compromise with Hapsburg. He relinquished the Hungarian crown but instead got Central Hungary as a fief for life. In that part of Hungary, which remained under Hapsburg rule, the Hungarian nobility was guaranteed autonomy and the protestants freedom of worship. Today Bethlen is being called, by a Hungarian historian, the first modern ruler of Hungary. He underlines that Bethlen did not suppress differences in the society but was in favour of peaceful pluralism, and that he tried to open up his country economically to Europe.[36]

We may summarise: skilful co-operation with adversaries, playing them one against the other, ideological tolerance and pluralism internally, contacts with the West externally: all this is cherished as 'modern', hence praiseworthy and of 'model' significance. Filling such a role as Bethlen did, a contemporary ruler of Hungary might receive some degree of legitimation. There is more to take notice of in this example, however: Bethlen's attempt to get himself crowned.

The crown Bethlen was striving for was St. Stephen's crown. According to tradition, it had been worn by the first Christian King of Hungary, Stephen (Hungarian István) in 996. The crown subsequently became regarded as the symbol of the Hungarian lands. In the 19th century it became a symbol of the struggle against Hapsburg domination: after the Hungarian defeat in 1849 it was hidden by patriots for a short time. It was then kept at the Royal Castle in Buda until the autumn of 1944. At the end of the war it was brought out of the country and fell into the hands of the US Army in Germany. In 1951 it was deposited at Fort Knox.

The political opponents of the Communist government among Hungarians in exile did not want the crown to be brought back to Hungary. During the Cold War the US administrations did not return it. The Carter administration, however, successfully negotiated the question of the return of the crown and other regalia. When these were at last delivered in Budapest by Secretary of State Cyrus Vance, they were solemnly received, in January 1978, by the political and cultural elite of Hungary, including the religious leaders of Christian as well as of Jewish creed.[37]

The return of the crown of St. Stephen was a confirmation of the fact that the Kádár regime was legitimate in the eyes of the West. The symbolic message was not lost on the Hungarian rulers, who used the regalia to demonstrate Hungarian unity and traditions.[38]

The Hungarian regime has risked a still more daring undertaking, in its use of historical myths, however, allowing the suggestion not only that it is an heir to the 'limited autonomy' tradition and the actual incumbent of St. Stephen's throne but also that it knows how to continue the tradition of defeat!

The defeat at the hands of the Turks at Mohács in 1526 has always been a very traumatic event for the Hungarians, in their collective memory. The Kádár regime decided to celebrate this defeat, however, on the 450th anniversary in 1976. The popular response to the preparations was strong.[39] At the former battlefield, a memory park in the shape of a huge cemetary was made. The outspoken purpose was to give the people a concrete reminder of the nurtured notion that those who had fallen for Hungary had not fallen in vain, even if defeat might have seemed total at first glance. In an official booklet of the Mohács memorial, one can read:

We have erected a monument to our bad I, the bitter past when disunity split our forces, because we want Mohács to become the source of our keeping together today and of our creative patriotism. We have erected the monument to the continuity of our past in order to be able to construct a model future from the example of the past.[40]

When history is perceived in a mythical perspective, names and dates take on a symbolic significance. As Mohács happened to be connected with a date ending in '6', Hungarians of course might think of another '6', which was not allowed to be celebrated in the same way: 1956.[41] This conclusion is no idle guess, as a popular joke in Hungary goes like this. It is about the answer to the question: why do we not hate the Turks? The answer is: the Turks did not force us to celebrate their victory at Mohács every year, they did not force us to learn Turkish, and they did not say that we and they were living in everlasting friendship. The Russians, of course, have been doing the opposite. The relevant question to ask does not have to be asked.

Accordingly, when the Hungarians 'celebrate' the defeat at Mohács they are celebrating that Hungarian nation and culture which survived Turkish rule: one will also survive Russian rule. Or as one of Hungary's leading intellectuals, the sociologist and novelist György Konrád, has formulated this experience in a novel, which was published in the West in 1979 but has not been published in Hungary. It is a parable of modern Hungarian history with the telling title *The Loser*:

At school I learned that our nation does not make history. Our revolutions have failed, we have lost all wars. Where one should assert oneself we are being subdued, but where one should keep a low profile, we are gaining advantages. My ancestors, serfs, hid in the reeds when the vagrant enemy troops were coming, sitting under the water and breathing through a reed. The horsemen left, the village had burnt down, but they crept back again with their kids. We have served Turks, Germans, and, now, Russians; two empires have fallen apart, the third one will fall apart as well.[42]

This theme may be recognised in Hungarian creative art. Reviewing the film 'The Trumpeter' by János Rózsa, which depicts the atrocities and lawlessness during the wars in Hungary in the 17th century, a critic underlined that what the film really described was the theme of military defeat and its effects. In spite of this, the film, or rather the director, seemed to be obsessed by the possibility of survival, of the energy which allows a nation to be resurrected again and again after having been, apparently, extinguished.[43]

The theme of defeat in Hungarian history thus is not only a matter of brave resistance and catastrophe. The antidote is survival. Here treason, collaboration of an indecent kind, enters the picture. It should be noted that those Hungarian princes who collaborated with the Turks were given absolution, as it were, by their descendants, as were also Széchenyi and Deák, who collaborated with Hapsburg in the 19th century. Even oppositionist Hungarians have pointed to the parallel from these historical precedents to János Kádár, who invited the Russians in 1956 but who was practically crowned with St. Stephen's crown two decades later.[44] It was hardly a coincidence when Rezsö Nyers, in the speech in 1981 referred to above, declared that the Hungarians in the face of actual economic and political problems should behave exactly as István Széchenyi and his reformist contemporaries had done.[45]

Hungarian literature and historiography keep repeating the theme that the Hungarians are a defeated nation and that they must consequently adapt to the existing state of affairs. The Kádár regime has allowed the creative intellectuals to treat this subject with few restrictions, however, and, which may seem paradoxical, gained in legitimation. The regime of the defeated nation collaborates with the oppressor in ways that have been tried earlier in Hungarian history and at least safe-guarded the nation's culture. It did not become Turkofied or Germanised — it will not become Russified either.

It is not only the old history, the relations with the Mongols, the Turks, and the Hapsburgs, which is being treated in the way outlined here. The interwar period is another subject area. The policy of the rulers then is seen in the light of the eventual catastrophic defeat, but it is described as a failure, not as illegitimate. Even the authoritarian Horthy regime is recognised as an integrated part of modern Hungarian history, as one of the bases for today's society. One Hungarian historian said in the early 1980s that the nation had begun 'a process of self-rehabilitation'. The point is that one breaks totally with the Stalinist treatment, i.e., falsification of Hungarian history. Under the Rákosi regime, the past was not described truthfully or realistically. The rulers aimed at instilling into the people the strongest sense of collective guilt possible: 'But only the prosecutor was heard, there was no case given for the defence'.[46]

Also the recent past has become increasingly a theme for intellectual discourse, though mainly in literature and film, not in historiography. In 1982 a literary critic could conclude:

> We have lived to see the fifties become a fashionable and popular literary subject: the years that we call, in a long-standing euphemism, the period of the personality cult in Hungary.[47]

The agony of the memories of this period is indicated by the fact, that it could take, in some instances, a decade or more for the works about it to reach a nation-wide audience. Péter Bácso's movie 'The Witness' was produced in 1968 but not shown publicly until 1978, Gyula Hernádi's novel *A Cry and a Cry* was finished in 1961 but not published until 1981.[48]

Básco's and Hernádi's works were of course unofficially consumed by a chosen public before their eventual release. The whole thing shows, however, that the boundary line between that which is allowed and that which is prohibited, i.e., the boundary between the 'first' and the 'second' culture, is as dim and fluent as the one between the first and the second economy. As in economics, the two spheres are mutually dependent upon one another. In this case, the second variety is of course also the more open one. The need for it was revealed by the creation of 'a flying university' in Budapest in the late 1970s, giving lectures on Hungarian history, politics, and social problems.[49]

The parallelism shows a remaining fault in the regime's endeavour to try to appear as 'protector of the national culture'. Hungarian history is perceived by the public as tragic, and the present regime is then viewed, probably, as just the latest instance of the play of fate, i.e., something that has to be accepted not because it is being actively willed by the nation but because it is a reminder of the fact that the nation owes its existence to the will of others. Hence the function of creative art and historiography in Hungary would be to provide a sociopolitical safety valve, letting the people live out its quest for freedom and dignity on the scene and in front of the screen, in poetry, epic, and history as myth, rather than act as a perfect alternative to legitimation in one of the Weberian senses. This kind of simulated legitimation is not geared towards the future and socialism, but towards a mythical eternity. This would be the more likely, as there are hardly any signs of Hungary developing towards socialism, at least not according to the Soviet definition of socialism.[50] It would also be likely, in a society where a comparatively high rate of suicide by individuals is considered to be the price to be paid for society as a whole not committing suicide. (The argument is that the alternative to the present society with all its strains on people is totalitarianism, when people do 'as they are told' and 'do not engage in dangerous introspection or speculation on their fate'.)[51] Similarly, the intellectuals are said to feel that there is a lack of valid and inspiring ideals and personalities that might govern development. Thus János Acs's staging of Weiss's 'Marat/Sade', referred to above, can be interpreted both as a measure of cultural freedom in Hungary and as a demonstration that it is all ending in a cul-de-sac:

> At the end of the play the walls of the asylum collapse, but the interpretation does not indicate a triumph, the awakening of the patients to consciousness or praise for the revolution. People languishing in captivity for this length of time are no longer

capable of winning freedom for themselves or others. But pressed together into a single mass this crowd will sooner or later obviously try to make use of its strength and exact revenge for its sufferings. The Herald stands apart out front holding a single flagstone torn from the road: he sobs.[52]

As has been indicated earlier in this study, the Hungarian economy must be said to be in a rather precarious situation in the early 1980s. Now we see that the same may be said of perceived history, i.e., of its capacity to integrate rulers and ruled. But what about the remaining possible outlets to be used, i.e., religion and nationalism?

Religion, nationalism and demography

The relations between the Catholic Church and the Hungarian rulers were sour both before and after 1956, but in the course of the 1970s and especially after the death of Cardinal Mindszenty in his exile, relations between the Vatican and Budapest became markedly better. The regime's own conclusion is that it has scored far better in this field than its unhappy Polish comrades. Thus János Berecz, Head of the Department of Foreign Relations of the Central Committee of the HSWP, stated in an article which was printed in May 1981, i.e., at the height of the revolution in Poland:

> The crisis of the People's Republic of Poland is a major one indeed and it occurred because one-sided grandiose economic measures offended objective economic laws thus producing uneven development. Furthermore, regardless of the name given, new systems of institutions must be accepted, especially if the masses think them important, and they act as valves at times of crisis or tension. Everything must be done to ensure that the new institution be integrated by society. That is one aspect of things. I could really go on to say that reading things that way also serves to justify Hungarian policy, for instance when it comes to Church and State relations. A reality which integrates the faithful, making them part of socialist national unity, taking note of church institutions, that is our reality and it justifies the soundness of Hungarian policy. . . . The formula which Poland presents today is that no sort of constructive experience or result can be defended if the basic institutional system of the nation, society, and the state is not defended, and its operation is not ensured.[53]

The pragmatic, cynical assertion of the Solidarity movement, which is

112

being referred to in an oblique way, should be noted. Of interest here, however, is that this phenomenon is combined with the question of church-state relations. Berecz is self-congratulating on behalf of the HSWP, but that need not mean that there is not any truth in his observation. We should take care to note that the Catholic Church is not as predominant in Hungary as in Poland; roughly 20 per cent of the Hungarians can be regarded as Protestants, nominally, while there are some 100,000 Jews. And it is evident that all three denominations are much better integrated with the state in Hungary than is the Church in Poland. This was demonstrated in connection with the return of St. Stephen's crown to Hungary.

Iván Boldizsár, the editor of official Hungary's cultural face to the West, the *New Hungarian Quarterly* (*NHQ*), wrote an article in his journal about 'The Crown's Day', i.e., 6 January 1978. On this day the crown arrived in Budapest, carried by an American delegation headed by Cyrus Vance. After underlining that the crown now symbolises the whole Hungarian nation and has become 'a symbol in a new and complete sense', Boldizsár goes on to declare that now 'it expresses continuity' as 'it has got back to its rightful owner, the Hungarian nation'. And then comes what is of interest in the present context, i.e., what Boldizsár is describing as the embodiment of the Hungarian nation. This was the scene when the American delegation approached the representatives of Hungary in the Parliament building's Domed Hall:

> The delegation, one after another, shake the hands of all those Hungarians whom the protocol Section had placed in the front row of the rectangle. First Cardinal László Lékai, Archbishop of Esztergom, then Antal Ijjas, Archbishop of Kalocsa and Bishop Cserháti of Pécs. The Protestants followed, Bishops Zoltán Káldy (Lutheran) and Tibor Bartha (Calvinist); then Bishop József Ferenc of the Unitarians and Imre Héber, representing the Hungarian Jews. Gyula Kállai, Chairman of the Patriotic People's Front was next, after him three ministers . . . .[54]

It would be hard to imagine a similar 'integration of the faithful' (cf. Berecz!) in Poland. Not only that, it seems that the Hungarians who express themselves in the official media appreciate the political role of the Pope far more positively, than do the Polish rulers. Thus the report by Boldizsár, in *NHQ*, from the consecration by John Paul II of the Hungarian St. Stephen's oratory in Saint Peter's crypt in Saint Peter's church in Rome on 8 October 1980 'in the joint presence of his cardinals, the Hungarian bench of bishops, and the representatives of the Hungarian People's Republic', took care to note especially:

This Pope has shown a feeling for the Hungarian past and he recognizes the Hungarian present. As a Pole he surely has as little fondness for the division of Europe as the national whose name the oratory bears.[55]

It is also of symbolic value that one of Hungary's greatest sculptors, Amerigo Tot, made reliefs for one of the walls in St. Stephen's oratory; back in 1969 it had been the very opposite, a 'secular Soviet saint', i.e., the cosmonaut Komarov, who was killed in a space-ship crash, who had been the object of Tot's creative work. Although the sculpture of Komarov is said to have had 'an enormous influence on monumental sculpture in Hungary after 1969',[56] this of course concerns the piece of art and not the person it was being made in memory of. In 1980 it was the act of homage towards St. Stephen and Hungarian history in itself that gave a wider cultural significance to the artefact.

We have seen above how anti-semitism has been used in communist Poland as a means of absolving the Party of its crimes in the eyes of the public, as an instrument to mould Poles together in an exclusive nationalism. Hungary's record was fairly good prior to the First World War, but the interwar years saw strong anti-semitism emerge. During the Second World War 'the destruction of the bulk of Hungarian Jewry . . . was tacitly abetted by most social strata'. The postwar period has not offered any clear evidence in either direction:

The evidence on the nature and the extent of anti-semitism is fragmentary and impressionistic, so that conclusions are bound to be tentative, but the distinction between Jew and non-Jew has re-emerged in Hungarian society as a source of division.[57]

All this said, however, there is no evidence of anti-semitism being supported by the rulers in the same way as in Poland, and while the Jewish cultural institutions in Poland are merely token ones — the Yiddish Theatre, staffed by Poles who learn their replies by heart without understanding them and the Jewish Historical Institute in Warsaw, singularly obsessed with the humiliation and annihilation of the Jews under Hitler — there is in Hungary a rabbinical seminary, and treasures of Jewish Hebraic culture are published, one example being the facsimile edition of Maimonide's Mishne Torah, published by Magyar Helikon and Corvina Press in 1980.[58] Of course all this may be compatible with anti-semitism in society. The point is, however, that the regime does not seem to use anti-semitism to fuel Hungarian nationalism, as a means of token legitimation. But the question of the Jews in Hungary raises more general questions regarding Hungarian nationalism.

We have seen above how the Hungarians relate today's experience with a rather special perception of the past. But how does one perceive the prospects of the nation for the future? Can one say that there is a general trust in the rulers, a belief that they will be able to protect the Hungarian people and its culture in the future?

As has been noted above, Hungarians do have a keen sense of being a defeated nation, but one which has always retained its hope for redemption. Some statements by Hungarian intellectuals show, however, the psychological tension which follows from this understanding of fate. In 1982, the situation was described in the following way by a Hungarian literary critic:

> The fact that for the first time in Hungary's history a population decline is taking place in peacetime does not in itself explain the anxiety bordering on despair with which some writers react to the declining graphs. . . . But since the beginning of the last century Hungarian writers have been haunted by the idea of the death of the nation to the extent of it becoming almost a cliché. The thought may be alien to a, say, West European but if account is taken of the traumas which the Hungarian national consciousness has suffered in the twentieth century alone, there will be some idea of what is involved. Hungary was on the losing side in both world wars; the Peace Treaty of Trianon in 1920 reduced the area and the population of the country by approximately two thirds, and over three million ethnic Hungarians became overnight citizens of foreign countries. (Today Hungarian minorities living in neighbouring countries approach four million.) In the thirties German influence grew apace; six to ten per cent of the population perished in the Second World War. The beginning of the fifties was both the period of official injustice and of forced industrialization, causing greater change to the social structure within a couple of years than the preceding one hundred years had done. Then came 1956. Yet within the economic and political stability of recent years, the suicide rate has been alarmingly high, and alcoholism has been on the rise.[59]

One should note in the quotation that demographic decline is put into the perspective of Hungary losing a large part of her population in and because of, world wars, and that the swift social change up to 1956 is also seen as a part of this 'threat to the nation'-process. And this process is viewed as continuing today. The suicides and the alcoholism obviously should be understood as symptoms of the feeling of insecurity and as dangerous to Hungary as war and high Stalinism.

Both the Stalinist regime in 1953 and the Kádár regime in 1973, tried to influence the birth rate by tightening the restrictions on abortions, and, in the latter case, by providing child care allowances for the mothers. The effects were short-run. In the early 1980s, optimistic demographic projections estimated that the country's population would diminish by some 350,000 within twenty years. In a debate in 1981 about this problem, the writer and literary historian Domokos Varga, connected it with the fate of the Hungarian minorities in the neighbouring countries:

> In a perspective of centuries, we cannot exclude the possibility that we may find ourselves in the situation of those who are to be assimilated gradually, just as this fate has already caught up with Hungarians living beyond our borders.[60]

Varga was referring to the idea that Hungary would have to accept immigrant foreign workers because of the population decline, and he was substantiating the alarm by quoting András Sütö, 'an outstanding Hungarian writer living in Transylvania, which belongs to Rumania' (note the expression!), who had observed 'We have to act so that we survive'.[61]

A statistician taking part in the debate summarised the phenomenon by the words 'never have so many given birth to so few'. He added that a viable population policy must be based on the ambitions, desires and ideas of people and that it was almost impossible to change this trend by orders 'from above'. The implication is that the Hungarians would not accept force in this matter. It is interesting to note that 'several people' in the debate, mentioned that the high birth rate in neighbouring Romania was an effect of an abortion law as strict as the one in Hungary during Stalinism.[62]

When the debate continued in 1982, the playwright Géza Páskándi showed that it was possible to see the demographic question as intimately linked with the fate of the Hungarian nation in the world, as he concluded that 'if the individual and the nation have no prospects, the population declines'.[63]

The point in drawing the demographic question into a discussion of Hungarian nationalism is that the demographic decline, as has been indicated above, obviously heightens the Hungarians' apprehension for the fate of the whole Hungarian people, i.e., including those four million living in neighbouring countries. It is especially Transylvania and Slovakia that have been of relevance here.

There seems to be general agreement among those who study the question that the situation of the Hungarians in Romanian Transylvania is that which causes greatest concern to the people of Hungary. What is important is that the general impression is that things have got worse from the late 1960s onward. In 1967 the Maros-Hungarian Autonomous Region in Romania was dissolved,[64] and at the same time Ceausescu launched his policy of seeking to obtain legitimacy by appealing to traditional Romanian nationalism. This apparently entailed discrimination against the Hungarians (and Germans) of Romania:

116

In his (Ceausescu's) educational reforms, economic development plans, employment policies, in short in the most important
areas of human existence, the nearly two million Hungarians
living in Romania are sharply disadvantaged.[65]

Relations are not being ameliorated by the fact that in the late 1970s
Ceausescu, in his attempt to use (mythologised) history as a means of
legitimation, began increasingly to emphasise the concept of 'free
Romania', i.e., the idea that Romania's road to statehood and independence goes back to 'those areas of Transylvania which escaped the Roman
conquest and were only marginally touched by the Turks or the Hapsburgs'. Although the Romanian patriotism is, according to a Western
researcher, Trond Gilberg, 'perceived as a uniting force, a banner around
which all ethnic groups can rally', the Hungarians naturally will tend to
understand the emphasis on Transylvania as the cradle of Romanian
statehood as an attempt to usurp their past. And the whole historical
controversy is taking place against the background of uncertainty regarding
the demographic data on ethnic assimilation in Romania (as distinct from
forced romanisation).[66]

The official reaction to this policy has been very muted from the Kádár
regime. However, two persons of political and cultural stature, respectively,
in Hungary and Romania have voiced their criticism quite openly,
obviously convinced of having the support of the majority of Hungarians
in both countries. In late 1977, the most prominent communist political
leader of the Hungarians in Romania, Károly Király, sent a letter to the
Romanian leadership, where he criticised the official policy as one of
national and cultural oppression of the Hungarians in the country. In early
1978 this criticism became known to the outer world, which also learned
that Király was supported in his protest by the prominent writer András
Sütö (cf. above) and the vice-Premier János Fazekas. The government
answered in two ways. It increased controls of the Hungarians but at the
same time Ceausescu tried to court them as well and made a tour of
Transylvania. In 1980, however, Király was forced to reiterate his
criticism,[67] and from the early 1980s on, Gyula Illyés, the Dean of
Hungarian writers (he died on 15 April 1983), started, in Hungary, to
express the deep concern and alarm of his compatriots for the fate of the
brethren in Romania.[68] An American historian of Hungarian origin, Ivan
Volgyes, goes as far as to say that the fate of the Hungarians (Magyars) in
Romania 'is now an issue on which the acceptance of the Hungarian
leadership by the entire Magyar population is dependent.'[69]

Volgyes's assertion would mean that to be able to play successfully the
role of 'protector of national culture', the Kádár regime must also take on
responsibility for the Hungarian minority in Transylvania. This thesis is
corroborated by what can be heard from inside Hungary, e.g. from a

'clandestine' survey carried out in 1980. Answering this, one respondent (who was not anonymous but a rather well-known dissident sociologist, János Kis) observed:

> The political situation (in Hungary) can deteriorate because of the situation of Hungarian minorities in Romania and Slovakia.[70]

Janos Kádár has however shown indirectly that he is aware of the problem, as he has expressed regret over the 'imperialist Trianon dictate after the Great War', when 'the territory of Hungary was reduced to one-third of its former size'.[71]

One should note that Slovakia is also entering the gloomy picture of bad neighbour relations — at the popular, not the state level. The communist regime in Czechoslovakia cannot be blamed for the harsh repression of the Hungarians in Slovakia up to 1948, although its own subsequent policy has become the object of rather sharp criticism from Hungarians.

During the reform period in Czechoslovakia in 1968, the representatives of the Hungarian minority (numbering c:a 560,000) i.e. the Cultural Union of the Hungarian working People (Csemadok) and the daily Uj Szó, demanded that the equality given to the minorities on paper in the Czechoslovak constitution of 1960, should become realised. One complained about the shortcomings in education and culture and actually demanded that the Hungarians and the other minorities should become the equals of the Czechs and Slovaka in the constitution as groups, rather than as individuals. Among the specific demands were that a Hungarian Scientific Institute, a publishing house, a national theatre, a national library, Hungarian television programmes, and special Hungarian organisations for youth should be established. There was also a demand that Hungarians should be appointed to leading posts in the ministries in proportion to their share of the population.

The Slovaks reacted with bitter protests: 'Passions increased in intensity on both sides', as Skilling summarises. At the same time, the mass media in Hungaria, 'showed considerable interest in the demands of the Hungarian minority and the plans for nationality reform'. When the whole game was changed by the Soviet-led invasion on 21 August the Hungarian minority kept quiet. The Nationalities law, adopted after the invasion, genuinely improved the legal status of the four recognised minorities (besides the Hungarians they were the Germans, the Poles, and the Ukranians), guaranteeing them 'participation in state power' and 'effective guarantees of their further development'. That tensions remained, however, is evident from the conclusion reached by Skilling at the very end of his well documented analysis of 'Czechoslovakia's Interrupted Revolution':

The nationalities law was greeted with relative satisfaction by Hungarian spokesmen and with considerable discontent by Slovaks. Csemadok, for instance, welcomed it as defining the nationalities, for the first time in a constitutional law, as 'constitutional factors' (státotvorní cinitelé) but regretted that it did not proclaim their political, economic, and cultural equality and did not guarantee their right to their own nationality organs or the right to proportional representation in executive as well as representative organs. Slovaks claimed that the law took no account of their earlier criticisms and hoped that the detailed provisions of the republican law would give protection to their interests.[72]

Thus the national appetite, so to speak, of the Hungarian minority was whetted at the same time as Czechoslovakia was heading for a period of increasing and eventually hardened political repression of subjects of all nationalities. In the course of the 1970s, relations apparently became strained between the Hungarians and the Slovak authorities. In 1982, a book written by a representative of the Hungarian minority in Czechoslovakia, Kálmán Janics, though being an analysis of the dark 1945–48 period, indicated that the Hungarians still felt that they were the subject of discrimination. The book has only been published in the West with a special preface by Gyula Illyés. In this, the latter answered the question about 'the good-neighbourly relations between Slovaks and Hungarians' in the following way:

1) The issue is not how to further 'improve' good relations but, rather, how to prevent or at least how to slow down, their further deterioration.
2) What should be done for such 'improvement' and by whom? Obviously, only those who are in positions of power to act can do something about the situation.
3) Speaking of past experiences? For many decades, we had no part in anything that was happening across the border; except, a little perhaps, intellectually.
4) As for literary activity? It should be twofold: to acquaint with our situation the outside world, and to educate our own people for setting an example by our virtues as Europeans and thus radiate hope.
5) How to encourage our friends on the other side of the borders? By telling them that, whichever of us should be 'up' or 'down', we both should do better in the future as our radiations go.
6) Finally, we should bury the ugly past.
Unfortunately, and Dr. Janic's book is a confirmation of it, the

ugly past is still very much with us. In many towns of Slovakia, once creative nests radiating Hungarian culture, the Hungarian language itself is banned.

Illyés did not content himself with criticising the Slovaks, and he took pain to underline the many common, positive traits in the cultural heritage of the two peoples, but levelled accusations at 'the official point of view in Hungary'. By overdoing Hungarian self-criticism after the war the official view was 'critical of the nationalism of the oppressed Hungarians rather than of the nationalism of their oppressors'. Illyés ends his presentation of Janics's work with an oblique reference to Transylvania:

> May similar situation reports spring up from all lands under oppression whose mother tongue is Hungarian! To inform the world — and to arouse its conscience.[73]

Apparently, Janics's book has a sequel that treats in detail the fate of the Hungarians in Slovakia after 1945. In early 1983, Amnesty International informed that 'one of the leading figures of the Hungarian minority in Czechoslovakia', Miklos Duray, was tried for 'hostile acts against the state', the crime being that he had prepared and sent abroad a manuscript on the mistreatment of his kinsmen in Slovakia. This is a corroboration of other information regarding the apparent deterioration of conditions perceived by members of the Hungarian minority. It is interesting to note that three well-known American leftist intellectuals, who tried to protest against the treatment of Duray, endorsing his complaints, addressed their letter of protest not to the authorities of Czechoslovakia, but to the Prime Minister of Hungary, György Lazar. They requested him and his government 'to use its influence and prestige to assure Mr. Duray's freedom' and, if necessary, 'take the responsibility of defending Miklos Duray upon itself'. The reason why they approached the Hungarian, and not the Czechoslovak government, was not only that the accused is Hungarian but also 'because in all of East Central Europe, the Hungarian government has paid the most attention, since the ratification of the Helsinki Agreement, to the principles of democracy and minority rights'. Finally, the tongue-in-cheek remarks of the three Americans is also worth noting:

> The Hungarian government was not afraid to intervene in Czechoslovakia's internal affairs in August 1968. It should not be afraid to raise its voice now on behalf of democratic rights guaranteed by an international agreement.[74]

Time has caught up with the Hungarian rulers. Now their reputation as 'protectors of the national culture' is such that they are requested by outside observers, speaking for 'world opinion', to also take upon themselves the role of protector of the Hungarians in Czechoslovakia (and Romania). However, this cannot be done.

In the balance: is pluralism possible?

A Western social scientist of Hungarian origin, George Schöpflin, while arguing that the Hungarian public's concern for the Hungarian minorities in the neighbouring states 'should not be equated automatically with irredentism', also quotes evidence substantiating the assertion that the overwhelming majority will not recognise that the Hungarian minorities 'are developing an autonomous nationality-consciousness of their own'.[75] The obvious conclusion must be that what Hungarians still consider to be the 'real' Hungary includes the alienated territories, inhabited by Hungarians. The general attitude would be that any 'real' protector of the Hungarian nation and culture should be able to effectively defend the interest of the Hungarian minorities abroad.

It is obvious that the Hungarian perception of the nation's past is a tragic one, focusing on historical defeats. It is also obvious that many Hungarians are concerned with the decline in population growth, which some regard as a threat to the nation's survival. It is equally obvious that many Hungarians feel frustrated in face of the impossibility of doing anything substantial for their oppressed brethren (as they perceive it) in Transylvania and Slovakia. Seen from the perspective of the Kádár regime, and granted that it wants to base its relations with the population on mutual trust, it would be very important to try to influence the value system of the Hungarians in a direction which would lead the attitudes away from the great interest in the national question in the ethnic sense.

If one analyses recent Hungarian literary works and social science, one is led to the hypothesis that a possible outlet for the frustrations and tensions is pluralism. I will now discuss this assumption.

One of Hungary's best known modern playwrights is István Örkény, who died at the age of 67 in 1979. His play 'Pisti a vérvizatarban' (Pisti in the Bloodbath), though grotesque in style and really a peace of fiction, was deliberately meant to be 'a survey . . . of recent Hungarian history'. A summary of the play illustrates very well the historical need to recognise plurality and pluralism in Hungary, a country which is a microcosm where 'the world has somersaulted several times' and nothing, consequently, can be unambiguous:

> If Pisti is taken as specifically Hungarian, one will not be surprised to see him, in 1944, commanding the firing squad and at the same time as one of those up against the wall; to see sometimes two Pistis, one pro-Soviet, and one pro-German,

and witness this state of things as long as one cannot know who will win the war; to see Pisti going into hiding, distributing pamphlets, making propaganda, campaigning, being afraid, being executed, liberated, reborn, educated, improved, and set up as an example; a statue is erected in his honour and he is respected as a standard, and then it emerges that he does not exist at all, but this must be kept secret and three days' mourning is proclaimed in honour of his memory. Every time he rises from the dead and starts from scratch, even if he must start from ruins, paying the price of disappointments; although disillusioned he starts afresh with new faith, and the indestructibility of the resourceful. . . . Pisti is the jolly joker of the age. He can be substituted for everybody who has experienced the last 40 or 50 years in Hungary.[76]

The summary quoted above was written in 1980 by a Hungarian literary critic, Tamás Koltai, himself in his late thirties at the time of writing. It seems to me that his understanding of the play, which can be called a modern classic, and his assertion that it expresses a universal Hungarian experience can be considered as representative of today's Hungarians. It is not a coincidence that Örkény's hero is called Pisti, which is the nickname for István and 'István' is the Hungarian equivalent to the British 'Smith'. Any regime wanting to obtain active support of such a population with the experiences described by Örkény would have to show that it is, at least tacitly, admitting the historical relativity of its own role. Or, as the positive hero in another play by Örkény, 'Vérrokonok' (Railwaymen), that according to the author, should be interpreted as an allegory, declares:

Everything would be different if doubt split open these closed systems in some place. Without doubt no change is possible.[77]

Hungarian social scientists of official stature, i.e., who are not being treated as 'dissident' and are allowed to represent Hungary for foreign readers, also recognise the need of a value system that is not tied exclusively to either consumerism ('economic compensation') or nationalism ('protector of national culture'). In a book which was published in 1980, the sociologist Zsuzsa Ferge concluded from her studies that the prevailing social attitudes among the Hungarians 'can hardly be seen as eminently socialist ones'. This was explained with reference to the influence of traditional values and to the fact that actual economic practices (at the individual level) reinforced these values. This is standard common sense Marxism. More interesting, however, is that Ferge acknowledged that the future was not foreclosed and hence must be open to a certain pluralism:

An additional factor leading to the present problems is that positive standards are rather hazy, so that the modelling of conditions and attitudes moves on uncertain grounds. . . . So we come back to what the positive alternative should be — and this is exactly what we cannot find out in advance, purely on logical grounds. The 'positive' approach does not consist of working out the 'ideal' models for a new way of life. Instead, I apply . . . the assumptions about social determinants, to the future.[78]

We are meeting here a basically Popperian attitude, which treats utopia negatively and points into the direction of piece-meal engineering.[79] There is no direct reference to Sir Karl Popper in Ferge's work, but the pluralist implication of her view of 'constructing' society is much closer to his conception than to the traditional Marxist one.[80]

The importance of what Ferge calls 'social determinants' was stressed in 1982 by the economist Béla Kádár, in an article with the intriguing title 'Preparing to Meet the Challenge' (interestingly enough, Ferge's book bore the title 'A Society in the Making'.

Kádár noted that the decisions of the CC of the HWSP in 1977 on the continuation of the New Economic Mechanism and the reform policy in general, were given new emphasis in a Party resolution in June 1982. According to Kádár, the choice of economic policy would have important consequences for the value system of Hungarians:

The reform policy has to take into account that a switch to a more competition oriented growth course or social environment clashes with the conditioning of several decades, and in the absence of suitable preparation is likely to produce more, and make more visible successes and failures. Society has to be psychologically prepared, and armed with a new set of values to accept the more conspicuous success of a few, and to bear the inevitable failures and conflict situation. That is, a broad transformation of social views has to take place. . . . It is increasingly recognized today that the success of the reform, cutting short the phase fraught with the more severe ordeals, ultimately depends on the extent to which society is able to shape the non-economic conditions of progress.[81]

One should note that Kádár, when referring to 'the conditioning of several decades' obviously had socialist indoctrination in mind, whereas Ferge was concerned with the vitality of 'bourgeois' values. This can be viewed as pluralism in practice, i.e., two evaluations suggesting rather different futures being put forward simultaneously by Hungarian scholars.

The difference between what is called in this study 'economic compensation' and the kind of differentiation to which Béla Kádár was referring, is that the former one would work, if it worked, in an authoritarian or patriarchal context, the regime 'giving' its subjects material goods, while the latter would mean that citizens were free to pursue their own interests and thereby raise their material standards. Our thoughts naturally return to Adam Smith . . . or to the Weberian notion of legitimation of the legal, rational kind.

The contemporary Hungarian trend towards a development which faintly resembles the market and rationality pattern, has its most outspoken protagonist in the economist Tibor Liska. His ideas about 'entrepreneurial socialism' became widely discussed in Hungary in the early 1980s when they became, as one Hungarian journalist expressed it, 'part of official economic policy'.[82]

While Liska's programme takes so called 'socialist ownership of the means of production' for granted, it has money, the market and freely moving prices as its motor. Thus freedom of competition is deemed as crucial. According to Liska, the essence of socialism is that 'it enables everyone, freed from the limitations of private property, to make use of the opportunities of enterprise'. He criticises the traditional large enterprises as being of a 'feudal character' with a 'decision making hierarchy', and he is in favour of a 'contractual system' where every individual is free to test his/her abilities:

> The substance of socialist enterprise is that the utilization right of the land or of any social property should not necessarily go to the person who happens to cultivate or manage it, but whoever takes it upon himself to manage it more successfully than any other competitor should be able to cultivate, manage, or develop it if he subsequently proves by financial results that he will be able to increase this social property most effectively also in the future.[83]

The means of production — land, machinery, transportation vehicles, etc. — under this system are utilised on the basis of 'competitive bidding', i.e., a kind of leasing of them from society. So far, the system has been tried on the Szentes farmers' co-operative and in small business.[84] Although Liska was reported to be treated with considerable suspicion by the Hungarian authorities in early 1983,[85] his ideas have already become part of Hungarian reality. In the economic field, the so called system of contractual operation, which was introduced in 1981, is based on Liska's ideas. It means 'transfer by auction, to private persons of a large number of specific shops and public catering units'.[86] In the same year Liska's friend, the writer Gyula Hernádi argued that cultural policy should be run on similar lines. His contention was that cultural products are commodities, as they are intended for exchange. According to Hernádi, the prevailing system, however, which subsidises culture over the state budget, did not

124

produce the best results. He was obviously tacitly referring to the well known shortcomings, especially as regards quality, of the nonmarket socialist economy. As regards culture, he argued that people should not be given cheap books and so on, but instead be able to earn more money and buy books etc. that were expensive but considered worth buying:

> By selling tickets cheap we also exempt the arts from the constraint to win their public, to produce something which interests and attracts people.[87]

Hernádi was of course criticised from an orthodox Marxist position, theory of labour as the only source of value included, but it seems that he managed to move public debate in the commodity competition, hence pluralist, direction, also as regards culture. Or as one writer and critic, János Széky, summarised the debate in early 1982, after quoting the opinion that 'rentability, market research, the mapping of requirements' could not be banished from the cultural sphere: 'To be more blunt, it is necessary to increase fees and, in some cases, also prices'.[88]

The point in Hernádi's 'transfer' of the idea of entrepreneurial socialism to the cultural sphere and, hence, the sphere of value formation is, in our context, that the authoritarian 'protector' legitimation substitute should give way to a cultural pluralism which would make the regime only a rational co-ordinator and mediator on certain legal grounds. It would acquire legal legitimation in the Weberian sense. This conclusion has been drawn in the Hungarian public debate, which is evident from the following quotation from the sociologist Kálmán Kulcsár:

> Society started the building of socialism at the end of the 40s, the socialist reorganization of agriculture emerged in the late 50s. The new economic mechanism started functioning in the late 60s. The social and economic problems which had accumulated by the end of the 70s constitute a challenge which, in turn, demands social innovation. This challenge manifests itself in the exhaustion of the possible means for solving the accumulated problems inherent in the former structure.

The authorities and intellectuals were reported to be in agreement that risktaking and innovation must become the rule in economic and social life. One such innovation is the Innovation Fund of the National Bank of Hungary. The Fund operates on a semicommercial basis, taking risks but also getting some dividends from economically successfully applied innovations in enterprises.[89] For this risk taking and innovation to work properly, actors must be able to count on predictability and the absence of arbitrary interference in business from the rulers. But what does this entail for the relations between the ruling Communist Party and the Hungarian people?

As has been noted earlier in this study, the HSWP did not come to power and did not remain in power thanks to popular support. Alienated from the majority of the population, it can be regarded as a 'counter-society'. The rift which separates it from society, i.e., its lack of legitimation, may partly be overcome through the mechanisms 'economic compensation' and 'protector of the national culture' discussed in this study. The ultimate step would be the Communist Party's acceptance of the limited role of society's 'manager'. The problem, from the legitimation point of view, is, however, that the Communist Party is obviously still perceived as a 'counter-society' and not as the 'manager' people would choose if they were free to choose. A survey carried out in 1976 showed that, if there was a free election, the votes would be cast in the following way (in percentages): Social-Democrats 42, Christian-Democrats 27, a peasant party 17, Conservatives 6, and the Communists 5.[90]

The ruling Party cannot get rid of either the history of its accession to power or its ultimate reliance on a force that was never voluntarily conceded to it by the people. Speaking of the force and coercion at the regime's disposal, one Western researcher of Hungarian origin, Miklós Molnár, has made the correct comment that 'in the last analysis, it does not matter much how it uses them. It has them'.[91]

While the reliance on economic and cultural pluralism instead of on 'economic compensation' and 'national protection', may not imply that 'governments are dispensable', as one Western reviewer of Liska's theory has suggested,[92] one may reach the conclusion that the question of political power has also been placed upon the agenda. Analysing the experience of Hungary and the other socialist states in Europe, the Hungarian sociologist Mihaly Vajda, a member of the so called Budapest school, reached the following conclusion regarding the prospects for political pluralism, i.e., democracy (this was in the late 1970s, but the problem has remained the same):

> The monolithic power of the single party of the state, of necessity suppresses every movement even if it is merely theoretical. Terror is a structural component of these societies and if it is not being employed at present, this is simply because there is no such movement in existence. A feature which constitutes an exception under capitalism is the rule under socialism as it exists today.
>
> In the light of what I have said — in however a superficial manner — it is quite clear that if we are to make genuine changes in the socialist system as it exists today, we must fight for political democracy. It may be that this step will not lead straight to socialism. But without it, it is surely impossible to achieve anything at all.[93]

Thus we are reminded of the fact that Hungary belongs to a class, the class of 'real existing socialism' and that there are barriers to genuine legitimation in the Weberian 'legal' sense, which cannot be overcome within the limits of the established system. The quotation from Vajda is from before the emergence of the Solidarity movement in Poland. It is evident, however, that this was a 'movement' of the kind Vajda was referring to: the crushing of it by the rulers corroborates Vajda's thesis of terror as a 'structural component'.

Against this background, it is interesting to note some statements of Hungarian politicians after the emergence and suppression of Solidarity in Poland. In an interview which was published in the Warsaw weekly *Polityka* on 12 February 1983, the leader of the Hungarian Trade Union, Sandor Gaspar, endorsed the notion that there was in Hungary 'an unwritten social contract' and that the leaders were against conformism and in the same number of the Polish weekly, the 'reform communist' of 1968 Rezsö Nyers, who is a member of the Hungarian Parliament, was reported to have declared that the political importance of the parliament would become increased. The parliament had not as yet found its proper place in the 'political mechanism' and it must be moved out of its 'second-rate role'. According to Nyers, the Hungarians did not have any 'ready made model' but the 'Western parliaments' could not be the ideal.[94]

It is evident that spokesmen for the Hungarian regime such as Gaspar and Nyers do see the need for a genuine legitimation, if the system is to be able to cope with the crises gathering ahead. The search for legitimacy that began in the early 1960s, has reached a new stage. The Polish 'solution' under Jaruzelski is most probably not regarded as the optimal one for Hungary. At the same time, the political leaders in Hungary, as well as anyone studying the question, must take cognisance of the fact that the degree of legitimacy that the regime really has, though it cannot be measured, depends on the population's 'positive orientation towards János Kádár'.[95] He is also perceived as a person keeping conservative forces, Stalinists, in the Party in check while being himself restricted by these forces. Therefore Toma and Volgyes conclude, in their major work '*Politics in Hungary*' that the Hungarian population accepts Kádár's rule believing that 'without Kádár's leadership the situation would very likely be much worse'.[96]

The portrayal of Kádár as a guarantee that 'conservative forces', i.e., the Stalinists, would not take power may be interpreted as just an instance of 'negative legitimation'.[97] According to a recent Western study of Hungarian politics, however, in 1981, at the time of the latest congress of the HWSP, the Stalinists 'had been completely eliminated from the highest leadership function' and thus, 'after 25 years, the battle against the Stalinists has been won'.[98]

To still be able to pose as the guardian against Stalinism and all that it stands for, Kádár should then, after 1981, have to appear as the one who fulfils this function with regard to those 'Stalinists' who remain in power, if not within Hungary, then outside her boundaries. Thus we are once again approaching the paradox that the very success of the regime leads to even greater demands being placed upon it by the population.

The dilemmas facing the Hungarian rulers in 1984 bear some resemblance to those of the Dubcek regime in Czechoslovakia in 1968. Economic decentralisation and pluralism are accompanied by a certain cultural pluralism, while the demands from below rather than receding are, on the contrary, being increasingly articulated. In Hungary, however, it has been a slow process, where developments which in Czechoslovakia were 'telescoped', have been stretched out over two decades. Moreover, after 1956 there has not been any dramatic turning point either in the economic or in the cultural sphere. Gradualism and pragmatism are the key words to describe these developments.

The HSWP has shown, both to its own subjects and to its brothers beyond the state boundaries, that it has retained control over developments by for instance clamping down periodically on 'dissident' intellectuals. So far, so good from the Soviet point of view. Far from criticising the Hungarian leaders, the Soviets have praised Hungary's policies, especially as regards agriculture (a field, where the Soviet record is far from successful).[99] In foreign policy, there has not been any reason for complaint from the Soviet point of view: Hungary has proved herself to be an impeccably loyal ally.

However, as has been indicated in this study, the whole Hungarian development points in the opposite direction to that of the rest of the Soviet bloc. In 1982, the country was accepted as a member of the International Monetary Fund. Although this is not without precedent for communist states, the conscious policy of attempting to make the forint, the Hungarian currency, convertible, is a new departure. Parallel to these developments runs the continuing cultural estrangement from Soviet communism and, as a corollary, Hungary's reintegration into European cultural life. While George Orwell's novels '*Animal Farm*' and '*1984*' are treated as anathema and ideological contraband in the USSR, a Hungarian critic could, in 1981, depict Péter Bacsó's film '*The Witness*', which is about the Stalinist show trials in Hungary, as 'a vitriolic and tempestuous satire, reminiscent at times of Orwell'.[100] The point is that the reference to Orwell came quite naturally, as it should do in a society which no longer resembles the Orwellian nightmare.

A decentralised economic system, accompanied by a certain pluralism in cultural life, while not incompatible with one-party rule, nevertheless diminishes the need for a party with a 'leading role'. Even if central agencies are controlling the largest enterprises, in a (socialist) market economy, the political influence over the whole societal development is indirect. While one cannot say that the Communist Party shows any signs of willingness to share power with other political parties, it is obvious that its own policies during the last twenty years have undermined the position of the HSWP. This is a logical consequence of the development, although it is not yet visible. The implication as such is recognised at the same time as there seems to be agreement to act according to the formula: 'As much pluralism as possible, as much Party as necessary'.[101] The problem is to decide what is 'possible' and 'necessary'.

As there are no signs that the majority of the Hungarian population regard the HSWP as a legitimate single ruler, political stability in Hungary is still based on rather fragile foundations. It is not improbable that a serious setback in the economy and a failure of the 'economic compensation' mechanism would entail increased self-organisation of society from below. So far the regime has shown acceptance of the unofficial or black economy. Part of official policy has been to legalise what people were doing anyhow.[102] But in the late 1970s, critical intellectuals arranged both an organisation for social welfare, for straight-forward material help to the numerous poor, and so called flying universities of the Polish model.[103] There is then, a certain preparation for a 'second society', the leaders of which might, in case of an economic crisis and of increased social tensions, acquire reputation as the true protectors of the national culture. But this would be in a situation rather different from the one in 1984 and more similar to the Polish one from 1976 onwards.

As the Party has controlled growth of economic prosperity and cultural revival, there has not been, in Hungary after 1956, any risk of a dynamic, self-propelling movement as in Czechoslovakia in 1968; and as the economic and cultural policies of the regime have not ended in disaster, as in Poland, there still is an important point, seen from the perspective of the nation as a whole, in letting the HSWP run the country. It is acceptable because it has not destroyed the country. The Party is needed for a role that only it can play: as protector against Soviet intervention. There were in 1983 no signs of Soviet discontent with Hungary. The Soviet leaders even expressed their confidence in the Kádár regime.[104]

Although official Soviet-Hungarian relations were considerably improved between 1956 — when, according to the official Soviet view, 'Imre Nagy, the new Chairman of the Council of Ministers, treacherously used the name of the government'[105] — and 1983,[106] the Soviet leaders have not managed to win the heart of the Hungarians (if that has ever been their objective). This is no official secret, as a survey showing 'wide spread anti-Russian sentiments' among a group of students was allowed to be published in Hungary in 1967, for example,[107] and as, on the other hand, prison sentences have been meted out now and then for 'incitement', which, according to a knowledgeable observer, George Schöpflin, 'almost invariably means abuse of the Soviet Union in a public place'. Schöpflin asserts that 'resentment and frustration over the Soviet Union's power over Hungary' are accompanied with 'passivity and reluctance to articulate that resentment'.[108] He thus points to a source of socio-psychological stress in Hungary, which is of relevance for any estimate of the effects of the Soviet security conception.

Toma and Volgyes, after asserting that to the Hungarians, the phrase 'the international socialist system', means simply the alliance with the USSR, go on to conclude that the possibilities of the Hungarians changing their negative attitude to this system are 'very slim'.[109] If this is true — and no evidence to the contrary is available — the Soviet-Hungarian alliance will remain basically unstable: for it to be stable, the Hungarian population must not be allowed to act in accordance with its value orientations in this question.

Notes

1 See Toma and Volgyes 1977, p. 31, Molnár 1978, p. 48.
2 Kende 1982, p. 6.
3 Kende 1982, p. 6, Molnár 1978, p. 119.
4 Vajda 1981, p. 141, Litynski 1980, p. 173 f. Cf. Földes 1979, p. 199, Kuttna 1979, p. 209 ff., Koltai 1980, p. 210 ff.
5 See Gitelman 1981, p. 138.
6 See Szamuely 1982 and Berend 1983.
7 Hare et al., p. 13.
8 Richet 1981, p. 26 f.
9 Vajna 1982, p. 182, 208.
10 Gati 1974, p. 29 f.
11 Vajna 1982, p. 181.
12 Csikós-Nagy 1982, p. 74 f., 83.
13 Nyers 1982, p. 22 ff.
14 Csikós-Nagy 1982, p. 74 ff.
15 Csikós-Nagy 1982, p. 85 f.
16 Puja 1983, p. 9.
17 Bognár 1980, p. 13 f., 20.
18 Gitelman 1981, p. 146 ff.
19 Schöpflin 1982a, p. 4.
20 Hernádi 1982, p. 153 f.
21 Bognár 1980, p. 9 ff., Bognár 1982, p. 20 ff., p. 34 (quotation).
22 Hernádi 1982, p. 151.
23 Tarján 1982, p. 187.
24 Hernádi 1980, p. 130 ff.
25 Schöpflin 1977, p. 152 writes of official celebrations on March 15: apparently the day was being celebrated without being an official holiday.

26 Kovrig 1979, p. 427.
27 Schöpflin 1977, p. 152.
28 Kovrig 1979, p. 427.
29 Földes 1980, p. 204 ff.
30 The myth as an important part in the perception of the past is stressed by Heller 1982b, p. 3 ff.
31 Klaniczay 1978, p. 140 ff. For a description of Hungarian historiography, see Fischer 1982. The book does not treat the dynamic relationship between historiography and politics.
32 Aczél 1983, p. 19.
33 See Seewann and Sitzler 1983, p. 95!
34 Illyés, E., 1981, passim, esp. p. 165 ff.
35 Bodnár 1980, p. 132 f.
36 Makkai 1981, p. 63 ff.
37 Dercsényi 1978, p. 53 ff., Boldizsár 1978, p. 65 ff.
38 Cf. Schöpflin 1982a, p. 22.
39 Klaniczay 1978, p. 143.
40 Pilaszanovich.
41 In a way this 'celebration' took place on the 25th anniversary, in 1981, when Népszabadság ran a series of articles on '1956'. When János Kádár, in 1972, spoke not only of the 'counter revolution' but also of the 'tragedy' of 1956, there was an obvious reference to earlier Hungarian historical experience. See Seewann and Sitzler 1982, p. 1 f., 17 f.
42 Konrád 1980, p. 60.
43 Kuttna 1979, p. 209 ff.
44 Litynski 1980, p. 175.
45 Nyers 1982, p. 24. Kossuth apparently is not conceived of as a 'model'. It seems that his messianic message has lost its impact on the Hungarians. (Cf. Deak 1979, p. 351).
46 Litván 1982, p. 104.
47 Györffy, M. 1982, p. 138. Cf. Seewann and Sitzler 1982, p. 1, who quote Hungarian sources on the 'gap' in historiography.
48 Gyertyán 1980, p. 218 ff., Györffy, M. 1982, p. 138 f.
49 See Schöpflin 1982a, p. 25 f.
50 Hann 1982, p. 149, reviewing Ferge 1980, notes that 'there is not much evidence to suggest secular trends leading in a socialist direction' (in Hungary).
51 Hernádi 1982, p. 152 f., reviewing Kunt 1981.
52 Tarján 1982, p. 188.
53 Berecz 1981, p. 21.
54 Boldizsár 1978, p. 73.
55 Boldiszár 1981, p. 142 ff.
56 Székely 1982, p. 177.

57 Schöpflin 1977, p. 146.
58 Scheiber 1981, p. 161 ff.
59 Széky 1982a, p. 123.
60 Quoted from Széky 1982a, p. 124.
61 Quoted from Széky 1982a, p. 124.
62 Széky 1982a, p. 126.
63 Quoted from Széky 1982a, p. 126.
64 R.F. 1979, p. 106.
65 Volgyes 1981a, p. 143.
66 Gilberg 1981, p. 193 f., 199 (first quotation), Gilberg 1975, p. 232, (second quotation). According to Száras 1983, p. 96 ff., the myth of Transylvania's Romanian past was vehemently propagated by Lancranjan 1982, a book which was 'enthusiastically' received by critics in Romania but 'astonished and shocked Hungarians who heard about it'. Already in 1979, Hungarian historians had dismissed the idea of ethnic continuity in the area as an unhistorical concept. (See Seewann and Spitzler 1983, p. 102.) As emphasised by Ronnås, 1982, p. 86 f., the question is open to subjective feeling: 'Few things have been subject to so much academic quarrel and so little serious investigation as the process of ethnic assimilation in Transylvania'. Ronnås himself came to the conclusion that romanization of the towns in Transylvania 'appears to have been accentuated in the seventies' (p. 118).
67 Illyés, E. 1981, p. 166 ff.
68 See Domokos 1983, p. 20 ff.
69 Volgyes 1981a, p. 144.
70 Kis 1981, p. 146 f.
71 Quoted from Száras 1983, p. 100. Although open revisionism (irredentism) certainly is out of question, the content of Száras's article does not validate the conclusion by Sewann and Spitzler 1983, p. 103 that nonrevisionism 'is today apparently a part of the political culture of the land'.
72 Skilling 1976, p. 608 f., 691, 744, 876 f. (quotation). Ulc 1974, p. 14 notes that 'The polarization continued during the eight pre-invasion months of 1968 and reached the point of demands that the Magyar-populated areas be incorporated into Hungary'.
73 Illyés, G. 1982, p. 20, 25 ff.
74 Howe et al. 1983, p. 44.
75 Schöpflin 1977, p. 145.
76 Koltai 1980, p. 203 f.
77 Koltai 1980, p. 208.
78 Ferge 1980, p. 319 f.
79 See Popper 1961.
80 Cf. Andropov 1983.

81 Kádár 1982, p. 98 ff.
82 Széky 1982b, p. 94. See also Antal 1983, p. 79, and Sitzler 1983, p. 471 ff.
83 Széky 1982b, p. 94. See also Széky 1982c, p. 113 (quotation).
84 Széky 1982c, p. 113, Széky 1982b, p. 97.
85 Macrae 1983, p. 23 ff.
86 Széky 1982b, p. 97 f.
87 Quoted from Széky 1982c, p. 113.
88 Széky 1982c, p. 113 f.
89 Quoted from Széky 1982c, p. 111 f.
90 Kovrig 1979, p. 430.
91 Molnár 1978, p. 143.
92 Macrae 1983, p. 26.
93 Vajda 1981, p. 146.
94 Jarnowski 1983, p. 12, 'Na Lewicy' 1983, p. 13 (quoting Nyers). See also Sperling 1983 and Swartz 1983.
95 Toma and Volgyes 1977, p. 149.
96 Toma and Volgyes 1977, p. 149.
97 Cf. Schöpflin 1982a, p. 4.
98 Kende 1983, p. 8.
99 Dyker 1983. An example of Soviet praise for Hungarian agriculture is Otsason 1983.
100 Gyertyán 1980, p. 218.
101 Sitzler 1982, p. 535.
102 See Csikós-Nagy 1982, p. 82. Volgyes 1981b, p. 153 warns that 'With the decrease in the standard of living that has been the sole support of the Party's legitimacy, the regime will face severe problems during the next lean years'. Hare 1983, p. 328 argues that 'the present direction of economic policy must be quite risky in political terms'.
103 See Engelmann 1981, p. 140.
104 'V Politbyuro TsK KPSS' 1983 says that the Hungarian-Soviet Party links shall become strengthened and that the political, economic, cultural and ideological cooperation between Hungary and the USSR shall be deepened.
105 Soviet Foreign Policy 1981, p. 253.
106 Cf. Korbonski 1980b, stressing that 'the last few years have witnessed a definite Hungarian-Soviet rapprochement'. The judgment is borne out by the wording in 'V Politbyuro TsK KPSS' 1983.
107 Kovrig 1979, p. 426, 491.
108 Schöpflin 1977, p. 142.
109 Toma and Volgyes 1977, p. 151.

5 The whole Central European scene

1956, 1968 and 1980–1981: a comparison

The Soviet reaction has been different during the three challenges to the Soviet order in Central Europe, in 1956, 1968, and 1980–81. While there are some non-Soviet memoirs as well as Khrushchev's mentioning the first two, not much has been revealed about the deliberations in the Politbureau of the CPSU in the Polish case in 1980–81.[1] Suffice it to note, however, that the outcome of the Soviet deliberations has been different each time: swift military action with Soviet troops against Hungary in 1956, increasing political pressure and eventual military action with Warsaw pact allies against Czechoslovakia in 1968, political and military pressure but no direct military action against Poland in 1980–81. And, last but not least, no overt military pressure or political action against Hungary in the period after 1968,[2] although the development in that country has, apart from obvious differences in the political sphere, shown some important similarities to what was underway economically and culturally in Czechoslovakia in 1968. Granting that the Soviet behaviour in each instance has been based upon a rational calculus of what would further Soviet security interests in a general sense, an analysis of the differences in the behaviour should give us a clue as to Soviet judgments. We need not try to speculate about motives of individual Soviet leaders and a possible bargaining within the Kremlin to be able to reach conclusions. What we have to rely on, is an analysis of actual Soviet behaviour in each case.

The most ruthless Soviet reaction against a perceived insubordination from a vassal was the treatment meted out to Hungary in 1956. It is necessary to take into consideration, in this case, the context of internal de-Stalinisation and external peaceful coexistence as the new guidelines of the post-Stalin Soviet policy under Khrushchev. 1955 saw a reconciliation with Tito's Yugoslavia as well as the remarkable Soviet action of giving up the partition of Austria and granting this country political freedom, through an agreement with the three other victors. When the Hungarian Premier Nagy, in October 1956, supported demands for a multiparty system and for neutralisation of Hungary, this most probably was perceived as a kind of 'domino threat' by the Soviet leaders. Peaceful coexistence should not mean giving up what was part and parcel of the security cordon established by Stalin.

Developments in Hungary up to October/November 1956 were obviously one effect of the de-Stalinisation and peaceful coexistence policy. It had to be unambiguously halted lest the whole Soviet security system should be eroded. The Soviet leaders could not accept a military strategic change, at a time when the British and the French were trying to regain a foothold in the Middle East (the Suez crisis).

At the time of the events in Czechoslovakia in 1968, the German question was not yet definitely solved. Czechoslovakia, with its boundary with the Federal Republic, was, together with the GDR, a front state of the WTO. Although Dubcek assured the world that Czechoslovakia would remain a loyal member of the pact, he was at the same time leading an internal policy, where differences of opinion were allowed to develop and flourish. The power monopoly of the Czechoslovak Communist Party was under threat, and hence also its ability to dictate the policy of the state in the future. Thus, while a challenge to the military security of the USSR could be perceived by the Soviet leaders to exist in Hungary in 1956, with the demands of Hungary's leaving the WTO, in Czechoslovakia in 1968, the immediate threat was of a political kind. The strike against Czechoslovakia was preemptive rather than reactive. The treatment of the challengers was, in the end, markedly different in the two cases. When Nagy and a few other Hungarian leaders were put to death by the Russians, Dubcek and his followers, though brutally treated in Moscow in late August 1968, were allowed to abdicate in an orderly manner and were not even imprisoned.[3] As the political line of the Dubcek regime was intimately linked with its attempts to reform the economy, the economic programme had to be abandoned with the political reform programme. The men that the Soviets could trust politically, turned out to be economically conservative. There is no evidence, however, that the Soviet leaders aimed at the economic reforms and deliberately set out to cripple Czechoslovakia economically. What they would not accept, was a political aberration.

The disturbances of the established order in Poland in 1956, 1968, 1970, and 1976 had been managed by the Polish communists and their security forces in a way which ensured continued loyalty to the WTO and retention of the political system of the Soviet type. Militarily and politically, Poland remained safe as seen from the Soviet leadership's point of view.

Developments in Poland between 1976–81 were not a violent process of the 1956 Hungarian kind. Nor was it a reform movement led by the Communist Party, as in Czechoslovakia in 1968. Instead one had the crystallisation of what Lenin labelled a 'revolutionary situation', i.e., a situation where the subjects are losing their patience with the rulers at the same time as the latter are losing their ability to rule.[4] This is another way of expressing that a regime has not secured legitimacy. We can follow this line of reasoning further and compare what happened in Poland in 1980–81 with what happened in Russia in 1917: the official registration of Solidarity as a genuine representative of the working people of Poland, on 10 November 1980, in practice meant the establishment of a 'dual power' in Poland, similar to the one existing in Russia between March (February) and November (October), 1917, with Solidarity playing the role of the Soviets, i.e., the councils as organisations from below, and the Polish communist leadership playing the role of the Provisional government. In Poland's case, however, the balance of forces were in favour of the government, as it could count on a loyal army and security police. And, there was the Soviet connection, the all-important Soviet perceptions of what happened.

The demands of the Solidarity movement in practice meant that the working population itself should gain influence over economic decisions. By implication, given the existing structure, this would mean influence over politics as well. One indication of the political implications of eventual labour influence on the economy was the hint, at the Solidarity congress in the autumn of 1981, that one should have to reconsider Poland's military expenditures.[5] The political implications were highlighted also by the Party's countering all reform proposals of a more radical kind with the argument that they could not be realised because of the 'geopolitical location' of Poland. Thus the dependence on the USSR became, in the eyes of the Solidarity leaders and their associates, not an asset but a liability, a barrier against all positive changes. The question of the power monopoly of the PUWP thus was linked to the question of Soviet supremacy. In the autumn of 1981, it must have been obvious to the Soviet leaders that if the PUWP began to share power with Solidarity, Poland could well become an ideologically, politically, and militarily unreliable area at the back of Czechoslovakia and the GDR, i.e., behind the front states of the Soviet security system.

As it became evident that the threats from the PUWP and police harassment of Solidarity people, as in Bydgoszcz in March 1981, could not frighten the Polish workers into submission, the PUWP, with apparent Soviet approval — the Soviet Commander-in-Chief of the WTO troops, Marshal Kulikov, visiting Warsaw and Jaruzelski in early December, 1981 — so to say 'abdicated' in favour of the top military men, the Polish generals around Jaruzelski (who were, of course, also Party members). As it were, the operation was a new version of Soviet interference, though of a more subtle kind than in either 1956 (in Hungary) or 1968 (in Czechoslovakia).

After Gomulka's return to power in Poland in October 1956, the Polish army seemed to become 'desovietised' and 'renationalised'. The Soviet Marshal Rokosovskii had to retire as Minister of Defence and from Polish politics in general. The Russian uniforms were exchanged for traditional Polish ones. Polish songs were sung instead of Russian ones in the army. The political control of the military became more discrete. The political commissars at the company level were withdrawn, for example.

However, the military's contact with the USSR remained intimate. A large number of Polish officers received their higher military education in the Soviet military academies. The Polish military organisation was divided into two parts, one consisting of 15 regular army divisions, about 4,000 tanks, the bombers, and the navy — with the aim of being deployed in an offensive against Scandinavia and Western Europe in case of emergency; the other of the so-called WOW forces, numbering 50,000–60,000 men — with suppression of internal disorder as its principal task. They fulfilled this task, in co-operation with the heavily armed, motorised police, the ZOMO, in 1970 (and in 1981).

Wojciech Jaruzelski was educated in the USSR. After becoming Minister of Defence in 1968, he managed to place his loyal followers in important posts. Under his custody, the general educational level of the officer corps was improved. In the 1970s, more than 40 per cent of the officers had received academic training. The political commissars were not only educated in military subjects but also in economics, sociology, and pedagogics. The salaries of the officers were raised and their privileges improved in order to attract able individuals. Poland got a well educated class of military officers, who were trained in the USSR and also members of the PUWP. In 1980 85 per cent of all Polish military officers, and 100 per cent of those at the colonel level and above, were members of the Party.[6]

What happened in Poland in 1980–81 was neither that the Party leaders who were loyal to the CPSU were put aside, as in Hungary in 1956, nor that the Party leadership took the initiative and objectively threatened to lead the country astray (as the Soviet leaders perceived it), as in Czechoslovakia in 1968. What happened was that the Party apparatus ceased to operate as a political body: it was not disloyal to the CPSU, but it could not dictate the policy of the country any more. The Polish military under Jaruzelski was both loyal to the CPSU and had the means to enforce the latter's will. Thus there was no need for the Soviet leaders to intervene militarily, as in Hungary in 1956 and in Czechoslovakia in 1968. They could count on General Jaruzelski, who 'happened' to be Premier and Party leader. Jaruzelski deployed so called 'operative field forces' of officers and conscripts in the country-side in late October 1981, and in the big cities in November. By propaganda tricks, he managed to foster hatred against Solidarity in the military.[7]

But why has there not been any direct or indirect brutal Soviet interference in Hungary after 1968, i.e., after the introduction of the NEM? It goes without saying that economic reforms as such are not perceived as being detrimental to Soviet security interests. In addition to the retention of political control inside Hungary, by the HSWP, the external political conditions of Hungary must be of importance for explaining the Soviet non-reaction. Although bordering on potentially instable Yugoslavia, Hungary is not a frontier state in the WTO–NATO confrontation. No military threat, no political challenge to the Soviet order — why intervene?

The nature of the relationship between the Soviet Union and states such as Czechoslovakia, Hungary, and Poland are of a feudal character. The CPSU is the seigneur and it can use and play the vassals against one another in any crisis situation. The vassals, the local leaders, do not acquire or keep their positions by election or promotion from below, by the people, but by appointment and approval from above, from the CPSU. The CPSU may abandon a vassal, i.e., an individual, and even have him killed, but it has never accepted a national leader with an independent standing and national backing. However, the whole scene is not static. As the Soviet leaders in 1956 made clear to the subordinate national rulers that they would be well advised to try to rule, not by terror and direct physical violence, but by consent from the subjects, a process of diversification was begun which revealed national differences. Hence the 1956, 1968, and 1980–81 disturbances can also be viewed as the unexpected and definitely unwelcome effects of a general attempt at indirect rule in the Soviet feudal empire.

Scholars' views, east and west

The Soviet security problem is, partly, a question of political legitimation of the regimes in the vassal states. A regime which is not viewed as legitimate by its own subjects has not got any inherent stability. It may enforce its will or the wishes of Moscow with the help of force, or it may try to compensate for the lack of legitimacy in the economic or the national cultural realm. But as soon as it chooses the compensatory way, it raises, if only in an oblique way, the question of legitimacy. It takes a certain responsibility upon itself and exposes itself to popular attitudes, feelings, and actions. It ceases to be the mere transmitter of wishes from above, from the seigneur, and has also to try to accommodate to a more or less outspoken pressure from below.

While the view being put forward in this analysis is that it would be beneficial to the Soviet leaders if their vassals had legitimacy in their own fiefs, as this would make Soviet costs and risks smaller, an opposite view can also be found in Western sovietology. In a study of Soviet influence in Eastern Europe (i.e., Central and South-Eastern Europe), Christopher D. Jones takes it for granted that it is perceived as a Soviet interest to keep vassals that are not popular with their subjects, as they thereby, because of their unpopularity, become more dependent on Soviet support and hence more attentive to the wishes of the Soviet leaders. Jones sees legitimacy and 'support from the centre', i.e., Moscow, as alternative bases of political power.[8]

Jones's opinion is shared by the Polish economist in exile, Wlodzimierz Brus, i.e., for Stalin's lifetime. The leaders Stalin imposed upon the Central and South-Eastern European countries were faithful to him 'and at the same time sufficiently alienated from their own people'. Brus calls this kind of rule 'delegated autocracy'.[9] His contention is that this is a birth-mark which cannot be obliterated as long as the basic contingency with the Stalinist system remains:

'Kádárism' is a child of Stalinism in the sense that it reflects both the need for change and the limits of change, imposed, among other things, by the political and ideological weakness of Communism emerging from the Stalinist experience. Would not the chances of transforming 'Kádárism' into 'socialism with a human face' be greater without this experience?[10]

In trying to evaluate Brus's assertion, one has to take into consideration the different traditions and the different political cultures in the respective countries. While Wojciech Jaruzelski in Poland most probably is seen, by his fellow countrymen, as the most recent incarnation of the Targowica men, and not as another Pilsudski,[11] Kádár may well be perceived by the Hungarians as a collaborator, making the best of an awkward situation and a follower, not of Rákosi, but of Bethlen or Széchenyi. 'Kádárism' would not be 'a child of Stalinism', then, but a bastard, the offspring from the forced liaison between Stalinism and Hungarian traditions.[12] As for Husák of Czechoslovakia, it seems superfluous even to pose the question of his chances of acquiring legitimation.

One of the Western researchers who has approached the question of the legitimacy of the Central and South-Eastern European regimes, Mary Hrabik Samal, even speaks of a 'crisis of authority' which does not recede after the end of (the original) Stalinism. She means that the regimes at least could get a minimum of credibility in the first years, i.e., into the mid-50s, by pointing to the hardships stemming from the Cold War East-West relationship as well as to the potential threat from the defeated domestic bourgeoisie. The overall decline in material standard could, in the early years, be compensated for by a social mobility that benefitted a considerable number of people. However, social, economic, ideological and political development exhausted all cultural and psychological foundations for even limited legitimacy for the regime, at the same time as dissidents began actively to question this kind of legitimacy. When the so called oil crisis hit the world economy in the mid-70s, the CMEA states showed themselves incapable of successful adaptation. Economic growth stagnated and the regimes could no longer pose as guarantors of economic welfare (this is the mechanism called 'economic compensation' in this study). The regimes were caught in the dilemma of having to try to placate both the Soviet leaders and their own subjects, the former ones demanding absolute loyalty, the latter ones demanding a decent life. Things were further complicated, for the leaders, as some of the demands of the dissident intellectuals were supported ideologically by communists outside the Soviet bloc, the so called eurocommunists.[13]

Hrabik Samal depicts three options for the local communist leaders in face of the continuing legitimation crisis: 1) allow the people to share power, 2) improve economic performance, and 3) increase repression. Experience has shown, according to Hrabik Samal, that the almost instinctive reaction of the leaders, when the crisis is deepening, is to use repression. The problem with the first solution is that it tends to get out of hand, as in Czechoslovakia in 1968 and in Poland in 1980–81. The dividends of the second alternative are uncertain, Hrabik Samal argues, quoting the GDR as an example: a relatively good economic performance has not been sufficient to obliterate dissidence. In the end it seems as if 'the communist leaders of Eastern Europe can choose only between different mistakes'.[14] 'Nothing fails like failure' is the gist of this argument. Once again we are brought back to the question of Kádár's Hungary as the possible exception to the rule, a successful instance of option number two.

While some observers of the Central and South-Eastern European scene believe that 'consumer demands' may 'prompt' some leaders 'to consider fundamental economic reforms'[15] and that 'Moscow' is aware of 'the potential linkage between economic wellbeing and the system's legitimacy',[16] there were no signs, in 1984, that either the Polish or the Czechoslovak leadership was able to implement anything of the kind: the very lack of legitimacy of their respective regimes leaves no alternative to continued repression. Any serious economic reform would mean intensified contacts with the West, as in the Hungarian case, but this is highly dangerous for these regimes, not least because of a particular consequence of thirty five years of communist mismanagement and propaganda:

> When these countries, the Central and South-East European regimes 'who see themselves as especially threatened', are coming into greater contact with bourgeois Western societies it is necessary, as the leadership sees it, to be even more vigilant against such potentially infectious ideas and practices as may permeate their societies. This is especially necessary since not only have certain of the ideologically based expectations, such as the imminent collapse of capitalism, failed to come about (so far), but the leaders are now dealing extensively with those very states previously characterized as the enemy . . . The more Europe returns to even a limited integrity, and the fewer the barriers to trade, travel exchanges and contacts of all kinds there are, the greater are the threats posed by the influence of uncontrolled and uncontrollable ideas, which inevitably accompany such contacts.[17]

One way out might be, according to the American political scientist Ronald H. Linden, who is the author of the quotation above, to try the first option suggested by Hrabik Samal, i.e., to share power with the people. Linden is also of the opinion, however, that this is rather risky, the dilemma of the regimes being to try to 'negotiate between the Scylla of too little legitimacy and the Charybdis of too much autonomy'.[18] Thus the regimes of the Husák or Jaruzelski type are trapped: economics are never 'pure'; either economic management is intimately related to internal policies and politics, especially in the case of attempts at reform, or it is combined with intensified contacts with the capitalist West.

As has been demonstrated above, the other 'compensation mechanism', i.e., the appeal to national culture, will hardly work if the regime fails in the economic dimension. Moreover, enhanced nationalism may very easily get out of control and usher in anti-Russianism or anti-Sovietism, as was the case in the Polish example of 1980–81. If anti-Sovietism has to be restrained, for obvious reasons,[19] the 'protector of national culture' device is turned into its opposite. It is exactly the bowing to Soviet wishes which is seen, by the Central European populations, as illegitimate. Nationalism 'can cause explosions' in a crisis originating in other sources,[20] and is thus a very dubious instrument for all vassal regimes. These are, as experience has repeatedly shown, operating 'on a much shorter fuse than their Soviet counterpart'.[21] Thus it is hardly true that the attempt to use nationalism is less dangerous, for the regime, 'in nationally homogeneous states such as Hungary and Poland'.[22] In the former case, the question of the Hungarian minorities abroad enters the scene, and in the latter, anti-Russianism.

The more profound significance of nationalism is that its reactivation will most probably remind the population of the differences between their own, European political culture, and the Russian/Soviet one. Of course, 'European political culture' is hardly a very clear or unambiguous concept. Not that one should neglect, in the Central European countries with a domestic communist tradition, what Skilling has called 'the domestic roots of Stalinism'.[23] The importance lies in the fact that a difference somehow exists between the traditional dominant political cultures in Russia/the USSR on the one hand, and in the vassal states on the other.

While the Soviet system, as distinct from the Soviet regime, has apparently acquired a kind of legitimacy among broad groups of the Soviet population,[24] similar circumstances do not exist outside the USSR. Thus the factors that would appear to have guaranteed political stability in the Soviet Union — autocracy and preeminence of the state over the civil society — have become a source of instability when imposed upon Czechoslovakia, Poland, and Hungary. The difference has been well verbalised by the Polish emigré sociologist Zygmunt Bauman (in 1981):

> Communist rule in Russia began without any vestige of a civil society. . . . Coming into a society which was lacking in a civil society of any importance – i.e., one likely to make its resistance felt – the new communist leadership slipped easily into the ready-made pattern of a mostly state-integrated system. . . . The post-war political colonization of Eastern Europe by the Soviet Union came on the top of a well-entrenched civil society in at least some of the colonized countries. There was already an institutionalized network of social debate mediating between the level of 'popular folklore' and the central value cluster supporting the state structure. The imported Soviet pattern squared ill with a society integrated in such a complex way. Hence, the post-war history of most East European countries can be seen as a series of efforts to subdue or eradicate civil society already in existence. . . . The battle for the transformation of civil society into an agency of political state is still ongoing and unresolved.[25]

Bauman viewed the struggle of the Polish workers as an 'attempt to regain the lost authority for civil society'.[26] The fact that such struggles repeatedly occur, is a proof that 'the old nationalist political cultures of Central and Eastern Europe are being mediated to the new working classes', as the British journalist and political scientist Neal Ascherson has observed, commenting on the 1956 upheavals as well as on the Prague spring of 1968 and the Polish August of 1980.[27]

The brutal and swift suppression of the Hungarian revolt in 1956 made clear that the Soviet leaders were well aware of the fact that they had to base their rule, and hence the stability of the system which should give them security, on military force. But as de-Stalinisation and peaceful coexistence continued after 1956, the prospects seemed a little brighter, from a Central European point of view. Perhaps gradual reform, a carefully monitored return to traditional values and beliefs, to non-Russian ways in the relations between the rulers and the ruled, was possible.

The relative 'liberalisation' at least made discussion, although not necessarily public, possible in the Central European countries. While the established communist leaders, such as Novotny, Kádár, and Gomulka and Gierek, and, basically, also Dubcek, must be perceived in a 'dialogue' situation as representatives of Soviet type communism, prominent intellectuals outside the party apparatuses (but not necessarily outside the Communist Parties), became the spokesmen of the national traditions, of the domestic political cultures.

In retrospect, it seems that it was not the brutal Soviet invasion of Hungary in 1956 that made the dissident intellectuals in Central Europe abandon all hope for a Soviet–Central European reconciliation based on mutual respect and trust. After all, the Hungarian revolt in 1956 was an open and direct challenge to Soviet rule. The Soviet reaction could be interpreted as a 'normal' great power conduct. No more and no less.

What made the Soviet–Central European divide appear insurmountable was what happened to Czechoslovakia in 1968–69, i.e., the so called 'normalisation'. It amounted to a gradual strangulation of the civil society and of the reawakened traditional political culture. In the Czechoslovak reform movement, the Soviet legacy had been negated in every respect; it was now reintroduced. What was at stake, i.e., what the differences were all about, has been well stated by, in addition to Skilling, the most erudite Western student of the Czechoslovak reform movement, the American-Israelian scholar Galia Golan:

> What ever the explanation, the values which prompted this rejection of Bolshevism, as evidenced by the proposals offered for a new model, were identical with those of the Hussite tradition as it developed over the centuries. Just a few examples from the 1968 demands demonstrate the relationship: the rejection of arbitrary authority and privileged elites; the proposals for a return to the rule of law with the re-institution of Constitutional and Administrative Courts and independence of judges; government responsibility to the parliament and parliamentary responsibility to the courts and the people; respect and tolerance for individual opinions and the right to express them, be it through elected organs, representative interest

groups, or individual creativity; Party leadership of society through persuasion and an appeal to reason; the Party's need to 're-win' or earn anew, continuously, its leading position through development of a realistic programme; a return to Europe and a Czechoslovak 'contribution'; and the very concept of 'socialism with a human face' which summed up the demands of the reform movement.

While Golan contrasts 'the Czechoslovak movement concentrated on legalistic programmatic achievements' with the 'speedier, but more nationalistic-orientated 'revolts' in Poland and Hungary after the death of Stalin' and asserts that the Czechoslovak movement was 'more thorough, disciplined, and realistic' than the Polish and Hungarian movements,[28] Poland and Hungary in a longer perspective. The post-1968 changes in Hungary and the 1976–81 process in Poland bear important similarities with the Czechoslovak reform movement.

The final disillusionment with the Soviet political and economic system and with Marxism of the traditional Soviet kind as well as that which was experienced by the intellectuals and others in countries such as Poland and Hungary, and in Czechoslovakia, of course, came after the debacle for the reformers in Czechoslovakia. The processes in the Hungarian and Polish societies from 1968 on have been analysed above. Here I will take up a perspective from within, concentrating especially on the Soviet-Central European differences, as it has been expressed by two fairly well known members of the dissident intelligentsia in the two countries, the Budapest school sociologist Mihály Vajda, and the former KOR activist, Adam Zagajewski, respectively. Their books in question were both published in the West in 1981.

Vajda was born in 1935. He has been an organised communist and a Marxist, a not atypical experience for a Central European intellectual of his generation. Zagajewski was born in 1945 and is thus part of a generation who experienced the repressions in Poland in 1968 and 1970, as well as the termination of the Prague spring, in its youth and never had time to nurture any illusions about communism and Marxism of the Soviet brand.

It must be put on the record as an important effect of thirty five years of communist rule in their countries that both Vajda and Zagajewski are of the opinion that Marxism is useless as a tool of analysis for anyone trying to understand the contemporary history of the Central European societies.

Vajda points to the reductionist economism of Marxism, which has entailed neglect of the subjective and traditional aspects of societal life, i.e., those aspects which create the human consciousness. Reductionist economism has made Marxists in East and West neglect the profound difference between the roots of the communist system in Russia/the

USSR, on the one hand, and in Central Europe, on the other. In Central Europe there were, when communism arrived, age-old traditions of pluralism, compromising and rational decision-making, all of which were missing from the Russian tradition. Russia's way of societal change had been one of despotic central rule and subjugation of the people. The masses suffered, rising up in violent upheavals when conditions seemed to be unbearable. It was never possible, however, for any distinct group in the society to exert influence on the rulers in a rational way, in a genuinely political way.[29]

Referring to the situation in Poland immediately after August 1980, Zagajewski views the Communist Party in a desperate struggle to preserve its position and the political status quo. But what the Party tried to preserve was not something that grew naturally or 'organically' out of Polish traditions, but the unnatural system, superimposed upon Poland.[30] Vajda's opinion is very clear regarding this difference. According to him, Czechoslovakia, the GDR, Poland, and Hungary 'are countries under occupation and their system is without any raison d'être in terms of their own past and thus without any organic unity'.[31]

According to Zagajewski, the birth of Solidarity in Poland meant the return of a whole people to political and cultural traditions that had survived beneath a communist ice cover. Democratic and pluralist traditions came to life again.[32]

Vajda points out that the 'progressive potential' of political democracy and socialism in Central Europe, which had been referred to by another Central European dissident, the East German Marxist Bahro, is to be found exactly where and only where, the communist system has been enforced through violence. The potential in question is based upon the domestic political democratic traditions of the countries themselves, rather than upon the 'modernisation' of the economy by Soviet type industrialisation.[33]

It is interesting to compare Golan's assertion, quoted above, that the Czechoslovak reform movement stressed legality, i.e., predictability and accountability in social and political life, with statements made by Vajda and Zagajewski in the same vein. For example, after paying tribute to the Russian people's traditional lack of 'servility' in spite of the despotism of the state, Vajda states:

> What was lacking in Russia — and I fear that this is still the case today — is the need and capacity for a democratic decision-making process, i.e., something which is not a question of character or tolerance. What in my view is lacking is the existence of a rational attitude.[34]

From his Polish perspective, Zagajewski views rationality as being represented by a completely different actor from that of the Soviet-type

Communist Party. When the Party created institutions that destroyed as much as they produced, hindered as much as they furthered production, the Catholic Church was seen in a new light, as the embodiment of rational organisation.[35] An expression of the irrational attitude of the Communist Party is, according to Zagajewski, that it can only tolerate communists, that the communists are dreaming of a 'one-colour world'.[36] Here one encounters neither respect for laws nor rational human behaviour:

> In Poland it was never as dramatic as in the Soviet Union under Generalissimus Stalin, but also here one could feel the cold gust of the same wind, an Asian wind which annihilated almost all values and achievements of the European civilisation: the freedom of the individual, the respect for truth and justice, the basic norm that political adversaries are not shot but attempted to reach a compromise with.[37]

Vajda's and Zagajewski's experiences and conclusions corroborate the general conclusion of the Brown and Gray research project on '*Political Cultural and Political Change in Communist States*', which states:

> Economists have pointed out that the idea of marginal utility is missing from Marxist economics. In the same way, and in a close psychological relationship, the idea of legitimate conflict and competition is missing from Marxist politics. The market place, whether for goods or ideas, is irrational and dangerous. Perhaps the most important conclusion which this book suggests is that in countries where there has in the past been experience of the fruitful play of competing ideas and competing interests, experience of Communist government has not weakened but actually strengthened the conviction among the population that political freedom brings both greater justice and greater efficiency.[38]

The Marxist view that the market place is 'irrational' has not stopped the market economies from working more efficiently as regards use of manpower, energy and material resources, than 'real existing socialism'. Small wonder that the Polish economist Stefan Kurowski observed in a speech in Warsaw in May 1979, that the economic theory of Marxism was the main cause of the 'permanent crisis' of the Polish economy and that this theory had damaged the Polish economy beyond repair.[39] Small wonder, then, that another Polish social scientist, the sociologist Jadwiga Staniszkis, considered that the roots of the 'waste and inefficiency in the Polish economy' were to be found in the 'economic philosophy and the methods of the institutions',[40] i.e., in Marxism and in the planning agencies. The point is that the Marxist theory imported from the Soviet Union is perceived, by Central European intellectuals, as another expression of the Russian lack of order and rationality, and not as a part of that Western civilisation in which Marxism was once born. Consequently, those concerned will tend to regard the economic mess in a country like Poland in the late 1970s or like Czechoslovakia in the mid-1960s and again in the early 1980s[41] as the ultimate consequence of the Soviet political model,[42] the irrational politicisation of economic life emanating from the Russian/Soviet tradition.[43] It is against this background that one should view the conclusion that the conflict between these political cultures is impossible to solve within the framework of the actual, existing conditions. Thus it has been expressed by an American political scientist of Polish origin, Seweryn Bialer:

> It is extremely difficult to imagine a peaceful solution to the Polish events and a peaceful transformation of the Polish system that would allow greater freedom for society while preserving the political monopoly of the Communist Party.
> . . . This gap between the necessary and the possible, is the reality of the Polish situation, and the measure of the gravity of the crisis.[44]

Similarly, Brown and Wightman note in their study of Czechoslovakia that the people's experience of 1968 and subsequent years, has effectively dimmed 'the prospects for the official political culture becoming the dominant political culture in respect of political knowledge and expectations . . .'.[45]

In his analysis of the Hungarian experience up to the late 1970s Vajda came to the conclusion that 'Kádárism', in spite of its popular acceptance as the least evil alternative, given Hungary's position as a defeated nation, has not succeeded in providing 'any real alternative nor qualitatively new model within "existing socialism".' But on the other hand, Vajda asserts, referring to the experience of intellectual life in Hungary under Kádár, that it is possible to create a 'public sphere' of critical intellectual discourse in Central Europe.[46] This may not seem to be very much to strive for. It is, however, an expression of confidence in a possible 're-Europeanisation' of Central European culture, of belief in the continued vitality of its non-Stalinist political culture.

Thus the tension between the Stalinist Soviet political culture and those of the Central European countries is a permanent source of conflict and a potential threat to the stability of the Soviet security system. As our study has shown, these domestic traditions have not become weakened over time. On the contrary, they have become reactivated and vitalised by events such as the Prague spring in 1968, the Polish August in 1980, and the Hungarian devolution from Stalinism from the mid-sixties onwards. There is more than a grain of truth in the bitter assertion by one of the Prague spring intellectuals in exile, Eduard Goldstücker, that the Soviet leaders can only receive Central European acquiescence by 'annihilating the collective memory, falsifying the national history and suppressing and manipulating the culture' of the vassals.[47]

International relations in Central Europe

Although Central European intellectuals often stress that the main dividing line in political culture runs between their own countries — the GDR, Czechoslovakia, Hungary and Poland — and the USSR, there is of course a number of differences between the former ones as well. Analysing the rather poor record of CMEA integration, Korbonski has pointed to these differences as a contributing cause, together with 'varying degrees of exposure and reaction to Western influences'.[48] However, it is not only a matter of domestic traditions and contacts with the West. Moreover, relations between the Central and South-East European states themselves have created obstacles to integration in the area.

Stalin's original Central and South-East European empire brought peace to the region in the respect of putting a very heavy lid on the traditional territorial disputes and ethnic conflicts between the countries. De-Stalinisation and peaceful coexistence, although leaving no space for irredentism and overt interstate conflicts within the system, allowed a certain re-emergence of national differences, including the actualisation of minority questions. The most obvious example was that of the Hungarian minority in Czechoslovakia in 1968, which demanded equal collective status with the Czechs and the Slovaks in the republic. As the three major serious challenges to the Soviet rule have come from Hungary, Czechoslovakia, and Poland, it is also of interest to examine as far as possible the attitudes of these nations towards each other.

It is evident that relations at an official level have also been poor between the three countries in question after 1956. This has been underlined by Linden, who has made the following remark:

> That the East European states actually threaten each other more than do the states of the West is born out by the undeniable, if brutal, empirical indicator of military action, used against Hungary in 1956, against Czechoslovakia in 1968, and, in a different form, against Poland in 1980–81.

The reasons were in each case, as Linden sees it, the fear of reformist contagion on the part of those who were hardliners at the moment.[49]

The problem is not confined to the actual perceptions of conflict. Historical traditions from time to time may reinforce mutual suspicion. A case in point is the old Polish-Czech confrontation over the Teschen area.

During the whole interwar period, the Teschen conflict effectively blocked any Polish-Czechoslovak co-operation in international politics. The former Hapsburgian Duchy was divided between the two successor states in 1920, but the Poles never gave up their claims to the major part of the Czechoslovak piece as well. When Germany took the Sudetenland from Czechoslovakia in 1938, Poland took 'Zaolzie'. The Lublin government in Poland, which by its very existence represented a definite break with prewar Poland and her policy, was slow in recognising the status quo ante Monachium (ante 1938). Only in 1947 was the matter settled as part of the Polish-Czechoslovak alliance agreement of that year.[50] However, the Teschen area has continued to be of some interstate political significance. In 1959, the 250th anniversary of an evangelical church (the building) was celebrated in the Polish part of Teschen. On this occasion, the increase in tension between Czechs and Poles was sufficient for the authorities to close the frontier, barring ethnic Poles of the evangelical creed who were Czechoslovak citizens from taking part in the celebration.[51]

In 1968, the Polish Gomulka regime, following in the footsteps of the Beck policy of 1934–38,[52] tried to play on the national feelings of the Polish minority in Czechoslovakia in order to embarass the government in Prague by demanding from representatives of the minority that they expressed dissatisfaction with Dubcek's regime. The attempt was a failure, as the Polish minority instead chose to express their loyalty with the regime.[53] In Poland proper, however, Gomulka was apparently more successful in trying to appeal to anti-Czechoslovak feelings. At the time of the invasion of Czechoslovakia, 'many Poles', Ascherson says, 'were extraordinarily unsympathetic to the Czechs and Slovaks', with the exception of 'intellectuals and students'.[54]

The abuse by the Husák regime of the Polish democratic movement in 1980–81 is proverbial.[55] According to general information from Czechoslovakia in this period, there was no popular support for the Solidarity movement in Poland.

Among the 'intellectuals and students', however, the late 1970s saw the emergence of mutual understanding between Poles and Czechs. The Czechoslovak human rights 'Charta 77' group and the Polish KOR in late 1977 exchanged letters stressing 'the solidarity of the two peoples in their striving for freedom' and expressing 'hope for a firm and lasting friendship between them in the future'.[56] Even if the assertion, made in 1978, of one scholar that the 'possibility of a chain reaction between events in Poland and Czechoslovakia is real',[57] was not borne out by what really happened in 1980–81, it points to a potential source of challenge to Soviet rule.

The relations between Hungarians and Slovaks have already been dealt with in this study. Suffice it to say in the present context that the Czechoslovak reform communists in 1968 avoided mentioning the Hungarian challenge in 1956 as a possible precedent of what they were doing themselves. In spite of Dubcek's early attempt to get cover from Gomulka and Kádár,[58] the Czechoslovakians stressed the exceptional nature of their undertaking,[59] thus signalling to Moscow that there was no real risk of concerted reform action between Czechoslovakia and her neighbours.

If relations between Poles and Czechs and between Hungarians and Slovaks leaves much to be desired, the record of Polish-Hungarian relations is brighter. Though there was sometimes rivalry between the rulers in the respective countries in the Middle Ages, the present generation of Polish and Hungarian intellectuals is stressing the common historical bonds, as, for example, the Transylvanian prince Stefan Bathory, who was elected king of Poland and ruled there from 1576–86, and the Polish officer Bem who fought together with the Hungarians in 1849 against the Russian troops. However, there are more recent events to be remembered.

After Poland's defeat by Germany and the Soviet Union in 1939, tens of thousands of Poles took refuge in Hungary. On the 40th anniversary of this event, in 1979, both Polish and Hungarian historians mentioned it as an example of a feeling of community and stressed that the Hungarian government on the 10 September 1939, declared that it was a matter of national honour not to take part in any military action against Poland; at the moment, the Hungarians were pressed in this direction by the Germans.[60]

In October 1956, the sense of a common fate was apparently widespread among the students in Warsaw and Budapest. There was also a direct connection between the two upheavals:

> The proximate cause of the Hungarian revolution, as a matter of fact, was an act of symbolic solidarity with Poland. On 22 October, a group of students decided to lay a wreath at the statue of General Bem ... it was this demonstration that attracted enormous crowds into the streets of Budapest on 23 October, when the wreath-laying took place.[61]

Even a researcher who asserts that the traditional Polish-Hungarian friendship 'has amounted to very little after 1945', Miklós Molnár, admits that what happened in 1956 was 'proving how durable collective mental structures can be'.[62]

A survey of the Poles' attitudes to other peoples, which was carried out by Polish sociologists in 1967, showed that among those who had visited both the USSR and Hungary, 60 per cent mentioned Hungary and 15 per cent the USSR as the nation which had the friendliest relations with Poland. Commenting on the survey, two Western political scientists find the explanation in 'certain shared insurrection movements, for example in 1848 and 1956'. They take care to add a sobering commentary, however, elaborating on the notion that contact is a necessary condition of conflict: 'The fact that the nations have no common border also contributes to harmony'.[63]

On the Hungarian side one may find assertions that similar experiences lie behind works of the Hungarian dramatist István Örkény and those of his Polish colleague Slawomir Mrozek, as well as behind Pál Gábor's movie 'Angi Vera' and Andrzej Wajda's 'The Man of Marble', both treating the impact of Stalinism on the society.[64] What is similar is the effect of the imposed Russian political culture on the social climate and personal relations in the two countries. These are perceived as two related instances of a common, terrible fate. Those who have been through all this will understand each other better than those without this experience can understand them. This is beyond politics, but it denotes a common frame of reference.

There were no signs of official Hungarian support for the Solidarity movement in Poland in 1980–81, although the Hungarian mass media were conspicuously restrained in their criticism, as compared with the East German, the Czechoslovak, and the Soviet media.[65]

All in all, the interstate relations in Central Europe have not been such as to constitute any threat to Soviet rule and security by way of concerted action by the vassal states. Viewed in a longer perspective, one may even conclude that cross-national co-operation against Soviet dominance has become weaker. In 1956, the popular upheavals in Poland and Hungary, if not co-ordinated, had at least inspired each other, and in 1968, there were Polish student demonstrations in support of the Prague spring.[66] In 1980–81 the Poles were virtually alone.

The threat to the stability of the Soviet security system in the ethnic dimension may come from internal conflict rather than from internal co-operation in Central Europe. In the area of concern to this study, Hungary's relations with her neighbours is the most interesting question. The geographical distribution of the Hungarian nation does not at all coincide with Hungary's state boundaries. We have treated this subject above, but a few remarks are necessary in the present context.

The Hungarian government and the HSWP do not lead or encourage irredentist policies against Czechoslovakia and Romania. On the contrary, it is an often articulated opinion that the regime's inability to take care of the interests of the Hungarian minorities in those countries, is the ultimate cause of its lack of legitimacy.[67] However, this is only one source of instability that stems from this question.

If the NEM and the whole process of Hungarian devolution are allowed to continue, the contrasts between the Hungarian economic and social fabric, on the one hand, and Romanian and Czechoslovak society, on the other, will increase. If not prospering in West European terms, Hungary may well look like a welfare country to her neighbours (not to the

Austrians, but this is beside the point). Even if the Hungarian minorities in Romania and Czechoslovakia are not discriminated against, they may well perceive themselves as disfavoured, comparing their general situation not with that of their co-citizens, but with that of their brethren in Hungary proper. It goes without saying that the effect of the choice of yardstick will be greater if the minorities in question feel that they are being discriminated against on ethnical-cultural grounds. We know that they feel that way. Thus one cannot disregard the possibility that unrest will increase and that the Hungarian regime cannot do much about it. The initiative is with the Ceausescu and Husák regimes. Judging from their previous record, they will react with suppression rather than with concessions to Hungarian nationalist demands. But to suppress a conflict is not necessarily to solve it for good. While this problem of the national minorities is not a direct threat to the stability of the Soviet security system, it may well seriously aggravate a crisis situation that stems primarily from other causes, for example economic breakdown in Romania or Czechoslovakia.

It seems that there is only one real common denominator among all the Central European peoples: their dislike of the Soviet regime and of the necessity of belonging to the Soviet system. Although all has been well at the formal, state level, after the Hungarian uprising in 1956 — the Czechoslovak leader in 1968, Dubcek, never made himself known as an opponent of the Soviet connection — viewed from the Kremlin's perspective, the popular attitudes have not changed for the better.

The Soviet security system in Central Europe remains inherently unstable. Although Soviet dominance can be said to have made armed conflicts between the vassals impossible, it can also be said that there is a permanent need for Soviet policing of the area. The stability of the vassal regimes may be affected by their relations one to another. Soviet military presence may be necessary to preserve the order. This must be considered a liability for the USSR rather than as an asset.

Notes

1 Micunovic 1980, p. 131 ff. gives a report from Khrushchev's and Malenkov's discussion with the Yugoslav leaders on 2–3 November 1956 (on Hungary), Mlynár 1980, p. 252 ff., one from the meeting between the Soviet and the captured Czechoslovak leaders in the Kremlin, Moscow, on 26 August 1968. Cf. Valenta 1981, p. 160, who stresses 'the internal dynamics of the Soviet Politbureau' in crisis situations. As Valenta shows, the fact that 'semi-insiders' such as fellow Communists from other countries also fail to see clearly what is going on inside the Kremlin (before they are brought there by force) should be taken as proof that Soviet decision-making in

questions of major importance still remains enigmatic.
2 See, however, Schulz 1981, p. 58 that Soviet pressure of a political kind lay behind the 'reform stop' in Hungary in 1972–75 and the dismissal of Nyers as Minister of Finance.
3 Cf. Eidlin 1980, p. 257.
4 See Istoriya i Sotsiologiya 1964, p. 8.
5 See Garton Ash 1983, p. 224. The tendency to question the military relationship to the USSR is also clear in the 'Foundation Proclamation' of the 'Club for a Self-Governing Republic' called 'Freedom, Justice, Independence'. Among the founders were former KOR members Jacek Kuron, Jan Litynski and Henryk Wujec. See Hirsch 1982.
6 See Johnson et al. 1980, p. 41 ff., p. 54., Sadykiewicz 1982.
7 See Arato 1981–82, p. 46 for a general interpretation. Mårtensson 1982 gives a detailed analysis, drawing on materials published after December 13, 1981, in the daily of the Polish Defence Ministry, Zolnierz Wolnosci.
8 Jones 1981, p. 12.
9 Brus 1977, p. 249.
10 Brus 1977, p. 256.
11 Cf. Michnik 1982, p. 8.
12 Cf. Vajda 1981, p. 141. Zimmerman 1981, p. 97, stresses the point that Kádárism represents both socialism and Hungary's 'Danubian' heritage.
13 See Adomeit 1979, p. 121, who is of the opinion that Euro-communism is a real challenge for the USSR as it aims at 'the legitimacy of these regimes (communist) both in the Soviet Union and Eastern Europe'. Although writing at an earlier date, Godson and Haseler have proved to be right in their dismissal of the influence of Eurocommunism in Central and South Eastern Europe as both ephemeral and superficial (Godson and Haseler 1978, p. 102 f.).
14 Hrabik-Samal 1982, 545 ff., 557 (quotation).
15 Larrabee 1981/82, p. 56 f.
16 Korbonski 1980b, p. 306.
17 Linden 1982a, p. 165. See also Pravda 1981, p. 183, drawing a balance sheet for the development over decades: 'But the 'Western option' has turned out to be far from the panacea for all East European ills. Whatever the early hopes for it as a substitute for structural reform, the whole Western connection has tended to exacerbate the problems it was meant to alleviate.'
18 Linden 1982a, p. 173.
19 See Schultz 1981, p. 57 f.
20 Schöpflin 1981, p. 67 ff.
21 Moreton 1981, p. 185.

22 Brown 1979, p. 158.
23 Skilling 1977, p. 257 f. See also Rupnik 1982, p. 309 ff.
24 White 1979, p. 189.
25 Bauman 1981, p. 52.
26 Bauman 1981, p. 52.
27 Ascherson 1981, p. 250.
28 Golan 1975a, p. 54
29 Vajda 1981, passim.
30 Zagajewski 1981, passim.
31 Vajda 1981, p. 123.
32 Zagajewski 1981, p. 172 ff.
33 Vajda 1981, p. 124 f. Cf. White 1979, p. 174 f., who stresses that there is not any empirical evidence of a correlation between modernisation and democratisation.
34 Vajda 1981, p. 115.
35 Zagajewski 1981, p. 62.
36 Zagajewski 1981, p. 59.
37 Zagajewski 1981, p. 204.
38 Gray 1977, p. 272.
39 Kurowski 1983, p. 73 ff.
40 Staniszkis 1982a, p. 241.
41 Mastny 1982 points to Czechoslovakia's economic crisis in the 1980s.
42 Moreton 1982, p. 89, 104, denotes this aspect.
43 Hedlund 1983, passim.
44 Bialer 1981, p. 538
45 Brown and Wightman 1977, p. 185.
46 Vajda 1981, p. 141.
47 Goldstücker 1982.
48 Korbonski 1980a p. 364.
49 Linden 1982a, p. 167. Cf. Ulc 1981, p. 154 who notes that the CC of the Czechoslovak Communist Party was summoned prematurely in October 1980, in order to allow the Czechoslovak leaders to take steps to counteract influences from the revolutionary Poland.
50 Müller 1977, p. 131 ff.
51 Patzelt 1972, p. 181.
52 See Gerner 1983 for the Beck policy.
53 Sikora 1972, p. 61. Schöpflin 1982b, p. 27 f. asserts, however, that the antagonism regarding Teschen Silesia — where the Polish minority in Czechoslovakia lives — spurred negative feelings among people at large towards the reform movements in the 'fraternal country' in 1968 and 1980–81, respectively. Hoensch 1982, p. 29 notes that the border dispute hampered military co-operation between Prague and Warsaw in the WTO.

54 Ascherson 1981, p. 97. Schöpflin 1982b notes that Warsaw students demonstrated in favour of the Czechoslovak reform movement in 1968, thereby reciprocating, so to speak, the students' demonstration on behalf of the Polish uprising in Budapest on 22 October 1956.

55 Cf. Linden 1982a, p. 168 (quoting Husák).

56 Bromke 1978, p. 753.

57 Bromke 1978, p. 758.

58 See Müller 1977, p. 244 f.

59 Vasari 1981, p. 381 notes this aspect, remarking that it proved to be of no avail.

60 Kozminski and Juhasz 1980, p. 105 ff.

61 Schöpflin 1982b, p. 26.

62 Molnár 1978, p. 129.

63 Kolankiewicz and Taras 1977, p. 106, 126.

64 See Koltai 1980, p. 210, Gyertyán 1981, p. 213 ff.

65 This difference is borne out in the study by Petersson 1982.

66 See notes 54 and 62 above!

67 Kende 1982, p. 12 f. Kis 1981, p. 147.

6 Soviet perspectives

Views of vassals: the Kazan tradition

We have seen how the Central European views of the Soviet Union are affected by the historical perceptions of the peoples concerned. Likewise, the Soviet Russian view of the smaller countries to the west of the USSR is partly determined by the Soviet leadership's understanding of the Soviet Union as an heir to Imperial Russia.

To enhance understanding of the Soviet policy towards Central Europe in our time, one should try to find out which images of the past that are likely to be held by contemporary Soviet decision makers. What one may find will not be historical causes of present Soviet external conduct in any direct sense, but an historically derived world view dominating the mind of the decision makers in question in the long run and apart from eventual personal idiosyncracies that may affect the outcome in specific situations.

To start from the present, it is quite obvious that the present Soviet leadership perceives the USSR as a global superpower (although they abhor the term) with a stake everywhere on the globe, from Nordkap to Angola, from Nicaragua to Afghanistan and Vietnam.[1] Seen in the context of the progressivist view of history common to all Marxists (and many others), it is not too bold to assume that the Soviet leadership looks upon the present status of the USSR as the natural outcome of a long historical process, a process of growth for Russia in territory, in economic potential, in military capability, and in political power.

While it has been argued that the past offers only partial insights into contemporary Soviet policy and that it cannot represent the new choices facing the Soviet leadership,[2] this is not really the point. The point is, rather, that there is a certain Russian legacy, of which the leaders feel they are in charge, and that they act accordingly. It is not a matter of historical precedence, but of continuity in history.

Though Soviet historiography is not a simple reflection of the will and orders of the political leadership, it is nonetheless true that historical works published in the USSR usually express views that are palatable for the leaders and in accordance with the general Party line. This is anyhow the case as far as the history of the Fatherland is concerned.

The picture of Russia's past that emerges from contemporary Soviet historiography is one of continuity, where the Muscovite principality of the late 15th century is seen as a direct continuation of the medieval Kievan state. Russia is also seen as an integral part of Western civilisation throughout history, in spite of the Mongol yoke.[3]

The gathering of Russian lands is seen as the natural thing to do for every Russian ruler, and this includes not only clearly ethnic Russian territories but, for example, the southern shore of the Gulf of Finland and the eastern shore of the Baltic Sea as well, not to speak of the Slav brethren of White Russians and Ukranians; all those territories are seen as being reunited with the Fatherland, be it in the 17th century (the Ukraine), the 18th century (the Baltic provinces) or the 20th century (the Ukraine and White Russia, the Baltic states). To this one should add the fact that also areas, which cannot possibly be labelled either Slavic or historically Russian, when they have been conquered are regarded as 'coming home' all the same, as they, thanks to incorporation in the 19th century (Transcaucasus, Central Asia) could pick the fruits and consume the delights of the Great Socialist October Revolution in 1917.[4]

The well known Russian and Soviet Marxist historian, M. Pokrovskii, once said of his adversaries in the profession that they were misusing history as they 'projected politics into the past'.[5] It is an irony of history that this indictment later has been used, and rightly so, to describe parts of Soviet historiography. It is possible to take one step further, though, and begin to think about the feed-back of this 'politics projected into the past' technique: the picture of the past, 'politicised' in the first instance, consciously or unconsciously, moulds the image of the present situation and of the 'natural' future of the state. The logic is one of the assumed suprahistorical validity of certain configurations in the international arena. A few examples will clarify the point.

The Soviet historian V. T. Pashuto wrote the following in a book about Russian-German relations published in 1976:

The brave defence of the Russian and Lithuanian peoples against the foreign, above all German, aggression in the 13th century is a page of fame in the history of national liberation struggles in the Middle Ages. The fiasco of the crusade against Rus' made possible the successful end of the struggle for independence of the peoples in East Europe. . . . In the 13th century the general preconditions were formed for a closer economic and political intimacy between Lithuania, Rus' and Poland, which in the further course of history was to be of the greatest importance for the successful outcome of the struggle of these peoples against the German aggression.[6]

In a book published in 1976 posthumously, the Soviet historian, B. F. Porshnev, wrote that the Livonian War, started by Ivan IV in the late 16th century, was necessary to try to break the isolation of, and to try to modernise, Russia. He added that the peace of Stolbova with Sweden in 1617, in Russia's hour of weakness, deprived the country of the 'invaluable treasure' of access to the Baltic Sea. In an article published in 1948 Porshnev depicted Russia's struggle against the Teutonic Order and Germany and the Roman-German emperor as a factor of great importance for the victory of the bourgeois revolutions in Western Europe, beginning with Holland in the late 16th century. Ivan IV certainly did not act in favour of the Dutch revolution consciously, Porshnev underlined, but objectively the Russian pressure on Europe and the Roman-German emperor made the success of the Dutch rebellion possible, although Muscovy hated the Dutch rebels and acted against them diplomatically. This 'contradiction' was to be 'the tragic element in all the subsequent history of Russia', according to Porshnev: the pattern repeated itself in connection with the treaties of Westphalia in 1648, which tipped the balance of power in favour of the progressive forces of Europe. Without the participation of Moscow, however, (on the Eastern front) the German empire would not have been destroyed, Porshnev said, noting in conclusion that Russia soon again became completely alien to the triumphant progressive powers of Europe.[7]

In the introduction of the 1976 book, a certain B. Veber underlined that Porshnev's 'main task' had been that of 'inscribing the Moscow state into the European system of states, from which historiography traditionally has amputated her'. Veber also stressed that exactly from this time, the late 16th century, the foreign policy of Russia became an integral part of, and a real factor in, the all-European political constellation. Porshnev himself in his introduction explicitly said that the Soviet-German war of 1941 was an inducement to the reinterpretation of the historical role of Russia in European politics.[8]

The point in Pashuto's, Porshnev's and Veber's argument is that Russia has a tradition of emancipating the nations surrounding her. In this case the beneficiaries were to be found in Central and Western Europe, but the pattern may well be generalised. The Pashuto and Porshnev texts may be regarded as messages, as signs showing the factual, conscious Soviet view of the history of Russian external relations. What is striking is the sense of continuity of Russia's mission and of Russian righteousness. This is in accordance with a national rather than a class perspective. One is led to question the importance for Russian perceptions of the past of the alleged break with the Russian tradition in 1917, the year of the socialist revolution.

The period immediately following upon the revolution and the Civil War certainly saw an attempt at Marxification and a sort of de-Russification of Russian history. But it has been established beyond reasonable doubt in recent Western sovietology that the attempted economic modernisation of the Soviet Union in the 1930s was undertaken with explicit references to the well-being of the old Fatherland, of the Russia which had happened to become the USSR, and that the thirties saw an active, purposeful return to traditional Russian models and examples in social (family) life and in the fields of literature, painting, architecture, and music. The pluralism and the modernism of the twenties in cultural life was upset. Part of this revival was an explicit comparison between Peter the moderniser and Stalin the moderniser. The continuity of Russian development and Soviet endeavours was stressed in historiography as well as in movies.[9]

The socialisation of people, the shaping of a nation's collective mind, is a process of *longue durée*,[10] a matter of generations. Any profound change in the socialisation pattern and in the cultural indoctrination of a people thus will have to last very long to have crucial effects on the images of the past. The change of perspective affecting the Soviet intelligentsia in the twenties did not have the time to establish itself in the minds of ordinary Russians during the odd ten years it was offered. The class perspective and the internationalism of the generation of Old Bolsheviks and of the futurist artists thus never had the opportunity of becoming more than a counter-culture embraced by a few. As the old generation of Marxist intellectuals was obliterated under Stalin in the thirties, those remaining were the peasants and workers with their minds steeped in traditional Russian forms, on the one hand, and a new generation of Party cadres and technicians socialised with the help of a deliberate revitalisation of the same Russian forms, on the other. Both cadres and the population at large came to belong to the same community of interpretation of the past. In an analysis, which according to the author herself may have been entitled 'The training of the Brezhnev Generation', Sheila Fitzpatrick has epitomised what happened in the thirties by quoting with approval a statement by Zhdanov in 1938 that the new intelligentsia was 'yesterday's workers and peasants and sons of workers and peasants promoted to command positions' as well as the following from Stalin's report to the Communist Party congress in 1939: 'The remnants of the old intelligentsia were dissolved in the body of a new, Soviet, people's (narodnaya) intelligentsia. Thus was created a new Soviet intelligentsia, firmly linked with the people and ready en masse to give it true and faithful service'.[11]

Soviet texts such as those referred to above by the historians Pashuto, Porshnev and Veber reveal the manifest Soviet view of Russian history. But to reach an understanding of latent, never questioned and perhaps even subconscious notions of Russian external conduct, one has to look elsewhere.

Let us attempt to highlight a model which the Russians, or Russian decision makers in the Soviet era, do not consciously regard as a 'model' but take for granted, as an integral part of the natural order.

In his book, *Russia and Kazan. Conquest and Imperial Ideology* (1974), J. Pelenski has analysed Russia's first major expansion beyond the Great Russian ethnic frontiers and the concomitant crystallisation of a conscious nationalist and imperialist ideology in Moscow.

Kazan was conquered by the Russians under Ivan IV in 1552. Pelenski shows that from 1547 and well into the 1560s, historical and ideological writings at the court and in the metropolitan's chancery elaborated the thesis that there was a continuity from Kievan Rus' through the Vladimir principality to the Muscovitian state. Relevant elements from Russian chronicles were skilfully amalgamated into historical justifications for the conquest of the Kazan (and the Astrakhan) Khanate. These 16th century historians tried to prove that Kazan had been a dependency of Muscovy before 1552. In the 19th century Russian historians wrote that a Muscovite protectorate was established over Kazan, and Soviet historians have reasserted this thesis. Pelenski shows that it was not so: the Muscovite court (and the Soviet historians later) simply adapted internal Russian legal terms and institutional concepts in its dealings with a foreign power as Kazan.

Muscovy, helped by its bookmen, claimed that the Russian rulers had the right to invest the Khans of Kazan. This simply was not true, as seen from the Kazan side. To counter the opposition, the Russian court propaganda, Pelenski shows,

> shrewdly divided the Kazan population into good and evil people. Those who were good asked the sovereign to establish order, those who were bad rebelled. The troops were sent supposedly upon the request of loyal servants, against those who refused to serve.[12]

Pelenski further shows that the Muscovite bookmen twisted or ignored facts from the chronicles that did not uphold the Russian claims. After the conquest, a certain *Kazanskaya istoriya* was compiled. This work is valuable as a remnant, i.e., as a source for the understanding of Muscovite political thought. The book signifies 'the introduction of an ethnic and national element into Muscovite imperial ideology'. It declared that Kazan was a Russian borderland occupied by the Tatars. Russia thus simply defended the border regions when she conquered the Khanate: Kazan 'had to pay for the bloody acts of its origins and history'. A peace under Muscovite auspices was regarded as the ideal condition in the *Kazanskaya istoriya*:

> Only after the Muscovite Tsardom was victorious and had achieved its political goals, would serenity and security prevail. Peace was also connected with the victory of Orthodox Christianity over alien beliefs and the establishment of the true faith in the conquered land. At the same time, the work advocated imperial growth and territorial expansion.[13]

The *Kazanskaya istoriya* was written post factum. But it was not only a justification of the conquest of Kazan but also a programme for the future. It would be wrong simply to regard it as a blueprint or manual for action, but it is safe to state that it became part of Russian imperial ideology and of Russian cultural world views. It was natural for any literate Russian to regard conquest of ethnically different but adjacent territories as an act of liberation, greeted by the true elements among the liberated people. It seemed unnatural to question that the Russians, Moscow, had the prerogative in defining what was good for neighbouring peoples. Moscow had the right to bring alienated territories back to the Fatherland. It was not just any 'imperial growth', not just any 'territorial expansion'; it was the territorial growth of a Russian orthodox empire which was the meaning of history. Thus there developed a stereotype of Russian external relations which could function as a perception filter. It could, of course, not cause anything by itself. But it undoubtedly could influence the range of options.

The so called 'Brezhnev doctrine', promulgated after the so called 'fraternal help' to Czechoslovakia in 1968, obviously was a justification and a direct response to an acute threat to Soviet hegemony in Central Europe. But the action itself, i.e., the invasion of Czechoslovakia by five Warsaw Pact states under the direction of the Soviet Union, was an option sprung from the same mind as that which shaped the 'Brezhnev doctrine': the action implied and the doctrine explicitly stated that Moscow defended the borderlands of the socialist system and the pure communist ideology and, furthermore, that the 'brothers' were invited by true, good relatives in Czechoslovakia against the rule of the villians, the rebels. The phrasing is reminiscent of the 'Kazan doctrine' and probably a proof of the deep commitment to the cause from the Soviet side. The whole story, justification and all, was repeated again with the Soviet military 'help' to Afghanistan in late 1979.

One should bear in mind also that the Soviet leaders keep repeating that they are not creating political upheavals in nonsocialist countries, as recently occurred in Ethiopia and Afghanistan, but that they cannot help that the socialist ideas (Moscow brand) are successful, and they cannot guarantee capitalism peace in this respect, the peace of the wrong, repressive, infidel kind. This is the other side of the Brezhnev doctrine and there is no reason to believe that it is not seriously believed in. In the late 16th century it was formulated:

> And [he] who does not wonder, and who does not praise God for this [conquest of Kazan] is a heretic and [like] the unfaithful foreigners, who are the only ones who do not welcome Christian well-being, and [who have] a brooding evil in their hearts, as they are gnawed by envy when they see the Christian faith expanding and their faith disappearing in the face of Christian power, and the Russian land extending and expanding and the people of the nation multiplying (*Kazanskaya istoriya*).[14]

The superimposition above has no predictive value whatsoever. But it helps one understand, post factum, the ease with which Soviet citizens greeted the action of August 1968. There are, apparently, no strong mental reservations to a repetition of it in the Russian collective mind.

It is important to underline that Pelenski makes no inferences to contemporary politics in his fascinating book. He actually de-emphasises the uniqueness of the Russian experience by declaring that the conquest of Kazan just

> helped to make territorial expansion and annexations of populations recognized national virtues and political goals, aims common to most centralized national states finding themselves in the process of transformation into multinational empires.[15]

The Russians were not necessarily worse than the others, nor are the Soviets. But here we are concerned with the Russians and the Soviets.

The Kazan model should not be conceived of as a universal principle of Russian and Soviet foreign policy, but rather as pertaining to political entities bordering on Russia which the Russians — Tsarist as well as Soviet — claim to be under their benevolent surveillance. A further qualification is that these entities should be under some Russian influence already, while at the same time bordering on important adversaries of the Russian or Soviet state. The erection of the People's Republics in Central Europe after the Second World War might be regarded as an elaboration of the Kazan model. In the case of Poland there was in fact a tradition of outright Kazanisation — the historical precedences to 1944–45 being the four partitions of Poland in 1772, 1793, 1795 and 1939. As has been discussed above, an intimate relationship with the socialist world is inscribed into the constitution of Poland of 1976.

The Stalinist attitude towards Poland was revealed, as we have seen, in utterances by Stalin and Molotov, i.e., whether Poland should be considered a legitimate and viable state at all. This view was matched, so to speak, by a Polish belief that friendship with the USSR would imply Soviet tutelage: in the Russian mind Poland was at best the same as Congress Poland (the Russian-supervised creation of the Congress of Vienna in 1815). The assertion, made in the 1930s, has been borne out by subsequent history. Thus Jiri Valenta, an American political scientist of Czech origin, is right in drawing a line from history to the present day, stating that the Russians have always regarded Poland 'as inextricably linked to the security of Russia'.[16]

Valenta's observation, which is based on an analysis of Soviet reactions to developments in Poland both in the past and in 1980, must be said to have received support from a source which ought to be well informed. Dimitri K. Simes is a Russian social scientist who worked at the Moscow Institute of International Economy and International Relations before settling in Washington, D.C. Commenting on the American-Soviet 'Clash over Poland' in the wake of Premier General Jaruzelski's introduction of martial law, Simes stated that 'most members of the Russian elite do not consider Poland an independent state but rather some sort of autonomous entity under Soviet supervision'. According to Simes, one may still hear Soviet decision makers speak of Poland as 'the Vistula provinces'.[17] This indicates that it is not even Congress Poland which is the model, but the emasculated creation that gradually took shape after the suppression of the rebellion in 1831.[18]

The Russian and Soviet treatment of Poland indicates that what counts is not the people, but the territory concerned. Thus one should not marvel at the fact that 'national sensitivity is not a quality in which the Soviets have excelled throughout their post-war history' but agree with the following conclusion:

> For Soviet political and military officials, maintaining the Polish connection is a central need. But in typical Soviet style, such needs have more often been pursued through the issuance of imperatives than they have through the nurturance of cooperation.[19]

The Soviet attitude to its Central European partners then is patterned upon the 'Kazan model' and classically imperialist. What matters is control of the territory. The feelings and strivings of the peoples inhabiting the territory are of secondary importance. They enter the picture merely as a nuisance, which has to be taken care of by proper emergency actions. It is now time for us to discuss how this control is carried out, not only in emergencies, but as a matter of routine.

163

Means of control: the Party network, the WTO and the CMEA

It should not be regarded as a mere coincidence that the Soviet leaders have chosen the term 'fraternal' to denote the nature of the relationship between the USSR and the other WTO and CMEA states. The action against Czechoslovakia in 1968, for example, was labelled 'fraternal help'. The popular Central European resentment in this matter is expressed in the saying 'you may choose your friends but not your relatives'. However, in the present context this is not the point. What is of significance is that the Soviet leaders do not refer to legal facts only, to contracts and autonomous decision making. What they do refer to is an 'organic' unity, i.e., something which is part of the natural or established order of things. Seen from this perspective, Central Europeans have no opportunity whatsoever to bail themselves out of the relationship. What nature has united, man should not try to separate. Thus Leonid Ilich Brezhnev, the late General Secretary of the CPSU, at the last Party Congress of the CPSU at which he presided, in February 1981 (which happened to be at the height of the Polish revolution):

> Comrades! In all these years the Party, her Central Committee, and Politbureau, have worked tirelessly to strengthen the friendship and cooperation with the socialist countries.
> Together with them we are building a new, socialist world and a type of relations between states as yet unparalleled in history, truly just, fraternal and based on equal rights. . . .
> During these years there have been thirty-seven friendly meetings at the highest level in the Crimea. Without any formalities of protocol and in a comradely atmosphere we have discussed the developmental perspectives of our relations and the crucial problems of world politics, and pointed out the tasks of the future. Every meeting brought something new and useful. I want to express my affection to the leaders of the fraternal countries and parties for this good cooperation. (Applause.)
> There has been a regular exchange of Party and government delegations. Meetings of the secretaries of the Central Committees on the questions of international relations and ideological and Party organizational work have been realized.
> The Party organizations of the Soviet Union and of the countries of the socialist commonwealth are united through a multitude of ties. They are united at all levels – from republics, territories *(krai)* and provinces *(oblasti)* to regions *(raiony)* and big enterprises. The cooperation between state organs, social

organizations and production collectives has acquired a vital and fruitful character. The spiritual communion and the intimate bonds in the ideological and cultural fields have become an established norm.

The relations between states have from times immemorial been called international. But only in our time, in the socialist world, have they really become relations between nations *(narody)*. Millions and millions of people take part in them directly. This, comrades, is the principal achievement of socialism, its great merit in the eyes of humanity. (Applause.) . . .

In the constitutions of the majority of the fraternal countries, the ideas of friendship and cooperation with the Soviet Union are underlined. This represents a great trust in our country, and we respond accordingly. The new constitution of the USSR proclaims friendship, cooperation and mutual help with the socialist countries as the cornerstone of the Soviet foreign policy. . . .

During these years a new organ for cooperation has been created: The Committee of Foreign Ministers. One can say that it has already justified itself: the effectiveness of the foreign policy coordination has been increased.

The building of United Armed Forces has been carried out harmoniously. Here as always a good job has been done by the Committee of Defence Ministers.

The Central Committee reports to the congress: the military-political defence union of the socialist countries truly serves peace. (Applause.) It has at its disposal all that is necessary to effectively defend the socialist achievements of the peoples. And we will do all for it to remain so! (Long applause).[20]

Brezhnev's words express a very strong commitment, as they were part of a high mass, the sacred ritual of the quinannual celebration of the CPSU, the Party Congress. The message is clear: the 'fraternal countries' are part of the Soviet system of power, as is expressed in the fact that both the Foreign Ministers and the Defence Ministers of the 'fraternal' countries are being co-ordinated by the Russians in especially created committees. One should also note Brezhnev's assertion that 'a multitude of ties' link the vassal parties to the CPSU. This may be interpreted as an indirect reference to the so called nomenclatura system, i.e., that every important post in the administration should be controlled by the CPSU[21] — apparently, the Communist parties of the 'fraternal' countries are themselves under Soviet surveillance in this way. Schöpflin, for example, has concluded from the course and outcome of the events in Czechoslovakia in 1968 and in Hungary in 1956 that 'the Kremlin actively participates in decisions on promotions and demotions' of the politbureaus of the 'fraternal' parties.[22] The clauses dealing with friendship with the USSR in the constitutions of the 'fraternal' states are not only an expression of legal norms but serve also as a pretext for Soviet interference in the political life of these '.raternal' states.

Regarding Czechoslovakia in 1968, it has been underlined that the reforms, which included change of personnel in the Party apparatus, the Ministry of Interior, and the Ministry of Defence, 'and other sensitive departments', were threatening to deprive the Soviet leaders of their ability to supervise and monitor 'day-to-day affairs inside Czechoslovakia'. Hence the notion of the leading role of the Party in the vassal states is not an expression of any general Soviet wish that all the 'fraternal' countries should be political copies of the USSR for aesthetical reasons or reasons of principle. The reason is very down to earth, as has been clearly expressed by a student of the Soviet conduct vis-à-vis Czechoslovakia in 1968, the British polical scientist Karen Dawisha:

> The argument over the leading role of the Communist Party should not, therefore, be seen as a sterile ideological polemic between Moscow and Prague, but rather as an absolutely vital and irreconcilable conflict over the issue of control, including not only by the Party of the state but also, through that mechanism, Soviet control over Czechoslovakia.[23]

The trick, as seen from the Soviet point of view, is to control certain key persons and not to be content with just ideological influence: when Nagy got out of hand, there was a Kádár available, in the case of Dubcek, a triumvirate of other Slovaks — Bilak, Husák, and Indra — and when the Party ceased to function altogether as an effective political body, as in Poland in 1980–81, a Party leader who happened to be a General, i.e., Jaruzelski. As Christopher Jones has underlined, 'to cede control of either policy or personnel is to cede control of the other', and to let both go, amounts to giving the subordinate party autonomy.[24]

It is in this light, i.e., the necessity for the Soviet leaders to control the personnel of the vassal Party, that the strong Soviet reaction against the attempt to create 'horizontal' links at base level in the Polish Party in the spring of 1981, should be viewed. Mikhail Suslov, the then chief ideologist of the CPSU, went to Warsaw on the 23 April to warn the PUWP leaders of the dangers, and the Moscow *Pravda* attacked the 'revisionist elements' who were trying to undermine the leading role of the PUWP.[25] The effect of the 'horizontalisation' of the PUWP would have been to enhance local autonomy and a merger with local Solidarity bodies, all of which would have meant a loosening of central control, and thus, indirectly, of the Soviet ability to monitor the development, any development, in Poland.

It is evident from developments in Hungary in 1955–56 and in

Czechoslovakia in 1968 that the control of personnel is not an absolute guarantee against deviation. The human incumbent of an important post may, for one reason or another, change his allegiance from his master to his subjects. Or at least he may try honestly to placate both, as apparently Dubcek was doing in 1968. Thus something else is needed. What remains, if ideological influence and political control are not sufficient, is economic and military control. The vassals must be kept dependent on the USSR as an addition to the other aspect, i.e., the political indirect rule. Let us look at the WTO and the CMEA against this background.

It is clear that in the 1970s, the Soviet leadership, now definitely consolidated under Brezhnev, was trying not to repeat the act of having to wreck the economy of a vassal country and completely alienate its population from the USSR, socialism, and Marxism, as had been the case with Czechoslovakia, in order to keep the WTO politically stable and militarily intact. In order to forestall the possibility of a national vassal army ever becoming a potential independent actor, it was obviously necessary to implement a policy of systematically integrating these armies into the supranational WTO network, the operative command of which is totally in Soviet hands. A connection was established between military organisation and the means of political influence over the vassal states. The national officer corps that consisted mainly of people who had received their higher military education in the USSR and who were accustomed to regard subordination to the Soviets as self-evident, provided support for those in the national communist parties who were loyal to Soviet interests, as expressed by the Soviet leaders. It is true that Romania, though a WTO member, remained outside the inner network.[26] However, the fact that this could take place must be interpreted as an indication that the Soviet leaders at least felt safe on this front since Romania is encircled by the USSR itself, Hungary and Bulgaria and borders on non-aligned Yugoslavia.[27]

Nominally, the WTO is an organisation of common defence against the enemy of the USSR, NATO. This does not, however, mean that it may not serve other ends as well, for example the one of safeguarding Soviet control of the vassals. Christopher Jones has underlined this dual function in his observation that the military barriers of the WTO, while giving protection to the member states, 'serve just as well to prevent the defenders from breaking out'.[28] This is the 'Al Capone type' alliance.

Like Jones, other Western experts such as the Britons Malcolm Mackintosh and John Erickson, stress the predominance of the USSR within the WTO, pointing to the fact that for all practical purposes, the Soviet High Command is also the WTO High Command (in the event of war, at least),[29] and that the USSR has a bilateral relationship with each of the subordinate states and effectively is barring any possibility of working out 'national' military doctrines by the latter.[30]

Of course there need not be any contradiction between the alleged dual aims of the WTO, as seen from the Kremlin. Discussing three different 'schools' among Western analysts, Lawrence T. Caldwell comes to the conclusion that their arguments are all compatible, i.e. that the WTO serves as a means of control and suppression of the vassals, that the WTO states are a buffer which gives the USSR 'tangential security', and that at least the East German, Polish, and Czechoslovak troops are an asset for the USSR, proving to be 'formidable opponents if Western forces should become involved in a conventional or tactical nuclear conflict with them'. Caldwell underlines the fact that the local elites, and their countries, may well be said to benefit, not only as regards military security, but also politically, from the WTO membership.[31] Caldwell does not distinguish between the interests of the ruling elites and the peoples (as they may perceive them). Linden, who does so, reaches a rather similar conclusion, however, but words it in a way that implicitly takes care of the 'Al Capone aspect' as well:

> At present the East European state's only source of protection from both West and East lies in military alliance with the Soviet Union. . . . the Soviet dominance of the postwar structure in East Europe has brought the latter partial nationstate security, at least from past Western enemies.[32]

The WTO network allows the Soviet leaders to always have their men on the spot in countries such as the GDR, Czechoslovakia, Poland and Hungary. This ensures that the Soviet leaders have got freedom of action at all times both against the West and against eventual internal disturbances. While the military and the political leadership may safely be assumed to be fully integrated within the USSR itself, one cannot postulate that the same relationship exists within the respective vassal states. The military leaders in these countries may very well have a dual loyalty, i.e., not only towards their Soviet comrades-in-arms and superiors.

Stalin made no bones at all about his intentions, as is evident from his treatment of the Polish army in 1939 and after the war. The 'renationalisation' of the Polish army under Jaruzelski did not represent, in the last instance, a loosening of the Soviet grip. Jaruzelski managed, apparently, to generate a degree of confidence among Poles by posing as a patriot, at the same time as he acted according to what he perceived as being in the Soviet interest. This hypothesis is compatible with the hypothesis that General Jaruzelski was, and is, a 'real' patriot (whatever that may mean) who just anticipated what he regarded as the inevitable next Soviet move: the military occupation of Poland with fresh troops. One need not hypothesise that Jaruzelski was directed on a day-to-day basis by the Soviet leaders. One need not even assume that he acted from lust for power. It was sufficient that he co-operated with the Soviet leaders voluntarily, proving that he had internalised the Soviet viewpoint.

However, mere military control of Central Europe might be burdensome and even precarious in the long run. In order to ensure that this security system becomes more stable, something more is desirable.

Already in 1949, a communist economic community had been set up under Soviet leadership. In the West it became known as 'Comecon'. Its real name was the 'Council for Mutual Economic Assistance', or CMEA. Originally it was declared to be a means to help the European socialist states overcome, with the help of the USSR, the drawbacks inflicted upon them by the US-inspired partial trade boycott and by the general hindrances to East-West trade at the height of the Cold War. The organisation became more or less a paper organisation, however. The USSR continued to exploit the East European states until Khrushchev launched his de-Stalinisation policy and tried to redefine the manners of intra-bloc relations.[33] Soviet exploitation of the other states ceased and instead the price structure became such that the USSR, an exporter primarily of fuel and raw materials, was being 'exploited' by her junior partners.[34] However, Khrushchev's attempt to integrate the economies of the CMEA states with the help of economical specialisation and 'division of labour' within the association, was a failure.

In the late 1960s not only Czechoslovakia but also Poland and Hungary were suffering from economic stagnation. The Czechoslovakian way of 1968 was not palatable for the Soviet leaders. But they seemed to admit that something had to be done in the economic realm, if the bloc was to remain economically viable and politically stable.

There seemed to be a general consensus in the Soviet block in the late 1960s that it had become necessary to modernise the economies to counter stagnation and the concomitant risks of political instability. Views differed, however, on which method to choose. In particular Hungarian economists were in favour of greater reliance on market mechanisms to promote integration within CMEA and thus advocated regional specialisation and wide national autonomy for each participant state, while Soviet economists pleaded for traditional socialist central (national) planning writ large. The outcome of the debate was the 1971 *Comprehensive Programme* for socialist integration. The programme was a compromise with its emphasis, however, on joint planning and joint investment projects.[35]

No real integration of the CMEA states took place. The mobility of capital and labour between the members remained very low and the traditional bilateral trade between pairs continued.[36]

As CMEA could not fuel self-sustained growth, the leaders of the respective states, obviously with the permission of the Soviet leaders, turned to the West for capital and new technology. While this meant an injection, it also strengthened centrifugal tendencies with CMEA.[37] Trade with the West soon became a substitute for CMEA integration.

As 'CMEA integration' did not work, the attempt by the Soviet leaders to create an economic prosperity that would entail political stability had ended in failure. The continuing political instability of the system was confirmed in 1980–81 by the Poles. Let us summarise the dilemma, i.e., the systemic Soviet bloc background to the events in Poland.

One can say that integration of the CMEA has been hampered by the preponderance of the USSR. The Soviet Union has got roughly two thirds of both the population and the total national product of the European CMEA aggregate, and more than 90 per cent of the crude oil, natural gas and iron ore resources.[38] Viewed superficially, this may appear as an asset for the USSR when dealing with the others. However, it has not worked in that way. The junior members have shown themselves to be very sensitive to further inroads into what is left of economic autonomy. They evidently tend to regard every Soviet proposal for supranational planning and co-ordination of production as a veiled threat of *de facto* incorporation into the Soviet Union. The heart of the matter, and the reason why the Soviet leaders did not succeed with their integration device, lies in the following paradox, or, rather, contradiction, which is inherent to the system: in order for centrally planned economies to integrate themselves with each other, they must either change themselves into one economy or cease to be centrally planned economies altogether. Without a single, central plan, national plans will not make sense, seen from the perspective of the whole system. And without a real market, regulated by demand and supply, there is no possibility of reaching the alleged goals of integration, i.e., effective, optimal, use of capital, labour, and natural resources.

However, the basic obstacle to CMEA integration, and hence to such a road to political stabilisation of the Soviet security system, is not that the Soviet Union is so big, compared to the others, or that the planners in the respective countries are incompetent. What has made the whole scheme unworkable is the lack of a meaningful, comparable price system and of currency convertibility within CMEA. The attempt with the 'transferable ruble' has been a distinct failure. In practice it has been a 'major barrier to CMEA integration' by furthering bi-lateralism.[39]

Drawing up a balance sheet of CMEA development up to the early 1980s, Jan Vanous has underlined the contradictory nature of the Soviet policy. On the one hand, the USSR has subsidised the other states in bilateral trade, thereby helping them to reach a higher economic level than otherwise would have been possible, given the existing economic model. On the other hand, Soviet subsidies can be viewed as a form of payment for continued restrictions on national sovereignty. The blessing thus has been mixed. Vanous argues that an independent Central and South-East Europe, free to restructure her internal and external economic relations, would be more productive than is the case today. Soviet trade subsidies probably do not compensate for the low productivity of the economic system, enforced upon the other states by the USSR. In Vanous's view this might be ominous for the future:

Without necessarily intending to do so, the Soviet Union may have seriously damaged the ability of East European economies to become competitive and thereby have threatened their long-term viability.[40]

Vanous's conclusion is borne out in another well-documented analysis of Soviet-East European economic relations, by Philip Hanson. He states that in the long term, Central and South-East European trade with the USSR 'has been detrimental to the growth of production and income levels in the region', although there is strong evidence to indicate that the economic benefits of the Central and South-East European states from the trade outweigh those of the USSR.[41]

The problem facing the Soviet leaders after the calling to order of Czechoslovakia in 1968 can be restated thus: What should be done to keep the vassal states politically stable without jeopardising Soviet control or being forced to bail out these states, economically, with the economic resources of the USSR and the help of the CMEA structure? Allowing the other European CMEA states to drain the Soviet Union of scarce resources is not a satisfactory solution in the long run. After 1973, the terms of trade agreed upon within the CMEA, began to change in favour of the Soviet Union. Following OPEC the USSR raised its prices on oil sold to the other CMEA states, although with a timelag.[42]

As the CMEA integration programme proved to be very slow, and not very effective, and as the poor performance that could be observed by researchers in the early 1980s, must have always been obvious to the interested parties,[43] it is not surprising to learn that the Soviet leaders accepted, willy-nilly, that the smaller states turned to the West for capital and technology. This probably was regarded as an alternative both to thoroughgoing reforms of the type envisaged in Czechoslovakia in 1968, and to the integration of CMEA which would not materialise. This loosening of the reins and opening to the West worked well during the entire 1970s with Hungary but not with Poland. But what about other kinds of economic control?

One way of keeping the vassals dependent on the USSR is through economic policy, by tying them to the Soviet economy. The 'administrative planned economy' is invaluable in this respect, to guarantee Soviet dominance:

The administrative planned economy ensures three things in this context: first, a considerable part of the economic potential of the smaller CMEA countries is tied to the USSR through bilateral plan coordination. Second, in this way the USSR can profit from technical progress in the more developed CMEA countries, notably the GDR and Czechoslovakia. . . . Third, and lastly, interstate plan coordination in Eastern Europe enables the USSR to plan a large part of its international economic relations. The transition to a socialist market economy in the CMEA countries, with the associated possibility of a freer choice of partners on Western markets, would endanger the economic and, furthermore, the foreign policy dominance of the USSR in Eastern Europe.[44]

It is a fact both that the Soviet leaders did not use any economic 'lever' against Poland in 1980–81 but supported her economically, and that the effect of the Polish economic breakdown was that the country's economic ties with the USSR became strengthened, at the cost of the relations with both the other CMEA states and the West.[45] As this development also meant that the USSR took upon itself an economic burden, as it had already done regarding Czechoslovakia,[46] the reason must be political. To be able to remain in power, the local leaderships are dependent on Soviet subsidies.

But one has to take into consideration also the fact that Hungary has been allowed to depart from the 'administrative planned economy' in favour of a market economy that certainly does not aim at further integration with the USSR and the other CMEA countries.[47] It is not least the agricultural sector which is market-oriented in Hungary. It was precisely this sector which was singled out for praise by Brezhnev in his report to the Party Congress of the CPSU in 1981. He referred to it as 'skilfully organised'.[48]

Hungary's diversion from the Soviet model has not met with open Soviet disapproval. This cannot be easily explained if one asserts that the 'administrative planned economy' is a necessary condition for keeping the Soviet empire intact. The West German economist Hans-Hermann Höhmann, who believes in that rationale, presents the following explanation, which can be regarded as an apt formulation of the argument:

It is scarcely likely that the Soviet Union will allow comprehensive economic reforms in the countries of the 'Council for Mutual Economic Assistance' as long as it is not prepared for thoroughgoing changes in economic policy itself. Even the Hungarian development does not contradict this assumption, for it must not be overlooked that Hungary received the green light from Moscow for its 'New Economic Mechanism' before the 'Prague spring' made it clear how far-reaching comprehensive economic reforms could be. Comprehensive reforms of the economy in Eastern Europe would not only weaken the economic and foreign policy influence of the Soviet Union there but also question the standing of Soviet socialism as the pattern to be followed.[49]

However, there is a catch in this argument. Green light or not, there is no reason to believe that the Soviet leaders would have let the Hungarians go on with their reform programme, had they (the Soviet leaders) perceived this as a threat to their control of Hungary. They have never hesitated, in the end, in the face of challenges: the 'fraternal aid' to Czechoslovakia may easily have been made to include 'brother Hungary' as well. No, the reason must be sought somewhere else.

If one asks Soviet decision makers, they are blunt on this point. Asked the question as to whether the Hungarian example was something to be emulated for the USSR, the Minister of Justice of the USSR, Vladimir Terebilov, answered with two arguments that showed above all else pragmatism. Firstly, the Soviet leaders were open minded and would even have adopted the Yugoslav model of workers' self-government, had it not proved to be hopelessly inefficient economically. Secondly, as for the Hungarian model, it was interesting but hardly suitable for the Soviet economy because of the latter's immense size.[50]

As monoparty rule and democractic centralism both have been retained in Yugoslavia as well as in Hungary, there is nothing to object to as far as the organisation of the economy is concerned — so one must interpret Terebilov's answer. One should keep in mind, in this context, that the Soviet-Yugoslav conflict in 1948 concerned politics, political subordination, rather than the economy. At that point of time, Yugoslavia's economic reform still belonged to the future. Its realisation did not stop the Soviet leaders from reaching a political accommodation with Yugoslavia. Although the USSR has not achieved control over Yugoslavia, and although the latter is not considered to be a 'fraternal country',[51] it was not differences over the economy that seemed to bother the Soviet leaders.

Hence the 'economic' argument must be reduced to the assertion that 'the administrative planned economy' may make Soviet influence and control easier. But it is, in itself, neither a sufficient nor a necessary condition. Hungary bears witness to the fact that it is not a necessary condition. Similarly, as we have already noted, Poland during the last days of Gierek proved that it is not sufficient. The Soviet leaders were unable to stop the disastrous economic policy in the latter country.

The ideal situation for the Soviet leaders would be if the whole Central Europe was just a military camp, packed with loyal soldiers and without any civilians to care about. As long as the civilians remain, the trick is to make them disposable, so to speak, i.e., to have a military network that operates against 'friends' and 'foes' alike all on its own. Granted that the

Soviet leaders view the situation in this light, one can also explain their indulgence of the Hungarian NEM. They are sure of the military connection and know that they can count on loyalty from the Hungarian officers corps in the case of emergency, exactly as they could rely on Jaruzelski when the rest of the control mechanism broke down in Poland.

Offensive security policy

The security system of the USSR in Central Europe has proved to be a security system for the USSR at the cost of the vassal states. As Linden has observed, the 'greatest threat to the autonomy of these states [is] the Soviet Union'. His conclusion, corroborated by the empirical facts is:

> But to discuss threats of invasion and occupation, to talk of forces with a demonstrated willingness and capacity for military moves against East Europe, is to talk primarily of the Soviet Union. The degree to which a particular state is threatened by the USSR is of course a direct product of the level of threat felt by the Soviet Union itself. The key aspect of that perception is the Soviet leadership's view of the level of danger existing within the state.

According to Linden, the Soviet point of view stresses the preservation in the vassal state of political control by the Communist Party, absolute commitment to the WTO, and the established social order. This is the conventional wisdom, and Linden quotes other researchers' results to substantiate his thesis.[52]

Linden admits that the limits of freedom of action for the vassal in each case are hard to know beforehand, an observation which has been expressed in a striking formulation by another American political scientist, Charles Gati, who has remarked that the USSR has 'a position towards Eastern Europe that combines traditional hegemonical habits and attitudes with an uneven and grudging pragmatism'.[53] The line of argument seems to be that if a vassal is allowed to pursue a certain policy for a length of time, this policy is accepted by the USSR: the possibility of a policy that is perceived by the Soviet leaders as detrimental to their interests, is ruled out.

It is a widely held opinion among researchers in the field that the Soviet leaders act to prevent ideological contagion from the West, both directly by sealing the Soviet frontiers,[54] and indirectly, by stopping any vassal from developing an alternative model.[55] While there is no denying the fact that the Soviet leaders try to bar direct Western influence from the USSR,[56] the assertion about the inadmissability of an alternative model is dubious. Given the hypothesis that military security and hence stability in

174

the vassal states are the overruling Soviet concerns, the 'model' argument becomes less convincing. Furthermore, this argument is weakened by the empirical fact that Hungary has been allowed to go a long way developing an alternative economic, and, what is also important, social model. The American journalist William Pfaff has perhaps provided the most succinct assessment of thirty-five odd years of Soviet dominance of Central Europe:

> Democracy is the one thing that is impossible to restore in the Soviet system. Nearly anything else is possible, so long as it is authoritarian and clothes itself in languages and forms resembling those of Soviet Communism — and so long as it scrupulously respects the demands of Soviet national security as Moscow sees them.[57]

It is Pfaff's contention, however, that the Soviet leadership 'is steadily losing power to control what happens' in the vassal states. He points especially to the developments in Poland from 1980 onward, and in Romania under Ceausescu.[58] What he is really indicating is that the attempt to govern the populations in the vassal states through indirect rule, has proved to be a rather hazardous undertaking. Here we come to a discussion of the basic rationale of the original Stalinist conception of a security system in Central Europe.

In retrospect it is easy to establish as a fact that Stalin did not care about people as human beings. He regarded them as tools, tools for building an armaments industry and for equipping an army. This was true of his own, Soviet, subjects. That his policy should be judged in this way was even admitted, for all practical purposes, by his successor, Nikita Khrushchev.[59]

As for Central and South-East Europe, the treatment meted out by Stalin and the CPSU to the peoples of the conquered states shows that he regarded these peoples more as a nuisance and a potential threat than as an asset. Stalin's major interest was obviously in the territories of the countries in question. His political line was to deprive the subdued populations, as well as their communist rulers, of every possibility of influencing their own fate, not to allow them to interfere with his wish to station Soviet troops in the middle of Europe. Stalin showed that he knew how to control a territory by converting its inhabitants into prisoners. This method was fundamental to ensure the system's stability. When Khrushchev admitted that not only his own countrymen but also the peoples of the vassal states were human beings, a new foundation for the system had to be worked out.

The method of finding a new basis for the stability of the Soviet empire proved to be trial and error. The Hungarians went too far under Nagy and had to be halted. Their ranks had to be purged of those communists or noncommunists, who mistook Khrushchev's recognition of their human nature for licence to act freely in their own interest. But there was no talk of returning to the dehumanisation policy of Stalin. The Poles were allowed to try to walk a 'national' path under Gomulka, and it was not Khrushchev and the CPSU that insisted in Novotny's retention of Stalinism in Czechoslovakia.[60]

The problem is that the political structure, with the Leninist theory of the leading role of the Communist Party and democratic centralism, had to be retained both in the USSR and in the vassal states, if the CPSU was to keep its monopoly of power and freedom of action as well as being able to control and to dispose of the resources of its vassals, if the need emerged. In the Soviet Union proper de-Stalinisation was not very difficult: no foreigners had to be withdrawn from state and security agencies — as was the case with the Soviet foreigners in some of the vassal states — and the Russian population had no intention of returning to the original Tsarism: in short, the Party dictatorship was fairly well anchored in Russian political culture, and the regime could draw on at least a minimum of legitimacy for the system in the Weberian sense (traditional legitimacy) and pose as the protector of the people against the imperialist West. It was of little significance that decisions were reached in an arbitrary manner, that the economy was wasteful and that the standard of living remained pitifully low, by Western standards. The Russians' standards were not Western. That things were better than under the Tsar as well as under Stalin, was enough for them. This is borne out by the fact that there has not been any major challenge to communist rule in the Soviet Union after Stalin's death, although terror has slackened.

In countries such as Czechoslovakia, Hungary, and Poland, things were very different. There, something had been destroyed under Stalin but not forgotten, i.e., political and cultural pluralism and, last but not least, there was a general popular resentment at the subordination to Soviet and Russian ways in economic, political, and cultural life. When terror slackened and the Stalinists were ousted from power, in Hungary and Poland in 1956, in Czechoslovakia in 1968, different interests were allowed to become expressed. However, the political system was unable to accommodate these expressions. Major disturbances followed, and a mellowed Stalinism had to be re-introduced, with Russian backing. In Czechoslovakia this happened in the course of half a year, between August 1968, and April 1969. In Poland the process dragged out and one cannot speak of full Stalinist control again until from 13 December 1981.

In Hungary under Kádár there was no eruption of popular discontent or any political reform communism. The political monoparty system has remained and there has not been any final showdown between democratic and Stalinist forces. However, one cannot say that the problem of transition from Stalinism to a pluralist political system has been solved.

In this study I have tried to show in depth both how the Soviet security system is unstable, and why it is unstable. The analysis has made the conclusion almost irrefutable, i.e., that the system cannot be stable. The reason is that once the Soviet leaders under Khrushchev started to behave as if they regarded the Central and South-East European populations as consisting of human beings, with human needs, and not as 'production factors' and potential cannon fodder they missed the point: Stalin had, apparently, thought in terms of territory. He was not interested in the well-being of the peoples, that is evident from his actions. Whatever he wanted to secure, it was not the defence of individual human beings. It was rather the great power interests of the Soviet state. Given the Soviet concept of security, to try to make stable Central Europe, and make it a solid security strip for the USSR, without either obliterating the population or frightening it into acquiescence, is like trying to square the circle. The actions of the Soviet leaders against Czechoslovakia in 1968, and their endorsement of Husák's policy thereafter, and of Jaruzelski's in Poland after 1981, show that they have understood this. But the premises, the basic rationale, is not the same as in Stalin's time. To Stalin, the Central European populations were nothing to fear. For his successors, the security problem has turned out to be how to protect themselves from the potential threat from these populations, from the perennial menace of their discontent erupting in anti-Soviet actions, forcing the Soviet hand in front of the principal adversary, the democratic West, led by the United States.

The ostensible Soviet foreign policy aim in Europe is, at the time of writing these lines in 1984, to further integrate the Central European vassals with the USSR. The 'fraternal' line and the idea of 'organic' unity, referred to above in this analysis, were further elaborated by Foreign Minister and Politbureau member Andrej Gromyko in April 1983. He said that 'the commonwealth of socialist states' shares adherence to Marxism-Leninism and socialist internationalism and is 'intensively' developing its economic integration and its co-operation 'in all spheres of life'. The relations between these states were characterised, according to the Soviet Foreign Minister, by 'fraternal friendship and comradely mutual aid'. Gromyko left no doubt as to the Soviet idea of the future structure of the system:

> The intimate cooperation between the states of the socialist commonwealth that are welded together by a political and socio-economic structure of a unitary type, and by unity in worldview and community of goals and ideals in the struggle for peace and socialism, now has grown into a fraternal union which is embodied in the Warsaw Treaty Organization and the Council for Mutual Economic Assistance and in a system of bilateral agreements of friendship, cooperation, and mutual aid that unite these states. It finds its expression in a process

which becomes deeper all the time and appears as an objective law, the process of comprehensive drawing together *(sblizhenie)* of the socialist states. On the basis of harmonious combinations the further unification *(splochenie)* of these states, still more intimate interweaving of the economies, mutual spiritual enrichment . . .

Gromyko gave further weight to his statement by including a quotation from the leader of the CPSU, Andropov, which declared that the 'commonwealth of socialist states is a powerful and sound organism'.[61] Compared to the result of our analysis, highlighting the importance of the traditional political cultures in Central Europe, the assessments of Gromyko and Andropov are inaccurate as a description of reality. Interpreted as statements of intent, however, the assertions receive a wide significance: the shaky structure of vassal states is hardly an adequate defence barrier for the Soviet Union. As Gromyko stated, in the article just quoted, that 'nobody should doubt that the fraternal states share a common resolve to defend their interests, to guarantee the stability of all links of the commonwealth, and to protect the socialist achievements'[62] and as he, in the same article, quoted Lenin to express his disdain at 'cheap pacifism',[63] one not only cannot rule out, but, on the contrary, has to reckon with the possibility that the Soviet leaders will attempt to make the Central European part of the empire secure in the same way as the USSR itself was once being safeguarded by the acquisition of Central Europe. As there is no war going on in Europe, both the opportunities and the means at hand for the Soviet leaders are different. But the logic of the situation is the same with regard to one basic aspect: the external protection of the empire must be reinforced if the foreign policy ambitions of the Soviet leaders are not to be jeopardised.

In Stalin's time, the anticipated area of direct confrontation with the main adversary, the USA, was Central Europe. Hence the salience of the German question and Stalin's need to consolidate his grip on the territory between the Soviet state boundary and the frontier of the US-led alliance, NATO.

Khrushchev's policy of peaceful coexistence meant a lessening of the East-West tension. It is evident from the fact of the agreement over Austria in 1955 that the Soviet leaders did not foresee any military showdown in Central Europe. The Hungarian revolt in 1956 and the invasion of Czechoslovakia in 1968 could not stop the development towards détente in Europe. This process reached its culmination in 1975, with the Helsinki agreement.

The Helsinki agreement meant a de facto renewed recognition from the United States and NATO of the Soviet empire and the invulnerability of its frontiers in Europe. In retrospect, it is easy to conclude that this enhanced the Soviet sense of security in Europe at the same time as the Soviet leaders embarked on a true and full-fledged global foreign policy, which soon manifested itself in Angola, in Ethiopia, and, in late 1979, in Afghanistan. The potential global conflict with the United States, which had been in the making ever since the Cuba crisis in 1962 and the US-Vietnam war a few years later, now became manifest. There followed a marked deterioration in Soviet-American relations. Soviet policy also became more offensive in Europe. This manifested itself in the deployment of the SS-20 missiles, which were targeted against Western Europe, and a concomitant propaganda campaign against NATO's planned deployment, announced in late 1979, of Pershing II missiles and cruise missiles in Western Europe, should the USSR not withdraw its SS-20 missiles.

This is not the place to anaylse the contest over the missiles or Soviet propaganda policy. Suffice it to note, in our context, that this whole development indicates an advancement, literally in a geographical sense, of Soviet security policy. The stated policy now is not only to defend the USSR and the other WTO states, but to try to weaken the defence capability of the European NATO states and their ties with the United States.[64]

Granted that the principal aim of the Soviet security policy in Europe is to impede NATO's possibilities of attack, granted that this aim is reached in Central Europe by preserving the political status quo and granted that South-Eastern Europe and the Balkans are not seen as an area where NATO may threaten the USSR, granted all this the Baltic area and the Nordic countries became important targets of the offensive Soviet security policy in the 1980s. This line of reasoning has the advantage of making Soviet policy against Norway and Sweden in the early 1980s intelligible.

There is one military-strategic background to the development sketched out above: the building up of a huge and modern Soviet navy and the construction of the major Soviet base area in the Murmansk district. Sweden and Norway do not lie in the periphery but in the centre, seen from a Soviet security perspective. Sweden may seem as disturbing to Soviet decision makers in the 1980s as Poland obviously did to Stalin in the late 1930s.

But there is one political ideological background to this development as well. By 1980, at the time of the Polish revolution, it must have become crystal clear to the Soviet leaders that they would never, never, succeed in getting loyal subjects, and hence inherent stability, in Poland.[65] Experience has shown the resilience of traditional non-Russian and anti-Soviet Polish political culture. Thus Soviet security can be enhanced not by making loyal partners out of the Poles but by widening the zone of Soviet predominance. But to develop this aspect would fall outside the scope of this investigation.

The militarised KGB party state

The period of Brezhnev and Andropov saw a gradual increase of KGB and military presence in the Soviet leadership. The ascendancy of Yurii Andropov to the post of Secretary General of the CPSU had been preceded by a hardening of the Soviet policy against dissenters; it was followed by a further 'KGB-isation' of the Party and state apparatuses, with an old KGB-hand, the Azerbaidzhan Party boss Geidar Aliev being elevated to full Politbureau member and Andropov's successor as head of the KGB Vitalii Fedorchuk, being appointed Minister of the Interior. Simultaneously, the then Chief of the General Staff, Ogarkov, kept repeating, in Party organs, the need for further armaments and for an adaption of the whole economy to the military prerogatives. Brezhnev in his last, and Andropov in his first speech as Party leader, both underlined that the military would get everything it asked for in terms of material resources.[66]

The KGB-isation and militarisation of Soviet politics has not been a dramatic and sudden change. Rather it is a slow return, *mutatis mutandis,* to the set up of Stalin's time — but without a personal dictator as Stalin. All in all, the development seems to have eradicated all traces of conflicts of interest between the Party apparatus, on the one hand, and the security and military establishment, on the other. The consequences for Soviet external conduct are unambiguous: military points of view apparently are given much weight in foreign policy decisions, as is evident in the 'solution' chosen to the Afghanistan disturbances of the Soviet peace of mind and in the activities of the Soviet navy in the Baltic Sea.

The question of an eventual widening of the Soviet security zone in the Baltic falls outside the theme of this study. It is of relevance here to discuss, however, why reliance on military means still is paramount in Soviet security policy almost forty years after the erection of the security system in Central Europe. It is obvious that there are some basic traits in Soviet politics which have to be highlighted before we enter our general conclusions regarding the Soviet endeavour in Central Europe.

Quincy Wright remarked several years ago that socialism had shown itself to be 'the war organisation of capitalism'.[67] The roots of this are to be found in Russian and Soviet traditions, in the state's political culture, as it were.

During the 18th and 19th centuries, Russian officers often played a prominent part in politics. The state-led modernisation of Russia, be it under Peter I, Alexander II or Nicolas II, always had as its principal goal the strengthening of military capability as a means for an active foreign policy. In his memoirs Sergei Vitte, Chairman of the Council of Ministers in 1905–06, recollected:

> In reality what was the Russian Empire based on? Not just primarily, but exclusively on its army. Who created the Russian Empire . . ? It was accomplished strictly by the army's bayonets.[68]

This tradition was continued by the Bolsheviks after 1917. As the American analyst William Odom has pointed out, the army was the first major institution that the Bolsheviks organised. From the very beginning, the army became an important administrative arm of the Communist Party.[69] Moreover, the economy was organised according to the principles of the German war economy (of the First World War).[70] It is true that the Soviet society and economy were somewhat 'recivilised' with the introduction of NEP in 1921. This period was followed, however, by one of enhanced militarisation in 1928, the year of the inauguration of the first Soviet five year plan for the development of the economy. Priority was given to heavy industry and defence.

Under Stalin it was not only a question of giving priority to heavy industry. The whole organisation of the economy became militarised. The workers were organised in *brigades*, one had *campaigns* to reach *targets*, the disciplinary measures were as strict as those in an army at war, and *traitors* and *spies*, accused of *sabotage* of the economy, were regularly shot.

The Soviet economy has retained the Stalinist structure and Soviet political culture has remained coloured by the old habits. The legacy is one of a militarised industrial state. At the same time, the Soviet military has always been controlled by the Communist Party. Within the Soviet political system there is limited scope for the military leaders to make policies on their own.[71]

The militarisation of political culture and the political leadership's obsession with military security and its inclination to rely on the armed forces have resulted in, however, military points of view, military priorities, and military rules of conduct playing an important part in Soviet foreign policy. As the foreign policy ambitions of the Soviet leaders have grown, and as their basic means to lead a successful foreign policy are military ones, the military aspect has become very important. The enhanced role of the military can be seen, for example, in the fact that two successive Defence Ministers, Marshals Grechko and Ustinov, respectively, have become full members of the Politbureau. It is also significant that the then Party leader and Soviet Head of State, Brezhnev, was made a Marshal of the Soviet Union as well as Head of the Defence Council in 1976 and that Brezhnev's successor as Party leader, Andropov, apart from being a former Head of the KGB, also had the rank of Army General and was also appointed Head of the Defence Council in 1983.[72] The process was repeated with Chernenko in 1984. But how should this development be evaluated? What are the implications for Soviet foreign and security policy?

There are no signs that indicate that the military-civilian relations are viewed as problematical in official Soviet sources. In the West, however, the matter has been discussed. In addition to what has been already referred to in this study, I find it appropriate to recapitulate some important arguments from the American academic debate.

The assessment of one seasoned expert in the field, Roman Kolkowicz is that the military as a professional corporation or bureaucratic interest group gained influence over Soviet politics under Brezhnev. His arguments are that the routinisation and bureaucratisation of government after the fall of the erratic leader, Khrushchev, meant that the military increased its ability to influence the decisions of the Central Committee and the Politbureau. At the same time,

> ... the enormously increased scope of Soviet political, diplomatic, and military involvement around the globe has given a correspondingly increased role to the military.

According to Kolkowicz, the combined effect of the two trends was that the institutional interests of the military were increasingly met, in modernisation of arms, in man-power, in top military leaders not only entering the Politbureau but also taking part in important international negotiations such as the SALT talks, and in an increase of military training in the civic educational system of the USSR:

> The present favorable position of the military represents the culmination of a twenty year trend of cumulative growth in institutional strength, corporate autonomy, professional sophistication, and political influence. ... The Soviet military is essentially a conservative, nationalistic, Party-loyal institution whose members share most of the important objectives and values of the Party. The Party's growing reliance upon the military in the pursuit of ever-increasing, global Soviet foreign and military policies creates a marked dependence, or interdependence, between the Party leaders and the military elites, thus enhancing the influence of military views and preferences. The persistence of collective leadership as a permanent coalition form of governance tends to reduce the Party's ability vigorously to resist the concerted bureaucratic pressures of the vast military machine.[73]

Hence Kolkowicz views these developments partly as a competition where the military as a corporation has gained influence at the cost of the civilian Party leaders. He does not speak of a conflict, but of 'an evolutionary adaptional process' of institutional accommodation between the Party and military leadership'.[74] Drawing basically on the same observations of Soviet development, William Odom, who stresses the long-time perspective, insists that 'the military is an administrative arm of the Party' and nothing more.[75] Although the outcome is the same, it is important to reach a judgment: if Kolkowicz is correct, there is no easy way back from the extreme militarisation of Soviet foreign policy which became so obvious in the late 1970s, but if Odom is right, the Party leaders could change this policy at will.[76]

Discussing Odom's and Kolkowicz's theses Dimitri Simes argues that both miss the point by failing to make a distinction between the Party and the Party apparatus. Simes holds that the Secretariat of the Central Committee, has no department for military affairs. The Politbureau, on the other hand, which is the top-level decision-making body not only of the Party but of the Soviet elite as a whole, has military representation, and what is more, in the Politbureau, the military 'has a virtual monopoly over crucial information related to its professional prerogatives, functions, and interests'. Simes quotes evidence from Soviet sources showing that the military elite is becoming a socially distinct group in the society, increasingly recruiting the new cadets from its own circle and giving them a much better general education than that available in the civilian institutions of learning. In addition to this, Simes can point to a demographic phenomenon which may further increase the self-esteem of the Soviet military elite; that the Party apparatus is getting older and older at the same time as 'the military is going through a rejuvenation process'. This observation may be interpreted as indicating that while the civilian Party elite grows more and more rigid and lacking in initiative, the military elite is becoming the dynamic, active factor in Soviet foreign policy decision-making. Simes mentions the sending of a 'limited contingent' of Soviet troops to Afghanistan in late 1979 as an indication that military points of view strongly influence political decisions.

Simes's conclusion is that it is neither a question of the military competing with the Party nor a matter of the military executing the will of the Party. What we have been witnessing is, instead, a 'steady if zigzag increase in the military's role in Soviet politics generally and in government councils in particular'. This Simes ascribes not to internal Soviet conflicts but to what he calls the pervasiveness of Soviet militarism in the society.[77]

According to Simes, military aspects and military solutions acquire an important role in Soviet security policy simply because the Party leadership is thinking about security policy exclusively in military terms and because the military has a monopoly of knowledge regarding all data pertaining to the military capability and armament needs of the USSR. There are no civilian experts on security policy. Simes underlines that, after all, there is nothing strange, for Soviet leaders, in taking refuge to force and violence in foreign policy, in security policy, as they are used to do so in their internal policy.[78]

Simes's conclusions regarding the role of the military in Soviet policy do fit very well with the facts that we have about recent Soviet foreign policy security actions, above all the one against Afghanistan in 1979. His stress on the pervasiveness of Soviet militarism also implies that it is not only the political elite which is affected by the militarisation. Another American analyst, Rebecca Strode, has pointed out that the affinity between the civil and the military aspects of life is underlined in the age of nuclear strategy:

> Time and time again, the Soviet media remind the population that it is only the military might amassed by the farsighted communist regime which restrains the aggressive imperialists from launching a surprise nuclear attack. This omnipresent threat provides a rationale for the continued militarization and mobilization of Soviet society. It may also explain in part the Soviet emphasis in civil defense. A population which is largely mobilized on a continuous basis for military production constitutes a military resource, and this confuses the distinction between the military and civilian sectors of society. The economy as a whole is viewed as a military resource, and hence, as a potential military target.[79]

We can conclude, then, from the arguments put forward by Simes and Strode and from the impossibility of finding substantial counter indications that the fact that the major Soviet asset in foreign and security policy is military power, together with the anticipated need to prepare for an eventual nuclear war, favour a militarisation of Soviet policy in general. The soundness of the conclusion is borne out, ironically, by a Soviet political actor, the then Komsomol leader B. Pastukhov. Writing about the 'Education of Patriots and Internationalists' he had the following to say, in early 1982:

> It is the lofty duty of the Leninist Komsomol to more actively make real the military-patriotic education of youth, to increase the moral-political, psychological and military-technical preparation for service in the Armed Forces, to imbue the youth with braveness, will-power, preparedness for heroic deeds, and love of the Soviet Army, to give it better knowledge of the heroic traditions of the Armed Forces of the USSR and of everyday campaign life, military techniques, and arms of today's Soviet soldier, and to arrange military-patriotic mass rallies and relays.[80]

184

At the same time as the Komsomol leader stressed the importance of paramilitary training for Komsomol members, i.e., of the Soviet youth, Marshal Ogarkov demanded active preparedness for a possible war. According to Ogarkov, it was necessary to strengthen the central direction of both the military and the economy to make the country ready for war in a very short time. The Navy and the Air Force must be modernised and the education of reservists improved.[81] There has been no official rebuttal of Ogarkov's demands and there has not been any sign of a re-orientation of Soviet economic policy after they were being forwarded, i.e., no change of priority away from heavy industry.

In the early 1980s the position of the military sector seemed to be stronger than ever before. The KGB also acquired a strong influence over Soviet politics during the Brezhnev era. Hence it does not seem farfetched to label the Soviet Union of 1984 'a militarised KGB Party state'.

Notes

1 Brezhnev 1979, p. 11 This part of the chapter is based upon Gerner 1980c.
2 Legvold 1979, p. 12.
3 See MacKenzie and Curran 1977, passim, Gerner 1978, p. 465 f.
4 See Tillett 1969, passim.
5 See Sokolov 1970, p. 259 f.
6 Pashuto 1976, p. 99.
7 Porshnev 1976, p. 18, 35, Porshnev 1948, p. 11 f., 25.
8 Porshnev 1976, p. 4 ff.
9 Golan 1975b, p. 19 ff., Fitzpatrick 1976, p. 211 ff, Barber 1981, p. 137 ff. See also Fitzpatrick 1979a, p. 212–54.
10 See Braudel 1969, p. 41 ff.
11 Fitzpatrick 1979b, p. 399.
12 Pelenski 1974, p. 80.
13 Pelenski 1974, p. 104, 135.
14 Pelenski 1974, p. 135.
15 Pelenski 1974, p. 304
16 Davies 1982, p. 393, Uschakow 1982, p. 37 (quoting an interwar source). Valenta 1981b, p. 50.
17 Simes 1982, p. 55.
18 For this process, see Davies 1982, p. 331 f.
19 Andelman 1981–82, p. 91.
20 Brezhnev 1981, p. 5 f.
21 The most exhaustive analysis of the Nomenklatura is Voslensky 1982.
22 Schöpflin 1981, p. 78.
23 Dawisha 1981, p. 15. Cf. Müller 1977, p. 263.

24 Jones 1980, p. 569.
25 See Ascherson 1982, p. 267 f.
26 Jones 1981, p. 226 ff.
27 It is hardly probable that Romania is able to lead a somewhat independent foreign policy because of the strength of her army, although Jones 1983 says so.
28 Jones 1981, p. 234.
29 Mackintosh 1981, p. 140 f.
30 Erickson 1981, p. 167 ff.
31 Caldwell 1982, p. 318 f.
32 Linden 1982a, p. 182 f.
33 Marer 1974, p. 144, Korbonski 1980, p. 379, Lidert 1982, p. 11 ff.
34 Zimmerman 1980, p. 174 ff.
35 Marer and Montias 1980, p. 23.
36 Cf. the conclusion 'bilateralism is still the rule inside the CMEA' by Bornstein 1981, p. 118. See also Vanous 1980, p. 189 ff.
37 Korbonski 1980a, p. 362.
38 Marer and Montias 1980, p. 28.
39 Brainard 1980, p. 136 f., Holzman et al. 1980, p. 139 ff.
40 Vanous 1982, p. 8.
41 Hanson 1981, p. 93.
42 Csikós-Nagy 1982, p. 76.
43 See Bykov 1983, p. 60 for an assessment from within!
44 Höhmann 1982, p. 12.
45 Ascherson 1981, p. 269. See also Gerner and Hedlund 1982, p. 322 f.
46 See Kusin 1982 and Mastny 1982.
47 Cf. Csaba 1983 who notes, on the one hand (p. 49) that 'worsening discipline of supplies from CMEA countries' necessitated the strengthening of 'the central, government-level supervision of the timing and carrying out of delivery obligations to and from CMEA trading partners', and, on the other hand (p. 62): 'It has become a majority conviction by now that a comprehensive reform is a package deal: piecemeal changes can only be a prelude but neither a substitute for, nor a way of implementation of, a set of measures that can bring about effects if realized concurrently. This is needed to alter enterprise behaviour in a fundamental way, so as to make them market, rather than hierarchy-oriented. This is the condition for Hungary's successful adjustment to the challenge of epocal changes in the world economy.'
It is evident that 'CMEA integration' is not the best development path for Hungary's economy in the eyes of 'the majority' of informed Hungarians.
48 Brezhnev 1981, p. 6.

49 Höhmann 1982, p. 15.
50 Terebilov 1983.
51 See Brezhnev 1981, p. 5, who, among 'fraternal countries' enumerates the WTO states and Cuba, Mongolia, Laos and Vietnam, but not Yugoslavia.
52 Linden 1982a, p. 167 f., 180. See also Moreton 1982, p. 86, 89, 103 f., Valenta 1981b, p. 51, and Caldwell 1982, p. 307.
53 Gati 1982–83, p. 294.
54 See, e.g., Voslensky 1982, p. 376, Zinoviev 1981, p. 19.
55 See, e.g., Skilling 1976, p. 736, Moreton 1981, p. 176 ff., Linden 1982a, p. 165 f., Larrabee 1981–82, p. 41.
56 See the declarations of the then First Deputy Chairman of the KGB, Tsvigun 1981 and the then Chairman of the Komsomol, Pastukhov 1982. See also 'Västs kultur är propaganda' 1983.
57 Pfaff 1982.
58 Pfaff 1982. Cf. Wesson, 1974, p. 193: 'The Soviet system is most vulnerable in its only partially incorporated fringes, in Eastern Europe. . .', and Seton-Watson 1979, p. 101: 'The discontents which the quasi-Russification policies of the Moscow rulers create within the Soviet empire and the Soviet semicolonies constitute one of the main dangers to world peace'.
59 In Khrushchev's 'secret' speech at the 20th Congress of the CPSU in 1956. See Chrusjtjov minns 1971, p. 531 ff. An interesting eye-witness account of what happened to the Russian peasants under Stalin was actually published by the *Manchester Guardian* in 1933: the reporter was Malcolm Muggeridge. An interesting point is that people in the West refused to believe him then: 'It was not until Khrushchev's famous speech ... that I was exonerated'. (Muggeridge, 1983.) The point is, of course, that the treatment meted out by Stalin to his subjects was literally incomprehensible for people living outside the confines of the Soviet Union.
60 It is vividly described by former Czech party members such as Mlynár 1980 and Kaplan 1982 how Novotny remained true to the Stalinist faith and only decided to follow Khrushchev in the early 1960s, i.e., just before the demise of the Russian ruler.
61 Gromyko 1983, p. 6. Cf. Mitchell 1978, p. 376, who notes that the doctrine of 'sblizhenie' of nations was extended to encompass the socialist states (and not just the Soviet republics) at the 25th Congress of the CPSU in 1976.
62 Gromyko 1983, p. 20.
62 Gromyko 1983, p. 28.
64 Cf. Gromyko 1983, p. 28 f.
65 Mastny 1979, p. 308 sees such a sad outcome as the unexpected effect of too much success for Stalin in the Second World War: '. . .

Stalin created the Soviet empire as a by-product . . . he saddled his country with a cluster of sullen dependencies whose possession proved a mixed blessing in the long run'.

66 See Ogarkov 1981, Brezhnev 1982b, Andropov 1982.

67 Quoted from Odom 1976, p. 34.

68 Quoted from Simes 1981–82, p. 126.

69 Odom 1976, p. 34 ff.

70 See Gerner, 1979, p. 532 f. who demonstrates how Lenin was fascinated by the German model, as expressed in his writings in 1917 and 1921. See also Szamuely 1974, p. 58 f.

71 Cf. the - so far - extreme case of General Jaruzelski in Poland, who became Party Secretary before he proclaimed a 'state of war' in his fief. Shtromas 1981, p. 121 even goes as far as to declare that the lack of political and economic change in the USSR will remain 'as long as the Party can retain the control over the army and use its force at discretion . . .'. Shtromas was a researcher of law in the Soviet Union before emigrating to the United Kingdom in 1973. He does not offer any direct evidence for his assertion (See Shtromas, p. 5).

72 In both cases, Brezhnev's and Andropov's, the assignment as General Secretary of the Party came first and the appointment as Defence Council Head second.

73 Kolkowicz 1977, p. 86 ff.

74 Kolkowicz 1982, p. 33. In this work Kolkowicz goes as far as to say that because of the Party's reliance on the military and the latter's continued loyalty, 'the Party becomes in a sense the captive of the military'.

75 See Odom 1978.

76 It is revealing for the trend, in the West, to regard the militarisation as a fact which need not be discussed that the volume by leading specialists in the field *Russia at the Crossroads: the 26th Congress of the CPSU* 1982 does not have any special chapter on the military, although Bialer and Gustafson 1982, p. 2 note that 'the economic strains of the 1980s will bring home to the leaders the full cost of their military programs and the burdens of empire', although Legvold 1982, p. 174 notes the implications for foreign policy of 'the historic and deeply embedded Russian tradition of equating increased power, principally military power, with increased security', and although Bond and Levine 1982, p. 106 conclude that it will be extremely difficult for the Soviet leaders to 'maintain their 4.5 per cent rate of growth of defense expenditures for very long'. The gist of the observations is that even if the military and the Party leaders agree on policies and the instruments to be chosen to implement them, economic reality itself might become a serious challenge, restricting the options for different policies.

77 Simes 1981/82, p. 131 ff.
78 Simes 1980/81, p. 97 ff.
79 Strode 1982, p. 326.
80 Pastukhov 1982, p. 54.
81 Ogarkov 1982.

7 Conclusions: from 1948 to 1984 — back to square one

This study has analysed why the security system established by the Soviet leaders in Central Europe after World War II is not politically stable. The basic cause of instability, as it has been manifested in Czechoslovakia, Hungary and Poland, has been the inability of the communist regimes imposed by the Soviet Union — the vassal regimes — to acquire political legitimacy, i.e., voluntary acceptance of their right to rule and active support from the population.

It is evident that the question of legitimacy became relevant for security and stability as a consequence of de-Stalinisation in the Soviet Union under Khrushchev. De-Stalinisation did not mean any dismantling of the Stalinist political structures in the Soviet Union and the vassal states. It meant, however, that terror was abandoned as the chief instrument by which the population would be kept obedient. In the Soviet Union itself, the communist regime could draw on tradition, i.e., acquire necessary consent by posing, and being perceived by the Russian population in general, as the rightful incumbent of the thrones of the Tsars and of Lenin.[1]

In the Central European countries Czechoslovakia, Hungary and Poland, however, it was revealed, when terror was slackened, that the communist regimes lacked legitimacy. Political stability was shaken.

As has been shown and discussed in this study, the kind of legitimation that the Central European communist regimes could and would acquire, when they perceived political challenge from their subjects, was goal-

190

oriented. The regimes could not possibly share fundamental moral values with their subjects, as the regimes had to adhere to Marxism-Leninism and the leading role of the Communist Party, while the populations cherished traditional Western values regarding the right and dignity of the individual, political democracy and legal rules.

Once the communist regimes had recognised, in practice, that they ought to act as instruments for the achievement of general goals such as material welfare and preservation of national traditions, they found themselves subject to pressures from below. These pressures found their outlets in forms that were taken from the countries' own pre-Stalinist national political cultures.[2] The influence of the political culture factor has been called, by the British political scientist Peter Summerscale, 'somewhat intangible and indirect'.[3] Although the operation of this factor may be difficult to assess, this is not a sufficient reason to disregard it, especially not if it is a concept of crucial importance for an understanding of (lack of) political legitimacy for a regime.

It should be evident from my whole investigation that I have not, in spite of my general 'pre-understanding' of national political cultures, a deterministic view which states that political cultures are given once and for all and are resistant to change. On the contrary, I have firstly made a distinction between a dominant political culture, in a given society, and political sub-cultures. Secondly, I have used the advantage of hindsight. This means that general historical knowledge of the societies under study, knowledge of a kind that is scarcely contested by anyone, such as that the Soviet Union is a monoparty dictatorship, has allowed me to dismiss certain aspects as irrelevant. A case in point is my notion that the Stalinist political culture is a continuation of the old Russian one. Of course there was a pluralist sub-culture in Russia at the beginning of the 20th century, when several political parties competed in elections,[4] but once the *duma* and then the Provisional government had fallen, this alternative political culture was nipped in the bud. With Stalin it was completely uprooted.

The analyses of the different cases have shown that once terror was abandoned it really became possible for the vassal countries to influence their own fate, to choose a national road within the Soviet bloc. It is evident that the limitations on their freedom of action were not known beforehand. Squeezed between anticipated Soviet demands and manifest pressure from their respective populations, the vassal regimes set out for a process of trial and error. The outcomes were different. I have discussed why the wider international context cannot be left out in terms of timing, i.e., especially the state of the Soviet Union's relations to the Federal Republic of Germany. In 1968, when the Czechoslovak party leadership embarked on a new action programme, on economic decentralisation and political democratisation, the Soviet Union had not yet reached a stable *modus vivendi* with the FRG. The Czechoslovak economic decentralisation implied modernisation of the economic structure and increased trade with the capitalist West, above all with neighbouring FRG. This might have been perceived as politically dangerous by the Soviet leaders. And when it seemed obvious that economic liberalisation would mean a diminished political role for the Communist Party, the Soviet Union intervened, rallying four other WTO states behind it. In 1971, when the PUWP under Gierek launched its economic modernisation programme, extended trade with the West, and allowed Polish culture to follow a national pattern, both Poland itself and the Soviet Union had reached a political settlement with the FRG. Moreover, the timid Western reaction to the intervention in Czechoslovakia a few years before had assured the Soviet leaders that the West had no intention of exploiting internal diversification of the Soviet bloc. During the whole period from 1968 on, when Hungary's Kádár embarked on the NEM, without the Communist Party losing its political control, there was no reason for the Soviet leaders to interfere and heighten tension in the Balkans, where Romania was perhaps a slightly disturbing factor with her independent foreign policy but where, also, non-aligned Yugoslavia showed no sign of trying to exploit the contradictions within the Soviet bloc.

However, the international setting cannot explain the whole difference between the outcomes in Czechoslovakia, Poland and Hungary, respectively. Internal factors also entered the picture, i.e., the patterns of action possible within the respective national political cultures and the ability of the national communist leaderships to utilise these possibilities. The details of the different processes have been described and analysed in the course of the study. Here I will highlight what proved to be crucial differences, relying, of course, on the advantage of hindsight.

Viewing the whole period 1953–81 one sees that Czechoslovakia was the last of the three countries trying to walk a national path and the first to fail. This was due to her political culture.

Czechoslovakia's first twenty years was an experience in parliamentary democracy, drawing on Western political doctrines and the traditions of the quest for national liberation during the late Hapsburg era. The national liberation movement was tied to a feeling of pan-Slavist community, with a benign view of Russia as the good, elderly brother. Also during the interwar years and, especially, during the Second World War, the Soviet Union was regarded as the natural ally against the German enemy. The Communist Party of Czechoslovakia was able to gain rather widespread support, as it was not a sign of national treachery to be a communist. During the first postwar years the Czechoslovak political parties that dominated the political scene opted for a pan-Slavic foreign policy under Soviet protection.

The communist take-over in February 1948, was a kind of coup, but it did not meet with concerted and whole-hearted opposition. However, the

Communist Party soon proved to be thoroughly Stalinised. Its rule of terror during the first years after the take-over forced the people into submission but also, which was to be revealed later, into strengthened appreciation of the traditional, non-Stalinist political culture. However, part of this culture was obedience to the government, and it took the reassertion of traditional political culture within the Communist Party once the Stalinists had lost their Soviet backing, to mobilise the population for democracy in 1968. It was the Communist Party leader himself, Dubcek, who in April 1968, referred to 'the specific national conditions' of Czechoslovakia, i.e., the democratic (and humanitarian) traditions.[5] At this juncture, in early 1968, the confidence in the goodwill of the Russians still remained, not least in the Party leader Dubcek personally. One did not foresee the Soviet reaction and had no strategy for coping with it. The Party leadership failed to mobilise the people against the Soviet pressures after the invasion. The reform programme was dismantled.

The Czechoslovak traditional political culture, rooted in history and developed in the interwar years, has not enabled the Czechs and Slovaks to accommodate to Russian rule while preserving autonomy and dignity. On the one hand, when this political culture was revived in 1968, it was clear that it contained political pluralism as a central trait. This was perceived by the Soviet leaders as a threat to their rule through the Communist Party. On the other hand, this same old political culture favours submission to external pressures and threats of violence, as long as these are combined with the use of the political institutions. It seems that, after 1968, the Czechs and Slovaks have relapsed into the subordination pattern of the Hapsburg era.

The Poles in 1956 were the first of the subjugated peoples to seriously challenge the regime imposed by the Soviet leaders and they have repeatedly challenged it over a period of 25 years. In contrast to the Czechoslovakia of 1968, the Communist Party has not guided the attempts at de-Stalinisation and in contrast to the conditions in Czechoslovakia, the pressure has been from below. The people at large could not stand what Polish sociologists have called, in 1982–83, the 'schizophrenic society' with its fake political institutions,[6] but rose in a political movement which they regarded as authentic, Solidarity. It is evident that the Polish workers, intellectuals and peasants, who have refused to accommodate to Stalinism, have drawn on national traditions and expressed traditional Polish political culture. The respect for government has never been great in Poland. During the partition period, and again during and after the Second World War, the Catholic Church acquired the role as the protector of the nation. At the same time, Polish nationalism has never had any pan-Slavist connotation. Russia, and then the Soviet Union, has been regarded as an arch enemy. This image was reinforced by the Soviet-Polish war in 1920, by the Soviet Union's collaboration with

Nazi Germany at the fourth partition of Poland in 1939, and by the attempted Russification under high Stalinism from 1949 onwards.

Time and again, Polish workers, intellectuals and peasants put the regime under pressure in different ways. The Catholic Church remained as an antidote to communism and preserved its influence over the life-cycle of the Poles: ritually, the people remained catholic. For a long time, the regime managed to handle the challenges by first yielding a little to specific groups and then gradually recovering the lost ground. This happened under Gomulka in 1956–58, and again under Gierek in 1971–76.

The year 1976 represented a new departure. For the first time, there was a change in the pattern of opposition, as intellectuals and workers began to support each other and co-operate. The democratic socialist tradition of the old PPS was revived with one very important difference from the old days. This time the Catholic Church, forced into opposition, of course, by the communist regime already in the early 1950s, found itself on the side, not just of that abstraction 'the nation', but of workers and intellectuals. Thus in the period 1976–80 one saw a merger of two different lines in Polish traditional political culture, i.e., democratic socialism with parliamentist values and a nationalist catholicism, with a Church which managed to integrate the interests of different social groups and was imbued with anti-Russianism and anti-communism.[7] The result of the merger was the Solidarity movement, which turned out to be not just a labour union but a whole polity, the incarnation of the — partly new — genuine Polish political culture. In addition the peasants, who had stubbornly resisted collectivisation in the early 1950s, were incorporated into the new political entity.[8]

In 1981, the regime could no longer placate the people with promises and carrots. The politically active part of the Polish population, not least the younger generations, had learned from the experiences of the earlier challenges and would not be talked into submission. But it was not only the opposition that had changed its nature. The regime had also changed. As the Communist Party as such had never managed to consolidate itself, a core of resolute Stalinists, or maybe Jaruzelski personally (we cannot tell whether he acted as a true Stalin or as a *primus inter pares*) in the course of the 1970s had developed a new instrument of power against the Poles, the army.

In Czechoslovakia, a form of neo-Stalinism was reestablished after the Soviet intervention in 1968. The major change in comparison to the previous, pre-1968 situation is the experience of 1968, namely that the Czechs and Slovaks could never place pressure on the rulers from below, only obey them. The country was unable to produce a political class that could stand up for the nation's sovereignty and dignity in the face of pressure from the outside.

Poland also saw the establishment of neo-Stalinism in 1981. But here it was the result of the suppression of a peaceful revolution, in which the Poles regained their national dignity. Bending their backs today, they know at least that they have made a serious attempt to make Poland sovereign again. Compared to the Czechs and Slovaks, they have won 13 years of close contact with that Western world to which they belong. The younger generation was reported to be, in 1983, wholeheartedly against the regime.[9] One cannot rule out the possibility that the Poles may rise again.

Hungary's challenge to Soviet rule in 1956 was the most serious of them all and the one that was most ruthlessly crushed. With the advantage of hindsight one can say that the defeat has proved to be beneficial, at least in the timespan that we have so far experienced after 1956.

The Hungarian revolution of 1956 had many aspects. It was evident, in any case, that the people at large wanted to get rid of both communist and Soviet rule. The Hungarians had been used to playing second string, both under the Hapsburgs and earlier under the Turks in Transylvania, but to be put under what amounted to a veritable occupation and economic exploitation was something else. This experience was added to the traumatic recent experiences of becoming, first mutilated as a state as a consequence of the Trianon treaty in 1919 and then humiliated as a nation by the Nazis and their puppet fascist regime in 1943–44. When the Soviet Union seemed indecisive during the de-Stalinisation campaign of 1956, part of the Communist Party in Hungary identified with the people and was carried along with the current.

The Hungarians learned that they had gone too far. Everybody understood after 1956 that there was no question of semisovereignty of the 1867 *Ausgleich* kind. Instead one adopted the strategy of the Transylvanian princes under Turkish rule.

One important legacy of the 1956 revolution was that both the people and the Party leaders had tried to change the situation. The actions were not very well concerted, but both were defeated. This is in contrast to both Czechoslovakia in 1968, where the Party was defeated and the people never summoned, and Poland in 1981, where the people were defeated but the Party was simply passed over by Jaruzelski. Kádár emerged as a representative of the defeated nation and not as the plenipotentiary of the Soviet rulers.

While for Poles, Soviet dominance is a new incarnation of age-old Russian oppression, the Soviet domiance for Hungarians is a new instance of foreign rule. The regime in Hungary can thus be perceived by the people, not only as an instrument of Russian imperialism, as the regime is viewed in Poland, but also as a necessary protection against hardships meted out by fate, the instrument of which now happens to be the Russians.

Compared to what the Czechs and Slovaks and Poles have achieved, what the Hungarians have achieved seems to be the best situation possible. A good summary of the situation in Hungary, as compared to the one in turbulent Poland, has been made by Maria Markus, who is of Polish origin but settled in Hungary in her early twenties and became one of the Budapest school of sociologists (in 1977 she left Hungary for political reasons):

> If Poland represents the one case of an open crisis of legitimation in East European societies, Hungary serves as an example not for the success of legitimation of the political *system*, but for an effective *compromise* between the population and the government. This compromise is based on the one hand on the nonexistence of any other practically available and politically realistic alternative, and on the other on the *relative 'effectiveness'* of governmental policies.[10]

What is 'realistic', 'practical' and effective' is to a certain degree a matter of perception, and the whole complex must not necessarily be constant over time. What Marcus calls 'relative effectiveness' refers to what I have labelled 'economic compensation' and, also, to what another member of the Budapest school, Agnes Heller, calls 'legitimation through substantive rationality', which is, both for me and for Heller, an 'auxiliary' form of legitimation but not legitimation in a proper sense. Heller and her compatriot Fehér even call the Hungarian experience 'pacification' only. Lacking formal rationality, namely one implying rules for the exertion of power and possibility to change government, which in turn implies political pluralism, the regime will have to rely ultimately on nonlegitimate power.[11]

But is political pluralism under limited sovereignty for the regime possible? In 1973, the Hungarian leaders dismissed the 'dissenting' sociologists of the Budapest school from their posts. The Party issued a declaration which said that the basic principles of the Party did not allow pluralism and the denial of the leading role of the Party and of the working class. In 1983, the Party's spokesman Aczél declared that one rejected 'the ideas, structures and forms of the political pluralism of classical bourgeois societies'. But Aczél added:

> We welcome with open arms everyone who cuts his links with opposition groups. As earlier we are ready to wipe the slate clean for anybody who wants to form part of the national consensus.[12]

It is clear that the Hungarian leaders have rejected political pluralism at the same time as they have tried to create a national consensus. Apparently they adhere to the notion, central to Marxism-Leninism, that

196

politicised conflicts of interest cannot exist in a socialist state. But then one cannot escape the conclusion that political stability in Hungary is precarious, since the logic of economic decentralisation and of the market mechanism is that conflicts of interests should be recognised. Tensions will grow if these conflicts are not channelled into ideological discussion and political life as well. The dilemma is that while the Kádár regime is aware of this logic, as the 1973 declaration shows, it cannot shed the principle of democratic centralism and monoparty rule. If it did, the Soviet leaders would either stage a coup of the Jaruzelski kind or send their troops. The dilemma is that as the official ideology declares that the Party is the leading force in the society and consciously leading the way towards a better state, the Party cannot recognise any alternative to its own rule as politically legitimate.[13] Thus Hungary is also caught by the Marxist and communist logic that there can be no legitimate alternative to the Party, as it is the Communist Party that legitimises the society and not the other way round.[14] The legitimation devices discussed in this study, 'economic compensation' and 'protector of national culture' therefore cannot, if they fail, remove the legitimacy of the Party in its own terms. If the devices succeed it is good for the Party, as this diminishes the need for rule by terror, which is rather impractical in a modern industrial state, but it does not mean, in the Party's understanding of itself, that the Party acquires legitimacy, it is just visible proof that it is legitimate.

The Poles, the Czechs and the Slovaks, and the Hungarians, all have tried to influence their own fate in spite of Soviet domination. The outcomes have been markedly different. The Hungarians have fared best, retaining much of their national culture and managing to increase material consumption. The Poles have, so to speak, saved their souls, but are very badly off materially.[15] The Czechs and Slovaks are comparatively well off materially but are, according to intellectuals in their midst, now running the risk of losing their souls.[16]

In this study, the various external and internal factors that have affected the respective outcomes have been analysed and discussed. Regarding the relationship with the main actor, the Soviet Union, one may make the following summary:

The Czechs and the Slovaks failed with their reform programme also because they had, and this was part of their traditional political culture, a too optimistic picture of the Russians and of the Russians' regards for their smaller Slavic brethren. They placed too much trust in the good will of the Russians.

The Poles have failed with their revolution because they have kept challenging the Russians without, apparently, realising that they are so much weaker. They have not, after 1945, been defeated as thoroughly and definitely as the Hungarians were in 1956. The popular risings, especially the one in 1980, have shown that the Poles have not learnt to put up with

197

the Russian determination and ability to keep the Soviet hold of Poland. Most probably, the Poles will not let General Jaruzelski develop into another Kádár. He will have to rule with oppression. If the worst comes to the worst, he will be remembered as a 20th century political reincarnation of the men from Targowica.

The Hungarians have not failed so far. Rulers and people alike have understood that any sign of political pluralism might trigger a Russian intervention of some kind and accepted that it is, in the final instance, the Russians, the Kremlin, who decides what Hungary must do to safeguard Soviet security. Do not trust the Russians but do not try to challenge them either. This is the memento on which both the leaders and the bulk of the population of Hungary seem to agree. The fate of Czechoslovakia and Poland cannot but have reinforced this attitude.

The Hungarian way makes sense if one assumes that the Soviet leaders are interested in security and are rather pragmatic. This means that the Soviet leaders insist on the vassals' copying their own system but only to the extent that this is necessary, as they see it, to safeguard Soviet interests. It also means that they take the reactions of the different peoples into consideration. Hungary's solution of the task that has only been defined in general terms by the Soviet leaders, has turned out to be better, so far, for the Soviet Union than either of the paths followed by the Czechoslovaks — under Husák — or the Poles — under Jaruzelski.

The worst fate has hit Czechoslovakia, as its survival as a culture is in danger. This is the nation which trusted the good will of the Russians. Apparently, this is a major error.

This study has discussed and answered questions about Soviet security policy in Central Europe. The scientific aim of the investigation has been to reach a well founded understanding of some important conditions and forms of this security policy. The aim has not been to try to test hypotheses of cause-effect relations between specific events. The object of the study has been abstractions, i.e., 'political stability', 'legitimacy' and 'political culture', concepts that have been investigated by means of an analysis of social events, processes and thoughts in print.

Interpreted as explanations of the causes of political instability and of threats to Soviet military security in Europe, the conclusions are, in the terminology of the the political scientist and theorist Morton A. Kaplan, 'overdetermined'. The number of possible constraints on a certain political actor is so great that 'explanations' shift with the choice of theoretical framework, with the perspective.[17] The 'cause' of Polish instability, for example, may be said to be the nature of the country's political culture, or the policy of the Soviet leaders, or the anti-Soviet

American policy, and so on. My ambition has been to try to examine and discuss how the interaction of many factors of different kinds has made the Soviet security system politically unstable and insufficient to guarantee by political means the degree of security which the Soviet leaders deem necessary. The analysis hopefully serves to deepen our understanding of why military factors and considerations have become so predominant in Soviet society and foreign policy. Direct military control in Poland and military pre-eminence in Soviet foreign policy is apparently necessary to guarantee the political stability of the Soviet security system in Central Europe. The buffer zone has changed into a front line as the 'zone' has proved to be, notably in Poland, a factor of political instability that threatens the security of the Soviet Union. An enemy image, i.e., that of the USA and NATO, has remained necessary to motivate the military control of the European periphery of the Soviet empire.[18]

Thus the outcome of four decades of Soviet security policy in Central Europe has been to increase the significance of the military factor in Soviet domestic and intrabloc politics. This outcome is due not only to the actions of the Soviet leaders but also to the reaction against Soviet politics in the countries of Czechoslovakia (1968), Hungary (1956), and Poland (repeatedly). Once the confrontation between the traditional political cultures in the latter countries and the imposed Soviet order became open, the differences between Czechoslovakia, Poland, and Hungary made themselves felt. The re-emergence of the traditional domestic political culture meant open (Czechoslovakia) or veiled (Poland) political pluralism in the two former countries but (only) economical reformism and cultural pluralism in Hungary. The Poles had no model of utilising submission to foreign power for peaceful and gradual devolution away from Stalinism. The Czechs and Slovaks had no tradition of managing their own affairs in the interest of the majority while accepting foreign dominance. For the Poles, defeat has repeatedly proved to be a challenge to rebel, for the Czechs and Slovaks a cause of relapse into despair. For the Hungarians, defeat was interpreted as a challenge to endure and regard the Russians as a temporary evil, to be outlived in the same way as at an earlier date the Mongols, the Turks and the Hapsburgs had been endured.

Thus the comparison of the behaviour of the three countries validates the conclusion that political culture matters. Political culture seems to be a crucial intervening variable responsible for the different outcomes. While Hungary hardly can set an example for anybody else, her fate shows that it is possible to reach a balance between Soviet security demands and own national interests, and, moreover, that this seems to be a way to render Soviet security less precarious.

However, history does not repeat itself. The political culture of Hungary in the 1980s cannot be said to be exactly the same as in earlier centuries. It is the activity of different actors in the Hungarian society

199

which has helped shape the political conditions of the present era. There are other legacies which Hungarian communists, workers, peasants and intellectuals have chosen to discontinue. The revolution in 1956 may be interpreted as a reactivation of the tradition of 1848, symbolised by the names of Kossuth and Pétöfi. When the 1956 revolution met with defeat, as in 1848–49, the tradition of rebellion was abandoned. That political culture which approved collaboration with the powerful alien power was instead regenerated.[19]

It stands to reason that both the Czechoslovak spring of 1968 and the Polish August of 1980 were nonviolent rebellions. The traditions of 1618 (of the Czechs) and of 1831, 1863, 1905, 1956, 1970 and 1976 (the Poles) were discontinued. But the political cultures of the respective nations did not generate any 'Hungarian' post-1956 alternative. Apart from what has been concluded earlier in this study about Czechoslovakia, one must also point to the fact that this country is not ethnically and culturally homogeneous to the same degree as either Hungary or Poland. Both the post-1948 and post-1968 developments witnessed competition between Czechs and Slovaks instead of concerted action against the Russians. In the first period, the Czechs got the upper hand, in the second the Slovaks. After the euphoria in the immediate postwar years and during 1968, the mutual distrust between the two ethnic groups re-emerged.[20] Stalinism and then neo-Stalinism, were able to reassert themselves. So while Stalinism did not serve as the only alternative political culture in the Hungarian case, it has apparently been the only alternative to political pluralism and democracy in the Czechoslovak case. The Soviet influence has been sufficient to bar democracy, but it cannot be said to have determined the precise form that Stalinism has taken in post-1968 Czechoslovakia. The Czechoslovak Stalinism has become the dominant part of the country's own political culture. The pluralist tradition is upheld by the small Charta 77-movement only.[21]

As for Poland, the parallel between the different trends within the Solidarity movement and the political groupings in the interwar period, has been noted in this study. Solidarity's congress in 1981 has also been compared, by the British historian Timothy Garton Ash, to the Polish Noble Democracy before the partitions of the 18th century. The loose federated structure was similar in the two cases, the Solidarity congress being the equivalent of the Noble Sejm. But as the 'anarchic democracy' in the 18th century kept the central government weak, the state was not able to resist its powerful neighbours. Likewise, the internal 'golden freedom' of Solidarity, which manifested itself in the diversity of opinions during the congress, made the organisation as such unable to resist Jaruzelski and his instruments of coercion.[22]

The regime in Poland superimposed by Stalin has been able to suppress both violent rebellions up to 1976 and the 'anarchic democracy' of

1980–81. Should the victorious neo-Stalinism of Jaruzelski be understood as a vigorous element of Polish political culture after the war? The answer must be in the affirmative. But it is a peculiarly fragile Stalinism, as it has to coexist with the tradition of pluralism and 'anarchic democracy', the traditional political culture which has obviously remained alive. Basically, Poland remains politically unstable. Consequently, Soviet security remains precarious on the Polish front.

Viewed from the perspective of the Soviet leaders, military power is the only means that safeguards their security. They used the military in Hungary in 1956 and were successful. They repeated the use of the military in Czechoslovakia in 1968 and once again their need for security became satisfied. In the latter case, military intervention took place in a politically earlier phase in the form of pre-emptive action.

In 1981, the Soviet leaders used their own military forces as a permanent threat. Once again they were successful, as General Jaruzelski in Poland could act under the 'cover' of the Soviet threat.

The Soviet experience of how the challenges of 1956, 1968 and 1980–81 were overcome makes it understandable why the military factor has remained so significant in Soviet politics. The Soviet security zone in Central Europe, established by Stalin, has re-emerged in almost original shape as part of an empire that is based upon military power. Militarisation of the Soviet Union itself is the outcome of the attempts to create military security at the cost of the nations of Central Europe. With one single exception — Hungary — the players have, in 1984, returned to square one.

Notes

1 It is necessary to stress the importance of the word 'Russian' in this context: for those people in the USSR that regard this state as a continuation of the Russian empire, the present system certainly has traditional legitimacy. There is no evidence that the Russians in the USSR do not, in general, view the Communist system in this perspective.

2 Remington 1982, p. 107 remarks that these nationalistic political cultures are, 'in some cases historically anti-Soviet'. This is an assessment which is more categorical than my analysis. One might argue, however, that in the case of Poland, its political culture really has anti-Sovietism as one constituent element: there was fertile anti-Russian soil available.

3 Summerscale 1982, p. 118. A similar objection to the use of the concept 'political culture' in macrosociological political analyses has been put forward by Lehman 1977, p. 32, who stresses that 'the

lack of short-term variation diminishes the explanatory potential of cultural variables'. As 'constants cannot account for change', Lehman asserts that the concept should be used only as one of the 'specifying variables for understanding political events'. I think it is proper to note this kind of objection at the conclusion of my own analysis: it should have shown by now that it is exactly the long-range operation of understanding which can provide a structural explanation as to why the Soviet security system in Central Europe has not been, is not, and cannot be stable.

4 Jensen 1982, p. 546 stresses this point.
5 Golan 1971, p. 317.
6 Tarkowska 1983, p. 44 f., Wnuk-Lipinski 1982, p. 88.
7 For the development of the Church, see Jerschina 1983, esp. p. 13 ff.
8 See Philipp 1982, p. 197 ff., for the role of the peasants. Cf. Potel 1982, p. 175 ff., 192. See also Ascherson 1981, p. 223 f.
9 Tsoppi 1983, p. 10. This hard-line Soviet observator should have reasons to state the opposite, had he found any signs to deduce from. He did not. Even Hungarian intellectuals are reported to envy the Poles for the experience of 18 months of 'democracy'. (See Garton Ash 1983, p. 303 f.)
10 Markus 1982, p. 191.
11 Heller 1982a, p. 62, Fehér and Heller 1983, p. IX.
12 Positionspapier 1976, p. 168 ff., Aczél 1983, p. 25ff.
13 See Konrád and Szélenyi 1978, p. 246 f., Schöpflin 1983, p. 2 for elaborations of this argument.
14 Berki 1982, p. 166.
15 Cf. the following lines from Herbert 1983, dated 'Warsaw 1982':

'cemeteries grow larger the number of defenders shrinks
but the defense continues and will last to the end
and even if the City falls and one of us survives
he will carry the City inside him on the roads of exile
he will be the City

we look at the face of hunger the face of death
and the worst of them all — the face of treason

and only our dreams have not been humiliated.'

(Translated by Czeslaw Milosz.)

Cf. also Touraine et al. 1983. They stress that 'the Polish sense of nationality . . . has its roots in consciousness and culture rather than in institutions and government'. Several of the members of Touraine's group were Polish sociologists: the statement may be considered to express an opinion from within Polish society.

16 Distinguished examples are the writers Kundera 1979 and Vaculik 1983.
17 Kaplan, M.A. 1971, p. 67 ff., 98 ff.
18 Touraine et al. 1983 argue that the Soviet Union 'no longer acts as the leader of the socialist camp, but as the master of an empire . . . above all concerned with its own power and security'. For a similar conclusion, see Mlynár 1983a, p. 199.
19 Cf. Dittmer 1983, p. 23 ff.
20 See Paul and Simon 1981, p. 38 f.
21 Rupnik 1982, p. 316 f.
22 Garton Ash 1983, p. 220 ff.

Bibliography

Aczél, G., 'The challenge of our age and the response of socialism', *The New Hungarian Quarterly*, vol. 24 No. 90, 1983.

Adomeit, H., *The Soviet Union and Western Europe: Perceptions, policies, problems*, Queen's University Press, Kingston, Ontario, 1979.

Andelman, D., 'Contempt and crisis in Poland', *International Security*, vol. 6, no. 3, 1981/2.

Antal, L., 'Carrying on with the economic reform', *The New Hungarian Quarterly*, vol. 24, no. 91, 1983.

Andropov, Y., 'Rech' tovarishcha Y. Andropova na plenume TsK KPSS 22.11.1982 goda', *Pravda*, 23 November 1982.

Andropov, Y., 'Uchenie Karla Marksa i nekotorye voprosy sotsialisticheskogo stroitel'stva v SSSR', *Kommunist*, no. 3, 1983.

Arato, A., 'Empire vs. civil society: Poland 1981–82', *Telos*, no. 50, 1981/2.

Arvidsson, C. and Fogelklou, A., 'Kontinuitet och förändring', in *Öststatsstudier: Teori och metod*, Arvidsson, C. (ed.), Liber, Stockholm, 1983.

Ascherson, N., *The Polish August: The self-limiting revolution*, Penguin, London, 1981.

Åslund, A., 'Den polska krisen är en systemkris', *Ekonomisk Debatt*, vol. 11, no. 3, 1983.

Azrael, J, 'Varieties of de-Stalinization', in Johnson, C. (ed.), *Change in Communist systems*, Stanford University Press, Stanford, 1970.

Bader, E–M., 'Das "polnische Modell" von 1980/81. Ein neues Regierungssystem und seine Schwächen', *Europa-Archiv*, vol. 37, no. 8, 1982.

Baranczak, S., *Facade and rear*, Typescript, London, 1979.

Barber, J., *Soviet Historians in Crisis, 1928–1932*, Macmillan, London and Basingstoke, 1981.

Barghoorn, F.C., 'Soviet Russia: Orthodoxy and adaptiveness', in Pye, L.W. and Verba, S. (ed.) *Political culture and political development*, Princeton University Press, Princeton, N.J., 1965.

Baryka, C., 'Polish Communists, 1937–1944', *Survey*, vol. 26, no. 4, 1982.

Bates, T. and Bates, B., 'The disintegration of Poland's economy', *Monthly Review*, February, 1982.

Bauman, Z., 'On the maturation of Socialism', *Telos*, no. 47, 1981.

Berecz, J., 'Detente and tension in the world today', *The New Hungarian Quarterly*, vol. 22, no. 83, 1981.

Berend, I.T., 'The first phase of economic reform in Hungary: 1956–1957', *The Journal of European Economic History*, vol. 12, no. 3, 1983.

Berki, R.N., 'The state, Marxism and political legitimation', in Rigby, T.H. and Fehér, F. (ed.), *Political legitimation in Communist states*, Macmillan, London, 1982.

Berndtson, E., 'Comparing political cultures. Politics as an agent of change in structured totalities.' Paper presented at the Polish-Finnish Colloquium on Political Culture, Sept.–Oct., Lahti, 1983.

Besançon, A., *Présent soviétique et passé russe*, Le livre de poche, Paris, 1980.

Bialer, S., 'Poland and the Soviet imperium', *Foreign Affairs*, vol. 59, no. 3, 1981.

Bialer, S. and Gustafson, T., 1982. Introduction, in Bialer, S. and Gustafson, T. (ed.) *Russia at the crossroads: the 26th Congress of the CPSU*, George Allen & Unwin, London, 1982.

Bingen, D. 'Die katolische Kirche im polnischen Sozialismus', in Uschakow, A. (ed.) *Polen — das Ende der Erneuerung?* C.H. Beck, München, 1982.

Blazynski, G., *Flashpoint Poland*, Pergamon, New York, 1979.

Bodnár, G., 'Kolozsvár, Paris, Budapest. An interview with Béla Köpeczi', *The New Hungarian Quarterly*, vol. 21, no. 78, 1980.

Bognar, J., 'Global economic security and growth', *The New Hungarian Quarterly*, vol. 21, no. 79, 1980.

Bognar, J., 'Hungary's progress in a world economic context', *The New Hungarian Quarterly*, vol. 23, no. 87, 1982.

Boldizsár, I., 'The Crown's day', *The New Hungarian Quarterly*, vol. 19, no. 70, 1978.

Boldizsár, I., 'Roman dawn — a personal account of the consecration of the Hungarian oratory in Saint Peter's crypt', *The New Hungarian Quarterly*, vol. 22, no. 81, 1981.

Bond, D. and Levine, H., 'The 11th Five-Year plan, 1981–85', in Bialer, S. and Gustafson, T. (ed.) *Russia at the crossroads: the 26th Congress of the CPSU*, George Allen and Unwin, London, 1982.

Borcke, A.V., 'Wie expansionistisch ist das Sowjetregime? Westliche Perzeptionen und östliche Realitäten', *Berichte des Bundesinstituts für ostwissenschaftliche und internationale Studien,* no. 6, 1981.

Brainard, L.J. 1980. 'CMEA financial system and integration', inMarer, P. and Montias, J.M. (ed.) *East European Integration and East-West trade*, Indiana University Press, Bloomington, Ind., 1980.

Braudel, F., 'Histoire et sciences sociales', in Braudel, F. (ed.) *Ecrits sur l'histoire*, Flammarion, Paris, 1969.

Brezhnev, L.I., 'Rech' tovarishcha L.I. Brezhneva na vstreche s izbiratelyami 2 marta 1979 goda', *Kommunist* no. 4, 1979.

Brezhnev, L.I., 'Otchetnyj doklad TsK KPSS 24 sezdu KPSS i ocherednye zadachi partii v oblasti vnutrennei i vneshnei politiki 23 fevralya 1981 goda', *Kommunist*, no. 4, 1981.

Brezhnev, L.I., 'Speech to Jaruzelski', *New York Times*, 2 March 1982a.

Brezhnev, L.I., 'Rech' tovarishcha L.I. Brezhneva na soveshchanii voennonachalnikov v Kremle 27 oktyabrya 1982 goda', *Kommunist*, no. 16, 1982b.

Bromke, A., 'Czechoslovakia 1968 — Poland 1978: A dilemma for Moscow', *International Journal*, vol. 33, no. 4, 1978.

Bromke, A., 'Policy and politics in Gierek's Poland', in Simon, M.D. and Kanet, R.E. (ed.), *Background to crisis: Policy and politics in Gierek's Poland*, Westview Press, Boulder, 1981.

Brown, A., 'Eastern Europe 1968, 1978, 1988', *Daedalus*, vol. 109, no. 1, 1979.

Brown, A. and Gray, J., Introduction, in Brown, A. and Gray, J (ed.) *Political culture and political change in Communist states*, Macmillan, London, 1977.

Brown, A. and Wightman, G., 'Czechoslovakia: Revival and retreat', in Brown, A. and Gray, J. (ed.), *Political culture and political change in Communist states*, Macmillan, London, 1977.

Brus, W., 'Stalinism and "The people's Democracies" ', in Tucker, R.C. (ed.) *Stalinism. Essays in historical interpretation*, W.W. Norton, New York, 1977.

Bykov, A., 'Novye rubezhi kooperatsii stran SEV', *Kommunist*, no. 18, 1983.

Caldwell, L.T., 'The Warsaw pact — continuity and change', in Keefe, E.K. (ed.), *Czechoslovakia: A country study*, Headquarters, Dept. of the Army, Washington, 1982.

Checinski, M., *Poland: Communism, nationalism, anti-Semitism*, Katz-Cohl Publishing, New York, 1982.

Chrustjov, N.S., *Chrustjov minns. Med inledning och kommentarer av E. Crankshaw*, Bonniers, Stockholm, 1971.

Csaba, L., 'New features of the Hungarian economic mechanism in the mid-eighties', *The New Hungarian Quarterly*, vol. 24, no. 90, 1983.

Csikós-Nagy, B. ,'Development problems of the Hungarian economy', *The New Hungarian Quarterly*, vol. 23, no. 88, 1982.

Czembor, H., Interview by *Kyrkans Tidning*, 19 May 1983.

Dabrowa, S., 'Poland, Europe and the world: 1980-82', *Polish Perspectives*, vol. 25, no. 4, 1982.

Davies, N. *God's playground. A history of Poland. Vol. 2. 1795 to the present.* 2nd ed. Clarendon Press, Oxford, 1982.

Dawisha, K., 'The 1968 invasion of Czechoslovakia: Causes, consequences, and lessons for the future', in Dawisha, K. and Hanson, P. (ed.), *Soviet-East European dilemmas: Coercion, competition, and consent*, Heinemann, London, 1981.

Deak, I. *The lawful revolution. Louis Kossuth and the Hungarians 1848-1849*, Columbia University Press, New York, 1979.

Dellenbrant, J., 'Polens partisystem', *Statsvetenskaplig Tidskrift*, no. 1, 1982.

Demus, R., 'The 1980 Polish strike and the strike cycles in the 1970s', *Telos*, no. 47, 1981.

Dercsényi, D. 'The Hungarian crown', *The New Hungarian Quarterly*, vol. 19, no. 70, 1978.

Dittmer, L., 'Comparative Communist political culture', *Studies in Comparative Communism*, vol. 16, nos. 1-2, 1983.

Documents. 'Antisemitism in today's Poland', *Soviet Jewish Affairs*, vol. 12, no. 1, 1982.

Domokos, M., 'A poet taking sides (the last TV interview)', *The New Hungarian Quarterly*, vol. 24, no. 91, 1983.

Dyker, D. 'Hungarian agriculture: a model for the Soviet Union', *Radio Free Europe. Radio Liberty Research Bulletin*, no. 8, 23 February 1983.

Eco, U., 'Looking for a logic of culture', in Sebeok, T.A. (ed.) *The tell-tale sign: A survey of semiotics*, The Peter de Ridder Press, Lisse, 1975.

Eidlin, F.H., *The logic of "Normalization." The Soviet intervention in Czechoslovakia of 21 August 1968 and the Czechoslovak response*, East European Monographs, no. 74, Distr. by Columbia University Press, Boulder, Col., 1980.

Elster, J., 'A note on hysteresis in the social sciences', *Synthese*, vol. 33, no. 2, 1976.

Elster, J., 'One hundred years of Marxist social science', *London Review of Books*, vol. 5, no. 11, 1983.

Engelmann, P., 'Hungary in autumn 1980', *Telos*, no. 47, 1981.

Erickson, J., 'The Warsaw pact — the shape of things to come?' in Dawisha, K. and Hanson, P. (ed.) *Soviet-East European dilemmas: Coercion, competition, and consent*, Heinemann, London, 1981.

Europa-Archiv, Letter from the CC CPSU to the CC PZPR, 17 September, 1981, *Europa-Archiv*, no. 4, 1982.

Fallenbuchl, Z., 'The Polish economy at the beginning of the 1980s', in *U.S. Congress, Joint Economic Committee: East European Economic Assessment*, Gov't Printing Office, Washington, D.C., February 1980.

Fallenbuchl, Z., 'Poland's economic crisis', *Problems of Communism*, vol. 31, no. 2, 1982.

Fehér, F. and Heller, A., *Hungary 1956 revisited. The message of a revolution — a quarter of a century after*, George Allen and Unwin, London, 1983.

Fejtö, F., 'Les Leçons de Varsovie', *Politique Internationale*, no. 15, 1982.

Ferge, Z., *A society in the making: Hungarian social and societal policy 1945-1975*, M.E. Sharpe, White Plains, N.Y., 1980.

Fischer, H., *Politik und Geschichtswissenschaft in Ungarn*, R. Oldenbourg, München, 1982.

Fitzpatrick, S., 'Culture and Politics under Stalin: a reappraisal', *Slavic Review*, vol. 35, no. 2, 1976.

Fitzpatrick, S., *Education and Social Mobility in the Soviet Union 1921-1934*, Cambridge University Press, Cambridge, 1979a.

Fitzpatrick, S., 'Stalin and the making of a new elite, 1928-1939', *Slavic Review*, vol. 38, no. 3, 1979b.

Friedrich, Carl J., *Tradition and authority*, The Pall Mall Press/Macmillan, London, 1972.

Földes, A., 'Inquest on a generation', *The New Hungarian Quarterly*, vol. 20, no. 75, 1979.

Földes, A., 'Time out of joint', *The New Hungarian Quarterly*, vol. 21, no. 79, 1980.

Garton Ash, T., *The Polish revolution: Solidarity 1980-82*, Jonathan Cape, London, 1983.

Gati, C. 'The Kádár mystique', *Problems of Communism*, vol. 23, no. 3, 1974.

Gati, C., 'Polish futures, Western options', *Foreign Affairs*, vol. 61, no. 2, 1982/83.

Gella, A., 'Resistance to totalitarianism', *Survey*, vol. 26, no. 3, 1982.

Gerner, K. and Hedlund, S., 'Problemet Polen — Kris eller Katastrof?', *Ekonomisk Debatt*, vol. 10, no. 5, 1982.

208

Gerner, K. and Hedlund, S. 'Fel på analysen eller fel på systemet? *Ekonomisk Debatt*, vol. 11, No. 5, 1983.

Gerner, K., 'Polen i sovjetrysk utrikespolitik 1920', in Jönsson, C. et al. (ed.) *Sovjets Utrikespolitik*, Studentlitteratur, Lund, 1972.

Gerner, K., 'The writings of Marx and Engels as sources on Soviet foreign policy', *Historisk Tidskrift*, no. 4, 1978.

Gerner, K., 'Marxismleninismen och naturmiljön i Sovjet-unionen' *Internasjonal Politik*, no. 3B-Supplement, 1979.

Gerner, K., *Arvet från det förflutna*, Liber, Stockholm, 1980a.

Gerner, K., 'Problems of information and central planning', in Jensen, J-J (ed.), *Sovjetunionen i forandring*, Sydjysk Universitetscenter, Esbjerg, 1980b.

Gerner, K., 'Kazan and Manchu. Cultural roots of Soviet foreign relations', *Cooperation and Conflict*, vol. 15, no. 2, 1980c.

Gerner, K., 'Politisk historia som arkeologi', *Historisk Tidskrift*, No. 4, 1981.

Gerner, K., 'Political groupings in Teschen Silesia in the interwar years. Paper presented at the 2nd Symposium of Swedish and Polish Historians, Gdansk, September 1983.

Gilberg, T., *Modernization in Romania since World War 2*, Praeger, New York, 1975.

Gilberg, T., 'Modernization, human rights and nationalism: The case of Romania', in Klein, G. and Reban, M.J. (ed.) *The politics of ethnicity in Eastern Europe*, East European Monographs no. 93. Distributed by Columbia University Press, Boulder, Col., 1981.

Gitelman, Z., 'Power and authority in Eastern Europe', in Johnson, C. (ed.) *Change in Communist systems*, Stanford University Press, Stanford, 1970.

Gitelman, Z., 'The world economy and elite political strategies in Czechoslovakia, Hungary, and Poland', in Bornstein, M., Gitelman, Z. and Zimmerman, W. (ed.) *East-West relations and the future of Eastern Europe*, George Allen and Unwin, London, 1981.

Godson, R. and Haseler, S., *Eurocommunism: Implications for East and West*, Macmillan, London, 1978.

Golan, G., *The Czechoslovak reform movement*, Cambridge University Press, Cambridge, Mass., 1971.

Golan, G., 'National traditions and Socialism in Eastern Europe: The cases of Czechoslovakia and Yugoslavia', in Eisenstadt, S.N. (ed.), *Socialism and Tradition*, Humanities Press, Atlantic Highlands, N.J., 1975a.

Golan, G., 'Elements of Russian tradition in Soviet socialism', in Eisenstadt, S.N. (ed.), *Socialism and tradition*, Humanities Press, Atlantic Highlands, N.J., 1975b.

Golan, G., 'Czechoslovak Marxism in the reform period', *Studies in Soviet Thought*, vol. 19, no. 7, 1976.

Goldstücker, E., 'Nationalitetsfrågan i ett delat Europa', *Listy*, no. 12, (Swedish ed.) 1982.

Gray, J., 'Conclusion', in Brown, A. and Gray, J. (ed.), *Political culture and political change in Communist states*, Macmillan, London, 1977.

Grazynski, W., Report. 7.1. 1939, *Protokoly Rady Ministrów,* Archivum Akt Nowych, Warsaw, 1939.

Gromyko, A.A., 'V.I. Lenin i vneshnaya politika sovetskogo gosudarstva', *Kommunist*, no. 6, 1983.

Gromyko, A.A. and Ponomarev, B. (eds.) *Soviet foreign policy 1945-1980*, vol. 2, Progress Publishers, Moscow, 1981.

Gross, J.T., *Polish society under German occupation: The general-gouvernement 1939–44*, Princeton University Press, Princeton, N.J., 1979.

Gyertyán, E. 'Tragedy in the looking glass', *The New Hungarian Quarterly*, vol. 21, no. 81, 1980.

Györffy, G., 'The thousandth anniversary of St. Stephen's birth', *The New Hungarian Quarterly*, vol. 11, no. 38, 1970.

Györffy, M., 'Books and authors', *The New Hungarian Quarterly*, vol. 23, no. 87, 1982.

Halperin, G., *Russian History*, vol. 5, no. 2, 1978.

Handel, M., *Weak states in the international system*, Frank Cass, London, 1981.

Hann, C.M., 'Social policy in the making', *The New Hungarian Quarterly*,vol. 23, no. 87, 1982.

Hare, et al., in Hare, P.G., Radice, H.K. and Swain, N. (eds.) *Hungary: A Decade of economic reform*, George Allen & Unwin, London, 1981.

Hare, P.G., 'The beginnings of institutional reform in Hungary', *Soviet Studies*, vol. 35, no. 3, 1983.

Hedlund, S., 'Stalin and the peasantry: A study in red', *Scandia*, no. 2, 1983.

Heiskanen, I., 'Political culture: A memory or an ego of politics?' Paper presented to the Polish-Finnish Colloquium on Political Culture, Sept.-Oct., Lahti, 1983.

Heller, A. 'Phases of legitimation in Soviet-type societies', in Rigby, T.H. and Fehér, F. (ed.) *Political legitimation in Communist states*, Macmillan, London, 1982a.

Heller, A., *A theory of history*, Routledge and Kegan Paul, London, 1982b.

Herbert, Z., 'Report from a besieged city', *The New York Review of Books*, vol. 30, no. 13, 1983.

Hernádi, M., 'Accelerating time: A non-fiction paperback series', *The New Hungarian Quarterly*, vol. 23, no. 87, 1982.

Hernádi, M., 'Festive behaviour in Hungary', *The New Hungarian Quarterly*, vol. 21, no. 79, 1980.

Herrmann, R.K., 'Comparing world views in East Europe: Contemporary Polish perceptions', in Linden, R.H. (ed.) *The Foreign policies of East Europe: New approaches*, Praeger, New York, 1980.

Hirsch, H., 'November 1981: Gründung von Diskussionklubs für eine selbstverwaltende Republik in Polen', *Osteuropa*, no. 3. A123-130, 1982.

Hoensch, J., 'The Warsaw pact and the northern member states', in Clawson, R.W. and Kaplan, L.A. (ed.) *The Warsaw pact: Political and military means*, Scholarly Resources, Wilmington, Del., 1982.

Holzman, F.D., Allen, M. and Zwass, A. 'Discussion' in Marer, P. and Montias, J.M. (ed.) *East European integration and East-West trade*, Indiana University Press, Bloomington, Ind., 1980.

Horowitz, I.L., 'The norm of illegitimacy - ten years later', in Denitch, B. (ed.) *Legitimation of Regimes. International Frameworks for Analysis*, Sage, London and Beverly Hills, Cal., 1977.

Hough, J.F., *The Soviet Union and social science theory*, Harvard University Press, Cambridge, Mass., 1977.

Höhmann, H-H., 'Economic reform in the 1970s - policy with no alternative', in Nove, A., Höhmann, H-H. and Seidenstecher, G. (ed.) *The East European economies in the 1970s*, Butterworths, London, 1982.

Howe, I. et al. 'The case of Miklos Duray, *The New York Review of Books*, vol. 30, no. 5, 1983.

Hrabik-Samal, M., 'Die Autoritätskrise in der Osteuropäischen Politik', *Osteuropa*, no. 7, 1982.

Illyés, E., *Nationale Minderheiten in Rumänien. Siebenbürgen im Wandel*, Braumüller, Wien, 1981.

Illyés, G., 'Beyond the introduction to a book', in Janics, K. (ed.) *Czechoslovak policy and the Hungarian minority, 1945–48*, Brooklyn College Studies. East European Monographs, no. 22. Distributed by Columbia University Press, New York, 1982.

Istoriya i Sociologiya, Nauka, Moscow, 1964.

Jablonski, H., 'Przemówienie', *Robotnik Slaski*, 18 September 1979. Also printed in *Pamietnik XII Powszechnego Zjazda Historyków Polskich 17-20 wrzesnia 1979 roku*, Uniwersytet Slaski, Katowice, 1982.

Jancar, B.W., Review of *The Soviet regime in Czechoslovakia*, by Krystufek, Z. *Slavic Review*, vol. 42, no. 1, 1983.

Jaruzelski, W., 'Speech to Brezhnev', *New York Times*, 2 March, 1982.

Jarnowski, M., 'Uniformizacija jest straszna choroba.' (Conversation with Sandor Gaspar.) *Polityka*, 12 February, 1983.

211

Jensen, B., 'Rit och politisk verklighet - en sovjetforskares dilemma', *Finsk Tidskrift*, no. 10, 1982.

Jerschina, J., 'Catholicism as the element of the political culture of Poland. Paper presented at the Polish-Finnish Colloquium on Political Culture', Sept.-Oct., Lahti, 1983.

Johnson, A., *Poland in crisis*, Rand Note-1891-AF, July. Rand Corporation, Santa Monica, Cal., 1982.

Johnson, A. et al., *The Warsaw pact Northern tier*, Rand Report-2417/r AF/FF. Rand Corporation, Santa Monica, Cal., 1980.

Jones, C.D., 'Soviet hegemony in Eastern Europe: The dynamics of political and military interaction', in Hoffmann, E. and Fleron, F. (ed.) *The conduct of Soviet foreign policy*, Aldine Publishing Company, New York, 1980.

Jones, C.D., *Soviet influence in Eastern Europe: Political autonomy and the Warsaw pact*, Praeger, New York, 1981.

Jones, C.D., 'The USSR, the Warsaw pact and NATO', in Oldberg, I. (ed.) *Unity and Conflict in the Warsaw Pact*, The Swedish National Defence Research Institute, Stockholm, 1984.

Jönsson, C., *Superpower. Comparing American and Soviet Policy*, Frances Pinter, London, 1984.

Kádár, B., 'Preparing to meet the challenge', *The New Hungarian Quarterly*, vol. 23, no. 88, 1982.

Kaplan, K., *I Centralkommitténs hemliga arkiv*, Ordfront, Stockholm, 1982.

Kaplan, K., 'Political persecution in Czechoslovakia 1948–1972', *Crisis in Soviet-Type Systems*, no. 3, Vienna, 1983.

Kaplan, M.A., *On historical and political knowing. An inquiry into some problems of universal law and human freedom*, Chicago University Press, Chicago and London, 1971.

Kende, P., 'The post-1956 Hungarian normalization', in Brus, W., Kende, P. and Mlynar, Z. (eds.) *"Normalization" processes in Soviet-dominated Central Europe. Hungary, Czechoslovakia, Poland. Crisis in Soviet Type Systems*, no. 1, Vienna, 1982.

Kis, J., 'Interview in "Hungarian Perspectives"', *Telos*, no. 47, 1981.

Klaniczay, T., 'Reflections on national tradition', *The New Hungarian Quarterly*, vol. 19, no. 70, 1978.

Kolakowski, L. 1982, 'Light in August', *The New Republic*, 14 April, 1982.

Kolankiewicz, G. and Taras, R. 'Poland: Socialism for everyman?', in Brown, A. and Gray, J. (eds.) *Political culture and political change in Communist states*, Macmillan, London, 1977.

Koleznikov, S., 'Pod znamenem nerushimoi druzhby', *Mirovaya Ekonomika i Mezhdunarodnye Otnosheniya*, No. 7, 1980.

Kolkowicz, R., 'The military in Soviet politics: From the perspective of the 25th party congress', in Dallin, A. (ed.) *The Twenty-Fifth Congress of CPSU: Assessment and context*, Hoover Institution Press, Stanford, 1977.

Kolkowicz, R., 'The military and Soviet foreign policy', in Kanet, R. (ed.) *Soviet foreign policy in the 1980s*, Praeger, New York, 1982.

Koltai, T., 'Bend over to see the world. (Örkény the playwright)', *The New Hungarian Quarterly*, vol. 21, no. 80, 1980.

Konrád, G., *Förloraren*, Alba, Stockholm, 1980.

Konrád, G.I., Szélenyi, I, *Die Intelligenz auf dem Weg zur Klassenmacht*, Suhrkamp, Frankfurt am Main, 1978.

Konstytucja 3 Maja 1791, Statut Zgromadzenia Przyjaciól Konstytucji. Opracowal J. Kowecki. Przedmowa opatrzyl B. Lesnodorski, Warsaw, Panstwowe wy dawnictwo Nankowe 1981.

Konwicki, T., *Lilla Apokalypsen*, Coeckelberghs, Stockholm, 1981.

Korbel Albright, M., 'Poland. The role of the press in political change', *The Washington Papers*, vol. 11, no. 102, 1983.

Korbonski, A.,'Poland and the CMEA: Problems and prospects', in Marer, P. and Montias, J.M. (eds.) *East European Integration and East-West trade*, Indiana University Press, Bloomington, Ind., 1980.

Korbonski, A. 'East Europe: Soviet asset or burden? The political dimension', in Linden, R.H. (ed.) *The foreign policies of East Europe: New approaches*, Praeger, New York, 1980.

Korey, W., 'The legal position of Soviet Jewry: A historical enquiry', in Kochan, L. (ed.) *The Jews in Soviet Russia since 1917*, 3rd ed., Oxford University Press, Oxford,1978.

Kossecki, J., 'Metody dzialania KSS-KOR', *Trybuna Ludu,* 24-25 April 1982.

Kostecki, M.J., 'Revolt of the incapacitated: Inter-and intra-organization consequences of the Polish summer 1980', *Journal of Peace Research*, vol. 12, no. 2, 1982.

Kovály, H. and Kohak, E. *Seierherrer og tapere*, Dreyer, Oslo, 1976.

Kovrig, B., *Communism in Hungary. From Kun to Kádár*, Hoover Institution Press, Stanford, 1979.

Kozminski, M. and Juhász, G., 'Hungary and Poland in 1939', *The New Hungarian Quarterly*, vol. 21, no. 80, 1980.

Krisch, H. 'Political legitimation in the German Democratic Republic', in Rigby, T.H. and Fehér, F. (eds.) *Political legitimation in Communist states*, Macmillan, London, 1982.

'The Kubiak Report', *Survey 26, 3*, 1982.

Kundera, M., *Le livre de rire et de l'oubli*, Gallimard, Paris, 1979.

Kundera, M., 'The tragedy of Central Europe', *New York Review of Books*, vol. 31, no. 7, 1984.

Kunt, E., *A halél tükrében*, Magvetö, Budapest, 1981.

Kurczewski, J. 'Solidarnosc od wewnatrz', *Wiadomosci Dnia*, 31 August 1981.

Kurowski, S., 'Doktrinen som förutsättning för Polens ekonomiska kris' in Wiberg H., Bertilsson, M., Gerner, K. and Kutylowski A. (eds.) *Konflikt och Solidaritet i Polen. Sociologiska analyser inifrån*, Prisma, Stockholm, 1983.

Kusin, V., 'Husák's Czechoslovakia and economic stagnation', *Problems of Communism*, vol. 31, no. 3, 1982.

Kusmierek, J., 'Szanowny Towarzyszu Zamiatin', Open Letter, Mimeo Warsaw, 15 October 1981.

Kuttna, M., 'I. Glittering shopwindow', *The New Hungarian Quarterly*, vol. 20, no. 75, 1979.

Kutylowski, A., 'Non-violence in the Polish breakthrough: An introduction', *Journal of Peace Research*, vol. 12, no. 2, 1982.

Lamentowicz, W., 'Legitimering av den politiska makten i efterkrigstidens Polen', in Wiberg, et al. (eds.) *Konflikt och Solidaritet i Polen*, Prisma, Stockholm, 1983.

Lancranjan, I., *Curint despre Transilvania*, Editura Sport-Turism, Bucharest, 1982.

Lane, C., *The rites of rulers. Ritual in industrial society - the Soviet case*, Cambridge University Press, Cambridge, Mass., 1981.

Larrabee, S., 'Instability and change in Eastern Europe', *International Security*, vol. 6, no. 3, 1981–82.

Legvold, R., 'The Concept of power and security in Soviet history', in *Adelphi Paper*, No. 151, 1979.

Legvold, R., 'The 26th Party congress and Soviet foreign policy', in Bialer, S. and Gustafson, T. (eds.) *Russia at the crossroads: The 26th Congress of the CPSU*, George Allen and Unwin, London, 1982.

Lehman, E.W., *Political society. A macrosociology of politics*, Columbia University Press, New York, 1977.

Lew, J., 'Ci, co siali wiatr....', *Zolnierz Wolnosci*, 13-14 March, 1982.

Levinson, C., *Vodka-Cola*, Stock, Paris, 1977.

Lewis, P., 'Obstacles to the establishment of political legitimacy in Communist Poland', *British Journal of Political Science*, vol. 12, no. 2, 1982.

Libiszowska, Z., 'From the Committee of Secret Correspondence to the Department of State. Some remarks on principles and achievements of the US foreign policy', in Rystad, G. (ed.) *Congress and American foreign policy*, Lund Studies of International History, 13, Scandinavian University Books, Lund, 1981.

Lidert, M., *Polen i kris*, Försvar och Säkerhetspolitik, Stockholm, 1982.

Lange, P.H., 'Poland as a problem of Soviet security policy', *Aussenpolitik*, vol. 32, no. 4, English edition, 1981.

Liess, O.R., *Sowjetische Nationalitätenstrategie als weltpolitischer Konzept*, Wien and Stuttgart: Braumüller, 1972.

Linden, R.H., 'The security bind in East Europe', *International Studies Quarterly*, vol. 26, no. 2, 1982.

Linden, R.H., 'East European Studies: Groups, gegs, and gaps', *Studies in Comparative Communism*, vol. 15, no. 4, 1982.

Lippe, P. and Heese, V., 'Kriegsrecht in Polen: Wie es dazu kam', *Osteuropa*, no. 3, 1982.

Lipski, J.J., 'The founding of KOR', *Survey*, vol. 26, no. 3, 1982.

Lipski, J.J., 'Two fatherlands — two patriotisms', *Survey*, vol. 26, no. 4, 1982.

Litván, G., 'The endgame of the Second World War', *The New Hungarian Quarterly*, vol. 23, no. 87, 1982.

Litynski, J., 'Wywiad Jana Litynskiego z G. Bence i J. Kisem. Wegry — od marksizmu do opozycji', *Krytyka. Kwartalnik Polityczny*, no. 5. London: Aneks 1980 (1982).

Lorentz, S., 'Muzea — kultura narodowa — spoleczenstwo', *Nowe Drogi*, no. 8, 1978.

Lüders, C.H., *Breshnew denkt anders. Ideologie und Machtdenken in der Aussen- und Sicherheitspolitik der Sowjetunion*, Nomos, Baden-Baden, 1981.

MacCannell, D. and MacCannell, J.F., *The time of the sign. A semiotic interpretation of modern culture*, Indiana University Press, Bloomington, Ind., 1982.

MacKenzie, D. and Curran, M.W., *A history of Russia and the Soviet Union*, The Dorsey Press, Homewood, Ill, 1977.

Macrae, N., 'Into entrepreneurial socialism', *The Economist*, 19 March, 1983.

Mackintosh, M., 'Military considerations in Soviet-East European relations', in Dawisha, K. and Hanson, R. (eds.), *Soviet-East European dilemmas. Coercion, competition, and consent*, Heinemann, London, 1981.

Makkai, L., 'Gabor Bethlen's European policy', *The New Hungarian Quarterly*, vol. 22, no. 82, 1981.

Martowa, I., *Marzec 1968: nieudana proba zamachu stanu*, No publisher given, Warsaw, 1981.

Marer, P., 'Soviet economic policy in Eastern Europe', in Joint Economic Committee, Congress of the United States, *Reorientation and commercial relations of the economies of Eastern Europe*, Government Printing Office, Washington, D.C., 1974.

Markus, M., 'Overt and covert modes of legitimation in Soviet-type societies', in Rigby, T.H. and Fehér, F. (eds.), *Political legitimation in Communist states*, Macmillan, London, 1982.

Mastny, V., 'Kremlin politics and the Austrian settlement', *Problems of Communism*, vol. 31, no. 4, 1982.

Mastny, V., *Russia's road to the Cold War. Diplomacy, warfare, and the politics of Communism, 1941-45,* Columbia University Press, New York, 1979.

Matejko, A.J., 'The structural roots of Polish opposition', *The Polish Review,* vol. 27, no. 1-2, 1982.

Meyer, A.G., 'Cultural revolutions: The use of the concept of culture in the comparative study of Communist systems', *Studies in Comparative Communism,* vol. 16, no. 1-2, 1983.

Michnik, A., 'What we want to do and what we can do', *Telos,* no. 47, 1981.

Michnik, A., 'Polska wojna. Warsaw', *Aneks. Kwartalnik polityczny* no. 27. Swedish translation by Maria Borowska, *Det polska kriget,* 1982.

Mink, G., 'Polls, pollsters, public opinion and political power in Poland in the late 1970s', *Telos,* no. 47, 1981.

Micunovic, V., *Moscow Diary.* Doubleday, New York, 1980.

Mitchell, R.J., 'A new Brezhnev doctrine: The restructuring of international relations', *World Politics,* vol. 30, no. 3, 1978.

Mlynár, Z., *Nattfrost. Om försöken att bygga en mänsklig socialism i Tjeckoslovakien,* Ordfront, Stockholm, 1980.

Mlynár, Z., *Krisen und Krisenbewältigung im Sowjet-System.,* Braumuller, Köln and Wien, 1983.

Mlynár, Z., 'Relative stabilization of the Soviet systems in the 1970s', *Crises in Soviet-Type Systems,* no. 2. Vienna, 1983.

Mojsiewicz, C., 'Concepts of political culture and researches in that field in Poland', Paper presented at the Polish-Finnish Colloquium on Political Culture, Lahti, Sept.-Oct., 1983.

Molnár, M., *A Short History of the Hungarian Communist Party,* Westview Press, Boulder, Col., 1978.

Moreton, E., 'Foreign policy perspectives in Eastern Europe', in Dawisha, K. and Hanson, P. (eds.), *Soviet-East European dilemmas. Coercion, competition, and consent,* Heineman, London, 1981.

Moreton, E., 'The Soviet Union and Poland's struggle for self control', *International Security,* vol. 7, no. 7, 1982.

Muggeridge, M., 'Behind the cruel propositions, an ancient greeting', *The Guardian Weekly,* vol. 128, no. 16, 1983.

Mushkat, M., 'The evolution of the situation in Poland in 1980', *Berichte des Bundesinstituts für Ostwissenschaftliche und internationale Studien,* no. 15, 1981.

Müller, A., *Der Tschechoslowakei auf der Suche nach Sicherheit,* Verlag Arno Spitz, Berlin, 1977.

Mårtensson, O., 'Militärtidning avslöjar planering inför kuppen. Medan regeringen talade om samförstånd med Walesa förbereddes officerare och säkerhetsmän för maktövertagandet', *Sydsvenska Dagbladet,* 10 February, 1982.

Mägiste, E., 'Polens partisystem', *Statsvetenskaplig Tidskrift*, no. 1, 1983.

'Na Lewicy.' Quotation by Rezsö Nyers, *Politika*, 12 February 1983.

Nilsson, G.B., 'Om det fortfarande behovet av källkritik', *Historisk Tidskrift*, no. 2, 1973.

Nowak, J., 'The Church in Poland', *Problems of Communism*, vol. 31, no. 1, 1982.

Nowak, S., 'Wartosci i postawy spoleczne', in Lewandowski, J. et al. (ed.), *Systemy Wartosci a Wzory Konsumpcji Spoleczenstwa Polskiego*, Instytut Filozofii i Socjologii PAN, Warsaw, 1980.

Nuti, D.M., 'The Polish crisis: Economic factors and constraints', in Drewnowski, J. (ed.),*Crisis in the East European economy*,Beckenham, 1982.

Nyers, R., 'The interaction of political and economic development', *The New Hungarian Quarterly*, vol. 23, no. 85, 1982.

Odom, W.E., 'The militarization of Soviet society', *Problems of Communism*, vol. 25, no. 5, 1976.

Odom, W.E., 'The Party-military connection: A critique', in Herspring, D.R. and Volgyes, I. (eds.), *Civilian-military relations in Communist systems*, Westview Press, Boulder, Col., 1978.

Ogarkov, N., 'Na strazhe mirnogo truda', *Kommunist*, no. 10, 1981.

Ogarkov, N., Review of work by Ogarkov, *International Herald Tribune*, 15 March, 1982.

Osadczuk-Korab, B., 'Von langer Hand vorbereitet. . . Zur Entstehungsgeschichte des Militärcoups von General Jaruzelski', *Osteuropa*, no. 4, 1982.

Otsason, R., 'Upravlenie sel'skokhozyaystvennymi predpriyatiyami v Vengrii', *Voprosy Ekonomiki*, no. 1, 1983.

Papée, I., Communication to the Ministry of Foreign Affairs in Warsaw from the Polish Ambassador in Prague, May 22, 1937. *Ministerstwo Spraw Zagranicznych PIII*, 5508. Archiwum Akt Nowych' Warsaw, 1937.

Pashuto, V.T., 'Die Rus', Litauen und Deutschland im 13. Jahrhundert', in Lemke, G. and Widera, B. (eds.), *Russisch-Deutsche Beziehungen von der Kiever Rus' bis zur Oktoberrevolution*, Akademie-Verlag, Berlin, 1976.

Pastukhov, B., 'Vospityvat' patriotov, internatsionalistov', *Kommunist*, no. 3, 1982.

Patzelt, H., 'Der Protestantismus in Teschener Schlesien in Vergangenheit und Gegenwart und seine Bedeutung für die evangeliche Kirche in Österreich', *Jahrbuch der Gesellschaft für die Geschichte des Protestantismus in Österreich* 88, 1972.

Paul, D.W., 'Political culture and the socialist purpose', in Shapiro, J.P.

and Potichnyj, P.J. (eds.), *Change and adaption in Soviet and East European politics*, Praeger, New York, 1976.

Paul, D.W.,'The Cultural Limits of Revolutionary Politics: Change and Continuity in Socialist Czechoslovakia', *East European Quarterly*. Distributed by Columbia University Press, Boulder, Col., 1979.

Paul, D.W. and Simon, M.D., 'Poland today and Czechoslovakia 1968', *Problems of Communism*, vol. 30, no. 5, 1981.

Pelenski, J., *Russia and Kazan. Conquest and Imperial ideology*, Mouton, The Hague and Paris, 1974.

Petterson, B., *Sovjetiska presskommentarer i Polen — frågan augusti 1980-december 1981*, Department of Political Science, Mimeo, Lund, 1982.

Pfaff, W. 'Eastern Europe is increasingly a danger zone', *International Herald Tribune*, 21 May 1982.

Philipp, A., 'Landwirtschaft und Nahrungsmittelversorgung', in Uschakow, A. (ed.), *Polen-Das Ende der Erneuerung? Gesellschaft, Wirtschaft und Kultur im Wandel*, C.H. Beck, München, 1982.

Piekalkiewicz, J., 'Polish local politics in flux: Concentration or deconcentration', in Nelson, D.N. (ed.),*Local politics in Communist countries*, Kentucky University Press, Lexington, 1980.

Pietraszek, E., 'Ethos polskiej klasy robotniczej (kilka wybranych zagadnien)', in Sicinski, A. (ed.), *Styl zycia, obyczaje, ethos w Polsce lat siedem dzieszatych — z perspektywy roku 1981*, Instytut Filozofii i Socjologii PAN, Warsaw, 1983.

Pilaszanovich, I., *A Mohácsi Történelmi Emlékhely*, Pécs. (No date).

Pistakowski, J., 'Notatka dla Pana Naczelnika Wydzialu Prawnego', *Protokoly Rady Ministró*, 5.1.1939, Archiwum Akt Nowych. Warsaw, 1939.

'Poles 80. Results of survey research. Conducted by W.W. Adamski et al.', in Adamski, W.W. et al. (eds.), *Sisyphus. Sociological Studies*. Vol. III, *Crisis and conflicts. The case of Poland, 1980-81,* Polish Scientific Publishers, Warsaw, 1982.

Polonsky, A., *Politics in independent Poland, 1921-1939*, Oxford University Press, Oxford, 1972.

Polskie Porozumenie Niepodleglosciowe. Mimeo. Warsaw, NOWA 1978.

Pomian, K., *Pologne: Défi à l'impossible,* Les éditions ouvrières, Paris, 1982.

Popper, K., *The poverty of historicism*, Routledge and Kegan Paul, London, 1961.

Porshnev, B., *Tridtsatiletnyaya voina i vstuplenie v nee Shvetsii i Moskovskogo gosudarstva*, Nauka, Moscow, 1976.

Porshnev, B., 'K voprosy o meste Rossii v sisteme evropeiskikh gosudarstv v XV-XVIII vekakh', in *Uchennye zapiski Akademii Obshchestvennykh*

Nauk, vyp II. Voprosy vseobshchei istorii, Moscow, 1948.

'Positionspapier des Kulturpolitischen Arbeitsausschusses beim Zentral-komitee der ungarischen sozialistischen Arbeiterpartei zu den anti-marxistischen Ansichten mehrerer Sozialforscher' in *Die Neue Linke in Ungarn,* Band 2. Merve, West Berlin,1976.

Potel, J-Y., *The summer before the frost. Solidarity in Poland,* Pluto Press, London, 1982.

Pravda, A., 'East-West interdependence and the social compact in Eastern Europe', in Bornstein, M., Gitelman, Z. and Zimmerman, W. (eds.), *East-West relations and the future of Eastern Europe. Politics and economics,* George Allen and Unwin, London, 1981.

Pravda. 12 June 1981.

Pravda. 13 Oct. 1981 (In *Osteuropa,* no.2.p.A 82. 1982.)

Programme of Solidarity, 7 Oct. 1981, *Europa-Archiv,* no. 4, 1982.

Przeworski, A., 'The men of iron and men of power in Poland', *Political Science,* no. 1, 1982.

Puja, F., 'Hungary's part in East-West relations', *The New Hungarian Quarterly,* vol. 24, no. 90, 1983.

Pye, L.W., 'Introduction: Political culture and political development', in Pye, L.W. and Verba, S. (eds.), *Political culture and political development,* Princeton University Press, Princeton, N.J., 1965.

R.F. 'National minorities — theory and practice', *The New Hungarian Quarterly,* vol. 20, no. 74, 1979.

Radio Free Europe. Radio Liberty RAD background. Report/210 (Poland), no. 22, July 1981.

Raeff, M., 'Seventeenth-century Europe in Eighteenth-century Russia', *Slavic Review,* vol. 41, no. 4, 1982.

Raina, P., *Political opposition in Poland 1954-1977,* Poets and Panters Press, London, 1978.

Raina, P., *Independent social movements in Poland,* LSE/Orbis Books, London, 1981.

Rakowski, M., 'Interview', *Guardian Weekly,* 31 August 1980.

Reddaway, N., 'Foreword', in Ruane, K. *The Polish challenge,* BBC, London, 1982.

Remington, R.A., 'Politics of accommodation: Redefining Soviet-East European relations', in Kanet, R.E. (ed.), *Soviet foreign policy in the 1980s,* Praeger, New York, 1982.

Rhode, G., 'Partei im raschen Wandel', *Osteuropa,* no. 4, 1982.

Richet, X., 'Is there an "Hungarian" model of planning?', in Hare, P.G. et al (eds.), *Hungary. A decade of economic reform,* George Allen and Unwin, London, 1981.

Rigby, T.H., 'Introduction: Political legitimacy, Weber and Communist mono-organizational systems', in Rigby, T.H. and Fehér, F. (eds.), *Political legitimation in Communist states,* Macmillan, London, 1982.

Rogowski, W., 'Zwiazki zawodowe — partnerzy czy oponenci?', *Nowe Drogi*, no. 9, 1981.

Ronnås, P., 'Ethnic structure and mobility in Crisana, Banat, Maramures, and Transylvania', *Bidrag till Öststatsforskningen*, vol. 10, no. 3, 1982.

Rosenfeldt, N.E., *Knowledge and power. Stalin's secret chancellery in the Soviet system of government*, Rosenkilde and Bagger, Copenhagen, 1978.

Rosenfeldt, N.E., *Stalinstyrets nervecenter.* Slavisk Institut, Copenhagen, 1980.

Rositzke, H., *KGB. The eyes of Russia*, Sidgwick and Jackson, London, 1982.

Rotschild, J., *Pilsudski's coup d'etat*, Columbia University Press, New York and London, 1966.

Rotschild, J. 'Political legitimacy in contemporary Europe', in Denitch, B. (ed.), *Legitimation of Regimes. International Frameworks for Analysis*, Sage, London and Beverly Hills, Cal., 1977.

Rupnik, J., *Histoire du Parti Communiste Tschécoslovaque: Des Origines à la prise du pouvoir*, Presses de la Foundation nationale de sciences politiques, Paris, 1981.

Rupnik, J., 'The roots of Czech Stalinism', in Samuel, R. and Stedman Jones, G. (eds.), *Culture, Ideology and Politics*, Routledge and Kegan Paul, London, 1982.

Ruane, K., *The Polish challenge.* BBC, London, 1982.

Sadykiewicz, M., 'Jaruzelski's war', *Survey*, vol. 26, no. 3, 1982.

Scheiber, S., 'A facsimile edition of the Maimonides Codex in Budapest', *The New Hungarian Quarterly*, vol. 22, no. 83. 1981.

Schulz, E., 'New developments in intra-bloc relations in historical perspective', in Dawisha, K. and Hanson, P. (eds.), *Soviet-East European dilemmas: Coercion, competition, and consent*, Heinemann for the Royal Institute of International Affairs, London, 1981.

Schöpflin, G., 'Hungary. An uneasy stability', in Brown, A. and Gray, J. (eds.), *Political culture and political change in Communist states*, Macmillan, London, 1977.

Schöpflin, G., 'The political structure of Eastern Europe as a factor in intra-bloc relations', in Dawisha, K. and Hanson, P. (eds.), *Soviet-East European dilemmas: Coercion, competition, and consent*, Heinemann for the Royal Institute of International Affairs, London, 1981.

Schöpflin, G., 'Hungary between prosperity and crisis', *Conflict Studies*, no. 136, 1982.

Schöpflin, G., 'Poland and Eastern Europe: The impact of the crisis', in Woodall, J. (ed.), *Policy and politics in contemporary Poland. Reform, failure, crisis*, Frances Pinter, London, 1982.

Schöpflin, G., 'Introduction', in *Censorship and political communication in Eastern Europe. A collection of documents.* Frances Pinter, London, 1983.

Seewann, G. and Sitzler, K., 'Ungarn 1956: Volksaufstand — Konter-revolution — nationale Tragödie. Offizielle Retrospektive nach 25 Jahre', *Südost Europa*, no. 1, 1982.

Seewann, G. and Sitzler, K., 'Ungarischer Nationalbewusstsein heute', *Südost Europa*, no. 2, 1983.

Shapiro, M.J., 'Interpretation and political understanding', *NUPI-notat*, no. 186, Norsk Utenrikspolitisk Institut, Oslo, 1980.

Seton-Watson, H., 'Nationalism, nations, and Western policies', *The Washington Quarterly*, vol. 2, no. 2, 1979.

Shtromas, A., *Political change and social development: The case of the Soviet Union*, Frankfurt A.M. and Bern: Verlag Peter Lang, 1981.

Sicinski, A., (ed.) *Styl Zycia, Obyczaje, Ethos w Polsce Lat Siedem dziesiatychz perspektywy roku 1981.* Instytut Filozofii i Socjologii PAN, Warsaw, 1983.

Sikora, F., *Sozialistische Solidarität und Nationale Interessen,*Wissen-schaft und Politik, Köln, 1972.

Simes, D.K., 'Deterrence and coercion in Soviet policy', *International Security*, vol. 5, no. 3, 1980-81.

Simes, D.K., 'The military and militarism in Soviet society', *International Security*, vol. 6, no. 3, 1981-82.

Simes, D.K. 'Clash over Poland', *Foreign Policy*, no. 46, 1982.

Simon, M. and Kanet, R., (eds.) *Background to crisis: Policy and politics in Gierek's Poland*, Westview Press, Boulder, Col., 1981.

Singer, D., *The road to Gdansk*, Monthly Review Press, London, 1981.

Sitzler, K., 'Interessenpluralismus und Einparteiensystem in ungarischen Reformmodell', *Südost Europa*, no. 10, 1982.

Siztler, K., 'Tibor Liska's Konzeption der "sozialistischen" Unterneh-mung', *Südost Europa*, no. 9, 1983.

Skilling, H.G., *Czechoslovakia's interrupted revolution*, Princeton, University Press, Princeton, N.J., 1976.

Skilling, H.G., 'Stalinism and Czechoslovak political culture', in Tucker, R. (ed.), *Stalinism. Essays in historical interpretation*, Norton, New York, 1977.

Sokolov, O., *M.N. Pokrovskii i sovetskaya istoricheskaya nauka*, Nauka, Moscow, 1970.

Sperling, V., 'Ungarn skal have större demokrati i parlamentsvalg', *Information*, 25 November 1982.

Sprawy Miedzynarodowe, no. 11, 1981.

Staniszkis, J., 'On some contradictions of socialist society: The case of Poland', *Soviet Studies*, vol. 31, no. 2, 1979.

Staniszkis, J., 'The evolution of working-class protest in Poland: Socio-logical reflections on the Gdansk-Szcecin case', *Soviet Studies*, vol. 33, no. 2, 1981.

Staniszkis, J., *Pologne. La Révolution Auto-limitée*. Pr. Un. de France, Paris, 1982a.

Staniszkis, J., 'Ökonomisch-Politische Zyklen in Polen. *Osteuropa*, no. 3, 1982b.

Staniszkis, J., 'Ett års fredlig revolution i Polen: en studie i polarisering', in Wiberg, H. et al (eds.), *Konflikt och Solidaritet i Polen,* Prisma, Stockholm, 1983.

Strode, R.V., 'Soviet strategic style', *Comparative Strategy*, vol. 3, no. 4, 1982.

Stroebel, G., Lecture at symposium in Sankelmark, West Germany, June 1983.

Suda, Z., *Zealots and rebels. A history of the ruling Communist party of Czechoslovakia*, Hoover Institution Press, Stanford, Cal., 1980.

Summerscale, P., *The East European predicament. Changing patterns in Poland, Czechoslovakia, and Romania*, St. Martin's Press, New York, 1982.

Swartz, R., 'Tjeckoslovakien säljer inte sin "själ". Liten skuld till västvärlden — men tekniken är föråldrad', *Svenska Dagbladet*, 22 November 1982.

Swartz, R., 'Ny vallag tillåter politisk konkurrens', *Svenska Dagbladet*, 30 September 1983.

Szamuely, L., *First models of the Socialist economic system*, Akadémiai Kiadó, Budapest, 1974.

Szamuely, L., 'The first wave of the mechanism debate in Hungary (1954-57)', *Acta Oeconomica*, vol. 29, no. 1-2, 1982.

Száraz, G., 'An odd sort of book on Transylvania', *The New Hungarian Quarterly*, vol. 24, no. 89, 1983.

Székely, A., 'Amerigo Tot Retrospective', *The New Hungarian Quarterly*, vol. 23, no. 87, 1982a.

Széky, J., 'Population growth and material welfare. A press debate', *The New Hungarian Quarterly*, vol. 23, no. 86, 1982b.

Széky, J., 'Entrepreneurial socialism' at the experimental stage, (The Liska Model), *The New Hungarian Quarterly*, vol. 23, no. 87, 1982c.

Széky, J., 'Innovation — from words to reforms', *The New Hungarian Quarterly*, vol. 23, no. 85, 1982.

Taborsky, E., *President Edward Benes. Between East and West 1938-1948*, Hoover Institution Press, Stanford, Cal., 1981.

Tarján, T. 'Madhouse', *The New Hungarian Quarterly*, vol. 23, no. 87, 1982.

Tarkowska, E., 'Kilka uwag o stylach zycia w wspólczesnej Polsce', in Sicinski, A. (ed.) *Styl Zycia, Obyczaje, Ethos w Polsce Lat Siedem dziesiatych — z perspektywy roku 1981*, Instytut Filozofii i Socjologii PAN, Warsaw, 1983.

Telos, No. 47, 1981.

Terebilov, V., Oral communication at the Department of the History of Law, University of Lund, Sweden, 14 April 1983. (Cf. 'Sovjetiska rättvisan besökte Malmö. Justitieminister Terebilov studerar domstolar', *Sydsvenska Dagbladet*, 15 April.)

Terry, S.M. and Korbonski, A., 'The impact of external economic disturbances on the internal politics of Eastern Europe: The Polish and Hungarian cases', in Neuberger, E. and Tyson, L. D'Andrea (eds.), *The Impact of International Economic Disturbances on the Soviet Union and Eastern Europe. Transmission and Response*, Pergamon, New York, 1980.

Tillett, L., *The great friendship. Soviet historians on non-Russian nationalities*, University of North Carolina Press, Chapel Hill, 1969.

Toma, P.A. and Volgyes, I., *Politics in Hungary*, Freeman, San Francisco, 1977.

Touraine, A. et al., *Solidarity. The analysis of a social movement: Poland 1980-1981.* Cambridge University Press, Cambridge, Mass., Editions de la Maison des Sciences de l'homme, Paris, 1983.

Treadgold, D.W., *The West in Russia and China. Religious and secular thought in modern times. Vol. 1. Russia 1472-1917.* Harvard University Press, Cambridge, Mass., 1973.

Tsoppi, V., 'Polskii reportazh. Preodolenie', *Literaturnaya Gazeta*, 12 October, 1983.

Tsvigun, S., 'O proiskach imperialisticheskikh razvedok', *Kommunist*, no. 14, 1981.

Tucker, R.C., 'Culture, political culture and Communist society', *Political Science Quarterly*, vol. 88, no. 2, 1973.

Tucker, R.C., 'Introduction: Stalinism and comparative Communism', in Tucker, R.C. (ed.), *Stalinism. Essays in historical interpretation*, W.W. Norton and Co., New York, 1977.

Tumarkin, N., *Lenin lives! The Lenin cult in Soviet Russia*, Harvard University Press, Cambridge, Mass., 1983.

Tägil, S. et al., *Studying boundary conflicts. A theoretical framework.* Lund Studies in International History. 9., Scandinavian University Books, Lund, 1977.

Ulc, O., *Politics in Czechoslovakia*, Freeman, San Francisco, 1974.

Ulc, O., 'Czechoslovakia and the Polish virus', *Current History*, vol. 80, no. 465, 1981.

Uschakow, A., 'Das Dilemma der polnischen Aussenpolitik', in Uschakow, A. (ed.) *Polen-das Ende der Erneuerung? Gesellschaft, Wirtschaft und Kultur im Wandel*, C.H. Beck, München, 1982.

V Politbyuro TsK KPSS. *Ekonomicheskaya Gazeta*, no. 32, 1983.

Vaculik, L., 'Thus spoke Schwejk', *The New York Review of Books*, vol. 30, no. 12, 1983.

Vajda, M., *The state and socialism*, Allison and Busby, London, 1981.

Vajna, T., 'Problems and trends in the development of the Hungarian new economic mechanism: A balance sheet of the 1970s', in Nove, A., Höhmann, H-H. and Seidenstecher, G. (eds.) *The East European economies in the 1970s*, Butterworths, London, 1982.

Vale, M. (ed.), *Poland. The state of the republic: Reports by the Experience and Future Discussion Group (DiP) Warsaw.* Pluto Press, London, 1981.

Valenta, J., *Soviet intervention in Czechsolovakia, 1968*, Johns Hopkins, Baltimore, 1981.

Valenta, J., 'Soviet options in Poland', *Survival*, vol. 23, no. 2, 1981.

Valenta, J., 'Soviet use of surprise and deception', *Survival*, vol. 24, no. 2, 1982.

Vasari, E., *Die Ungarische Revolution 1956*, Seewald, Stuttgart, 1981.

'Västs kultur är propaganda'. *Sydsvenska Dagbladet*, 26 January 1983. (Quoting the Soviet magazine "Zhurnalist".)

Volgyes, I., 'Legitimacy and modernization: Nationality and nationalism in Hungary and Transylvania', in Klein, G. and Reban, M.J. (eds.) *The politics of ethnicity in Eastern Europe*, East European Monographs, no. 43. Distr. by Columbia University Press, Boulder, Col. 1981.

Volgyes, I., 'The Kádár years in Hungary', *Current History*, vol. 80, no. 465, 1981.

Voslensky, M., *Nomenklatura*, Tiden, Stockholm, 1982.

Weber, M., 'Politics as a vocation', in Gerth, H.H. and Mills, C.W. *From Max Weber: Essays in sociology*, Oxford University Press, New York, 1958.

Wesson, R., *The Russian dilemma: A political and geopolitical view*, Rutgers University Press, New Brunswick, 1974.

Westoby, A. and Blick, R., 'Early Soviet designs on Poland', *Survey*, vol. 26, no. 4, 1982.

White, S. et al., *Communist political systems: An introduction*, Macmillan, London, 1982.

White, S., 'The USSR: Patterns of autocracy and industrialization', in Brown, A. and Gray, J., (eds.), *Political culture and political change in Communist states*, Macmillan, London, 1977.

White, S., *Political culture and Soviet politics*, Macmillan, London, 1979.

Wnuk-Lipinski, E. 'Dimorphism of values and social schizophrenia. A tentative description', in Adamski, W.W. (ed.) *Sisyphus. Sociological studies. Vol. III. Crisis and conflicts. The case of Poland, 1980–1981*, Polish Scientific Publishers, Warsaw, 1982.

Wojcicki, K., 'The reconstruction of society', *Telos*, no. 47, 1981.

Woodall, J., (ed.), *Policy and politics in contemporary Poland. Reform, failure and crisis*, Frances Pinter, London, 1982.

224

Wyka, A., 'O awangardowym stylu alternatywnym', in Sicinski, A. (ed.) *Styl zycia, Obyczaje, Ethos w Polsce Lat Siedem dziesiatych - z perspektywy roku 1981*, Instytut Filozofii i Socjologii PAN, Warsaw, 1983.

Zagajewski, A. *Polen. Staat im Schatten der Sowjetunion*, Rowohlt, Hamburg, 1981.

Zaslavsky, V., *The neo-Stalinist state. Class, ethnicity and consensus in Soviet society*, Harvester Press, Brighton, 1982.

Zielinski, H., 'Poczatki niepodleglosci', *Nowe Drogi*, no. 6, 1978.

Zimmerman, W., 'Soviet East-European relations in the 1980s and the changing international system', in Bornstein, M., Gitelman, Z., and Zimmerman, W., (eds.), *East-West relations and the future of Eastern Europe. Politics and economics*, George Allen and Unwin, London, 1981.

Zimmerman, W., 'Dependency theory and the Soviet-East European hierarchical regional system: Initial tests', *Slavic Review*, vol. 37, no. 4, 1978.

Zinoviev, A., *My i Zapad*, L'age d'homme, Lausanne, 1981.

Index

227